Chris

Enjoy !

Ken
Dec. 96'

WHAT THEY DIDN'T TEACH YOU ABOUT THE CIVIL WAR

WHAT THEY
DIDN'T TEACH
YOU ABOUT THE CIVIL WAR

Mike Wright

★

PRESIDIO

Published by Presidio Press
505 B San Marin Drive, Suite 300
Novato, CA 94945-1340

Library of Congress Cataloging-in-Publication Data

Wright, Mike, 1938–
    What they didn't teach you about the Civil War / Mike Wright.
        p.   cm.
    Includes bibliographical references and index.
    ISBN 0-89141-596-3 (hardcover)
    1. United States—History—Civil War. 1861–1865. I. Title.
    E468.W89   1996
    973.7—dc20   96-32970
                                                                CIP

Printed in the United States of America

As Ever ...
For my doctor, friend, and love:
Lin Joan Drury, D.N.Sc, R.N., M.A.

It is well that war is so terrible,
or we should grow too fond of it.
Gen. Robert E. Lee, C.S.A.
On seeing a Federal charge repulsed,
December 13, 1862, at Fredericksburg, Virginia

I am the man, I suffer'd, I was there.
Walt Whitman
"Song of Myself"

War is at best barbarism. . . . Its glory is all moonshine. It is only
those who have neither fired a shot nor heard the shrieks and
groans of the wounded who cry aloud for blood, more
vengeance, more desolation.
War is hell.
Gen. William Tecumseh Sherman
Address to the June 19, 1879, graduating
class of the Michigan Military Academy

CONTENTS

ACKNOWLEDGMENTS

Not every event and action in life can be enjoyable, but it's nice when they are. Writing this book has been one such enjoyable event. In researching the incidents I've written about, I met with and talked with many people who helped make the production of this project a pleasure. I've been to many of the sites, seen many of the locations. That, too, has been enjoyable.

I especially want to thank Publisher Robert Kane and Executive Editor E. J. McCarthy of Presidio Press for their enthusiasm, encouragement, and help.

An advertising flyer for an earlier book stated, "Mike Wright is a freelance writer and television producer. He resides in Chicago, Illinois." A good friend commented, "It should have said, 'He is a Virginian who now resides in Chicago.'" Butch, you're absolutely right. I don't often need reminding of my heritage, but thank you and Susie for nudging me now and then.

Above all, I thank my wife, Lin. When I am despondent, she cheers me up. When I feel lost, she helps me find my way. As Shakespeare says in *A Midsummer-Night's Dream,* "Though she be but little, she is fierce."

Thank you, Lin, and now we get on with your book.

A CHRONOLOGY OF THE WAR

1861:

Feb. 4: Seceding states meet in Montgomery, Alabama, to form government.

Feb. 18: Jefferson Davis inaugurated in Montgomery, Alabama, as provisional president of the Confederate States.

March 4: Abraham Lincoln inaugurated as president of the United States.

April 13: Fort Sumter falls.

May 23: Virginia voters ratify secession.

July 21: South wins at First Manassas (Bull Run); Rebel Gen. T. J. Jackson gains reputation as a "Stonewall."

1862:

Feb. 16: First meeting in Richmond of Confederate Congress.

Feb. 22: Davis inaugurated in Richmond as president of the permanent Confederate States.

March 8: Ironclad CSS *Virginia* sinks USS *Cumberland* and USS *Congress* at Hampton Roads, Virginia.

March 9: Drawn battle between CSS *Virginia* and Union ironclad USS *Monitor*.

March 17: Troops under Gen. George McClellan begin arriving at Fort Monroe, Virginia. Rain and mud delay. McClellan faked by Quaker guns.

April 6–7: South loses at Battle of Shiloh.

April 20: New Orleans formally surrenders to Union forces.

May 5: Battle of Williamsburg, Virginia—Rebels fall back toward Richmond; eight days later Davis sends his family to safety in North Carolina.

May 31: Confederates under J. E. Johnston attack Federal troops at Seven Pines (Fair Oaks), Johnston wounded; Gen. Robert E. Lee takes command the next day.

June 6–July 1: The Seven Days' Battles. Generally Confederate victories, and McClellan retreats.

Sept. 17: Drawn Battle of Antietam (Sharpsburg); Lee returns to Virginia but McClellan fails to follow up for decisive victory; Lincoln will relieve him.

Dec. 13: Lee wins major victory at Fredericksburg, Virginia.

1863:

Jan. 1: Emancipation Proclamation takes effect, freeing all slaves in captivity, in areas not controlled by United States.

Jan. 2: Drawn battle of Murfreesboro, Tennessee (Stones River).

April 2: Richmond Bread Riot.

April 29–May 3: Lee wins at Chancellorsville; Stonewall Jackson wounded, dies eight days later.

June 9: General Jeb Stuart wins Battle of Brandy Station, but it's the first time he's had difficulty with a rapidly improving Union cavalry. Largest cavalry battle on American continent.

June 15: Lee wins at Winchester, Virginia, then heads for Pennsylvania.

July 1–3: Union under Gen. George Meade wins Battle of Gettysburg; Lee returns to Virginia.

July 4: General Ulysses S. Grant takes Vicksburg, cutting the South in two.

Sept. 19–20: South wins at Battle of Chickamauga, Tennessee.

Nov. 25: Grant wins Battle of Chattanooga.

1864:

Feb. 9: 109 Union prisoners escape from Libby Prison in Richmond; 48 recaptured and two drown.

March 9: Grant assumes command of all Union forces.

May 4–7: Grant goes into the Wilderness to face Lee; widespread confusion, but Lee wins.

May 8–18: Grant and Lee face each other again, this time in Battle of Spotsylvania; on May 11, at Yellow Tavern outside Richmond, Stuart is killed.

June 3: Lee wins defensive Battle of Cold Harbor against Grant; 7,000 killed in first seven minutes.

June 18: After crossing James River, Grant loses Battle of Petersburg, begins siege.

July 30: The fiasco known as the Battle of the *Crater* is fought at Petersburg; the South wins.

Aug. 5: Confederate navy loses to Adm. David Farragut at Mobile Bay: "Damn the torpedoes! Full speed ahead."

Sept. 2: General William T. Sherman takes Atlanta.

Nov. 8: Lincoln is elected to a second term.

Nov. 16: Sherman burns Atlanta, then begins his March to the Sea.

Nov. 19: Gettysburg Battlefield dedicated, Lincoln delivers his Gettysburg Address.

Nov. 30: Sherman defeats Confederate general Hood at Battle of Franklin, Tennessee.

Dec. 21: Sherman captures Savannah, Georgia—Lincoln's "Christmas present."

1865:

Jan. 30: Lee appointed commander-in-chief of all Confederate forces.

Feb. 3: Peace commission led by Confederate Vice President Stevens meets with President Lincoln on a yacht in Hampton Roads; no result.

Feb. 17: Charleston, South Carolina, falls to Sherman; that same day, Sherman's army burns Columbia, S.C.

Mar. 18: Last Confederate Congress in Richmond adjourns.

Mar. 25: Lee fails in attempt to take Fort Stedman at Petersburg; it's his last attack of the war.

April 1: General Philip Sheridan's cavalry overwhelms Confederates at Battle of Five Forks.

April 2: Grant breaks through Lee's forces outside Petersburg; that night, Lee abandons Petersburg; Confederates set fire to Richmond.

April 3: Richmond falls to Federal troops.

April 4: Lincoln visits Richmond, sits in Davis's chair at Confederate White House.

April 9: Robert E. Lee surrenders to Ulysses S. Grant at Appomattox Courthouse, Virginia.

April 14: President Lincoln is assassinated in Washington, D.C.

April 26: General Johnston surrenders to General Sherman.

May 8: General Taylor surrenders to Gen. Edward Canby at Citronell, Alabama.

Aug. 23: Confederate surgeon Maj. Aaron Brown surrenders wounded in Upson County, Georgia, the last Rebel ground forces to surrender.

Nov. 6: Confederate Capt. James Waddell of the CSS *Shenandoah* surrenders to the British in Liverpool, England, preferring not to hand over his ship to the U.S. It's the final surrender of the war.

Many more battles, many more skirmishes, many more events that may have changed the way the war went could be added to this list. Some others might be deleted. These are, however, among the most important incidents of a war that saw almost exactly four years of important events.

PREFACE

This is history with the drama left in, rawboned and rawhide. It is real life, human existence, the story of people and their passions. This is about their jealousies, their hatreds, and their loves. It is about how they lived life with the bark left on.

This is not some bland tale of the past as told in History 101, that desiccated husk of life many of us suffered and often slept through in high school or college. Nor is it history taught at its lowest common denominator with the drama dried out: learn this date; remember who won what battle during what war; don't forget who did what to whom and where.

This is not history on a grand scale, either. This is not all about battles and numbers; instead, it is about people. You'll find as few dates and numbers as possible in what follows. You will find here some of the stories and motives, some of the economic, moral, and philosophical accounts, the tidbits and trivial events of America's Civil War.

History is today's news wound out over an extended period of time, but what you are about to read is *not* the illustrated news of television. There are very few pictures. These essays fall in no particular order, so you may end up skipping around.

You may find some of what follows amusing. Some may border on the gruesome; some of it may sound irreverent. It may leave you with questions. That is good; find your own answers. This book only scratches the surface.

You know who won the shooting war. Or at least you think you know, but read on. These are the emotions, the passions, the stories of America's Civil War.

INTRODUCTION

For four long years, America's Civil War raged on. More than six hundred thousand soldiers, sailors, nurses, and doctors were killed, North and South. Gettysburg, Shiloh, Antietam, Chickamauga. Place names that became as familiar as that of our own hometowns. Abraham Lincoln, Robert E. Lee, Ulysses S. Grant, "Stonewall" Jackson. Heroes spoken of by everyone from New York to New Orleans, from Chicago to Charleston.

These places and individuals are written about in the bold strokes of history. We seldom hear about Pauline Cushman or Harry Buford. David Van Buskirk and John Beauchamp Jones rarely show up in History 101 lectures. Seldom are we taught about the Crater at Petersburg, Virginia, or the raid on St. Albans, Vermont. Often as not these names—human and geographic—are ignored by all but the most dedicated Civil War buff.

We need a few numbers to put the war in perspective, and right here we get into trouble. We don't know how many served in America's Civil War, but one figure often used places the total at about 3,713,000. Others disagree, especially on the number of Confederate troops. Some estimates place the number who fought for the South as low as 600,000: others as high as 1,400,000. A middle-ground figure of 900,000 may be about right. One historian takes "the number of surviving veterans of the Union and Confederated armies counted by the census of 1890," notes that Confederate veterans "totaled 42 percent of the number of Union Veterans" and comes up with a figure of 882,000 Rebels who served, basing this on a total of 2,100,000 Union soldiers. Since the ratio of Confederates slain was higher than Union killed, we'll nudge the total Confederate figure a bit higher.

We can adjust downward the number of Union troops, since the North counted the number of enlistments, not the number of men. Some men served their enlistment, then re-upped, as the modern saying goes, enlisting again. This leaves us with the actual number of those who served the Union at fewer than 2,100,000. This downward adjustment shouldn't be made for African-Americans, since they weren't allowed to enlist prior to late 1862 and their three-year enlistments didn't have time to run out.[1]

Since we don't know how many fought, we don't know exactly how many died. We do know the war was devastating, its numbers mind boggling even compared to the other wars we fought. It was a most *un*civil civil war.

• America's Civil War lasted almost exactly four years, and almost one third of those who served died. The death rate in America's Civil War was ten times higher than our second most deadly war. At least 600,000 American troops (360,710 Federal and 258,000 Rebel) were killed, a 13.4 percent mortality rate.

• The Vietnam War lasted eight and a half years and counted at least 58,152 deaths.

• The Korean War ran for just over three years, from June 25, 1950, to July 27, 1953; 33,651 died.

• In the three and a half years of America's involvement in World War II, more than 405,399 were killed.

• World War I was responsible for about 116,516 American deaths.

• And the six years and six months of fighting during the American Revolution tallied about 4,435.[2]

Other wars accounted for 15,506 deaths. The point of this is not to wow you with figures but to show one thing: The Civil War took almost as many American lives as all of the other wars we've ever fought. Combined.

America's Civil War ended more than 130 years ago, yet it remains one of the most talked about, most written about, certainly the most sung about, war of all times. Generation after generation of would-be historians scribble, gush, and pour out torrents of words telling stories about the years of conflict and the decades preceding and following the actual fighting. Historian David Donald claims, "There must be more historians of the Civil War than there were generals fighting it." He adds that "of the two groups, the historians are the more belligerent."

Nothing, with the possible exception of religion, causes more arguments, evokes greater emotion, than does America's Civil War. Even calling it that—the *Civil War*—can cause trouble. One of my sons shudders each time he hears me refer to it as the "Civil War." "Pop," he says, "it's 'America's War'; won't you ever get it right?" Well, I probably won't. I recognize the various terms used about the war and count more than two dozen names given the four-year conflict:

The War for Constitutional Liberty, the War for Nationality, the War for Southern Nationality, the War for Southern Independence, the Second American Revolution, the War for States' Rights, Mr. Lincoln's War, the War Against Slavery, the War for Abolition, the Southern Rebellion, the War of the Rebellion, the War for Southern Rights, the War of the Southern Planters, the Civil War, America's Civil War, the War Between the States, the Civil War Between the States, the War Against Northern Aggression, the Yankee Invasion, the War for Separation, the War for the Union, the Confederate War, the War of the Southrons, the War for Southern Freedom, the War of the North and South, and the Lost Cause.[3]

Often, half jokingly, it's called "The Late Unpleasantness." There never was an official name for those years of conflict; I was reared by a grandmother to whom the fighting occurring between the years 1861 and 1865 was *The War,* despite the two world wars that came later. I generally refer to it as the "Civil War" or "America's Civil War" simply because they're easiest to say or write.

The two sides themselves couldn't even agree on what to call the many battles. Generally, the North named the battles after a nearby body of water, if such existed. Therefore, up North it was the Battle of Bull Run, while down South it was Manassas. The Union named it Antietam after the creek, while the Confederacy called it Sharpsburg after the town. Federal troops fought the Battle of Stones River, while the Rebels in the same combat were at the Battle of Murfreesboro. They fought to a draw at Fair Oaks (U.S.A.) or Seven Pines (C.S.A.).

While Confederate armies were named for states, the Union

called its armies after the streams and rivers. The Confederate Army of Northern Virginia fought the Union's Army of the Potomac. Sometimes it sounded as if they fought each other. The Rebel Army of Tennessee did battle with the Yankee Army of *the* Tennessee. All very confusing.

I sometimes refer to Confederate troops as "Rebels," knowing Jefferson Davis himself said it was a revolution, not a rebellion; the *Richmond Daily Dispatch* apparently disagreed and, on May 12, 1862, carried the following poem: "They call us Rebels, if you will,/ We glory in the name,/ For bending under unjust cause,/ We count as greater shame."

I often call Union troops "Yankees," knowing to some it's a derogatory word. The word, however, goes back at least to 1638, but no one has yet determined just where *yankee* originated. It may have been taken from a Dutch association whose members were known as Yankeys. It may have begun when someone stumbled over the French word for English, "Anglais." In the Revolution it meant Americans. In America's Civil War it meant those who fought for or who sympathized with the North. So there.

It doesn't take much to cause a rumpus when you talk about the war or any of its events. In researching these essays, I telephoned the librarian at the Norfolk Navy Yard Museum in Portsmouth, Virginia; it was in Portsmouth that the first ironclad was built. Without thinking, I asked if the library had any artifacts from the battle between the "*Monitor* and *Merrimack.*" "Wash your mouth out with soap," I was admonished by the librarian. "It was the *Virginia*, not the *Merrimack*," I was reminded. Pardon, ma'am, you're absolutely right. The *Merrimack* was a Union vessel; the *Virginia* was Confederate. I just forgot myself there for a moment.

Nearly everybody is an "expert" on the Civil War. Waiting for the start of the filmed version of Michael Shaara's *The Killer Angels,* titled *Gettysburg* in an oversimplification of life, I warned my wife there undoubtedly would be a lot of talk during the show—audience talk, that is. I was correct; whenever something happened on the screen with which some self-proclaimed expert in the audience—almost invariably one of the male persuasion—disagreed, we'd hear a loud, vocal objection. Be it to dialogue, makeup, uniform, how many men, how few, who did what to whom, where, and how often, someone spoke out. And this was in Chicago. I could only imagine the backtalk during the showing of the film in, say, Richmond or Atlanta. There had to have been times when the audience couldn't hear the soundtrack for its own clamor.

Most of us love trivia, even the bit of trivia about the word itself. It comes from two Latin words, *tri* (meaning "three") and *via* (meaning "road"). Seems that whenever the Roman army came to a point where three roads met, they'd place a post at the junction. And then nail small (trivial) notes to the post, events at home, trivial dispatches to friends and loved ones, asking about someone or telling about other events.

Little things such as this make life breathe. Example: The great impact the war had on shoes; more shoes had to be mass-produced rather than handmade, and more sizes had to be offered. Example: The war changed men's hair tyles; sideburns came into widespread favor, taking their name from Union general Ambrose Burnside's rather long locks. Example: Hardships caused by the war changed the way flour was sold; instead of buying it by the barrel, for the first time homemakers could buy it in five-pound bags.

The war sometimes greatly changed great men. As the war progressed, Confederate Gen. Pierre Gustave Toutant Beauregard's hair turned more and more gray. Perhaps not unexpected, you might think, due to the fighting and all. But some so-called experts claim the black-to-gray change came because the Yankee blockade of Southern ports prevented Beauregard from receiving his regular supply of hair dye.

Your teacher didn't tell you that, and it's certainly something to fight about.

CHAPTER ONE

Fort Sumter: The First Shot

I shall await the first shot, and if you do not batter us to pieces, we shall be starved out in a few days.

—Maj. Robert Anderson, U.S.A.
April 11, 1861[1]

They were the gangs that couldn't shoot straight, both the Union and Confederate armies. We should be glad they couldn't; they did enough damage as it was. Imagine how bloody it would have been if they *could* have shot straight.

In 1862, George McClellan and the Union Army of the Potomac slogged their way up the rain-clogged Virginia peninsula, chasing a Confederate army slowly retreating toward Richmond. A regiment from Mississippi stumbled onto a unit from Georgia, each side thinking the other was the enemy. They opened fire—Mississippi Rebels blasting away at Georgia Confederates. Since neither group could shoot straight, the only casualty was a horse.

Ulysses S. Grant once complained that his Northern troops were so green, so poorly trained, most of them couldn't load their muskets. Many who did know how to load them didn't know how to shoot them. Or maybe they tried to fire them but either the poorly made muskets didn't work or the powder wouldn't fire. Maybe the soldiers just thought they fired their rifles, but the battle raged around them so loudly they couldn't hear whether they did or not. In any case, a lot of times, nothing happened. This worried the Union army brass, so after the three-day Battle of Gettysburg, they checked weapons left on the field. They found at least thirty-seven thousand discarded rifles. Sometimes the troops ran off without firing their rifles; sometimes their muskets misfired. Twenty-four thousand weapons were still loaded. Many of the weapons left behind—eighteen thousand—were loaded with not one, but at least two minié balls. Six thousand had a lot more, as many as ten unfired cartridges rammed down their barrels. The others were improperly loaded, sometimes backward, the lead bullet facing the rear of the weapon. If loaded backward, or loaded with more than one cartridge, the rifle would not fire. One poor soldier had managed to stuff nearly two dozen minié balls down his rifle, and then probably wondered why it didn't fire. He was lucky the damn thing didn't blow up in his face.

Troops on both sides were not only poorly trained; in the case of the South, they usually were poorly armed. The tactics they used were left over from the Napoleonic wars, but the weapons weren't. Whether it was Johnny Reb or Billy Yank, the technique was the same: march side by side, row after pitiful row, until you were about seventy-five to one hundred yards from the enemy. Then you'd fire point-blank at the other side.

Modern rifles often are automatic weapons, firing multiples of small-caliber projectiles. In the Civil War, soldiers faced hordes of weapons that resembled high-caliber, low-velocity shotguns whose bullets often broke bones rather than simply going in and out of the unlucky victim's body. This was a primary reason for so many amputations during the war, and a primary reason for so many one-legged, one-armed veterans in the years that followed. The mangled and maimed individuals seen at reunions or limping down Main Streets North and South were the ones who, against all odds, managed to survive.

Most of these shotgunlike weapons were muzzle loaders, which was a reason Civil War soldiers often looked so dirty. Loading their weapons called for troops to bite off one end of a paper cartridge packed with powder and ball, then ram the cartridge down the rifle barrel. When they bit off the end of the cartridge, some of the black powder plastered itself over their faces. The dirtier a soldier's face, maybe, the more rounds he fired off.

Often, Southern troops forgot to bite the end off the cartridge, which meant they couldn't fire their weapons. Why this was a problem for Southern troops, we don't know, especially since the Rebels generally were more accustomed to firearms.

Maybe it was the excitement of war or fear at "seeing the elephant," a phrase used to mean "seeing combat for the first time." The phrase has a legend all its own. Since most people of the mid-nineteenth century had never seen such an animal, to "see the elephant" originally meant to see something unusual or large. Most of the men and women who fought during the Civil War had never been in battle, had never witnessed anything so large, had never seen an elephant. They put the words and meaning together.

A second version of the phrase says it goes back to 217 B.C., during the Second Punic War, when Hannibal of Carthage invaded Italy by crossing the Alps. Hannibal used elephants the way modern armies use tanks and, in the battle, beat a vastly superior Roman army with this new invention. For most of the Roman troops, it was the first time they had "seen the elephant."

Weapons in hand, soldiers on both sides of America's Civil War frequently aimed (if you can call it that) at a 45-degree angle, meaning that even if their weapons *did* fire, they probably missed the enemy. Twentieth-century Civil War reenactors often do the same thing, and initially it appears ludicrous—mock soldiers firing into the air. While it looks ridiculous, and we're not sure the reenactors are aware how correct they are, what they're doing today apparently is what their ancestors did more than a hundred years ago. Occasionally, art really does imitate life, and it all works out for the best.

Neither side had enough weapons to go around when the shooting match started. When Abraham Lincoln called for volunteers to put down the rebellion, many of the weapons the Union had on hand were the old "Brown Bess" variety, not much different from the type used by both sides in the American Revolution. Of the estimated 275,000 weapons the Union army owned at the start of the war, only about 22,000 were rifles, the rest were smoothbore muskets.

Almost half—47 percent—of Union soldiers were farmers or farm workers. Sixty-one percent of Confederate soldiers were farmers or planters and, therefore, more likely to be familiar with rifles and shotguns. This may account for the South's initial success in the war.

For troops on both sides, being away from home was a new experience. America's Civil War was a great and grand adventure for the three million–plus men and women who took part in it.

War trains soldiers for other wars, and sometimes that's the main reason they're fought. The Black Hawk War, the Seminole Wars, and the Mexican War all were training grounds for America's Civil War. All saw men fight side by side with future enemies.

By the 1830s, almost all American Indians, including the so-called five "civilized nations"—Cherokee, Choctaw, Creek, Chickasaw, and Seminole—had been forcibly removed from the eastern part of the United States, approximately eighty-five thousand in all. Black Hawk, chief of the Sauk and Fox, tried to retain his ancestral tribal seat at the mouth of the Rock River in Illinois, near what would later be one of the worst Civil War prisons on either side, Rock Island, in the northwest corner of the state.

In 1832, a regular army officer just seven years out of the U.S. Military Academy at West Point signed up a lanky young lawyer from Illinois to command a militia unit in the Black Hawk War. Abraham Lincoln was in Springfield, Illinois, when he heard the call to arms. He borrowed a friend's horse and went off to war. He more or less went off to war. Lincoln's militia unit elected him captain, an event that apparently surprised him. They marched off, slogged through the rain, then—like soldiers before and since—they waited around. Finally, Lincoln's militia unit was put under a regular army regiment headed by Capt. Zachary Taylor. They marched again and stole anything they could find near to hand—food, clothing, you name it. Lincoln's men once got hold of some whiskey and went on a rampage. As their officer, Lincoln was in charge, so to punish him, he was made to walk around all day carrying a wooden sword for all to see.

Apparently, Lincoln never saw combat. In the meantime, Chief Black Hawk was chased into Wisconsin and captured by someone else.

The regular army officer who recruited Lincoln was Robert Anderson. Their paths crossed again nearly three decades later when Lincoln lived in the White House in Washington and Maj. Robert Anderson commanded the Federal garrison at Fort Sumter, South Carolina. One was killed by a single bullet to the head; the other survived unscratched despite four years of combat and hundreds of rounds of artillery fire aimed his way.

The calendar turned from 1859 to 1860; then came 1861 and the heady atmosphere of the times captured Americans North and South, young and old. War fueled a nation's fever with impassioned oratory, heart-moving songs, and choking clouds of dust rising from the feet of what, in a later age, we would call America's best and brightest, all marching off to slay a nineteenth-century dragon.

Patriotic fever ran so high, the desire to display the flag so strong, cloth manufacturers couldn't weave enough red, white, and blue bunting to make flags. It was especially scarce, since flags of both North and South shared those colors, just as the people the banners represented shared much else in life and death.

Now came war. Old men railed and told stories of their own fighting days. Young men cheered, eyes gleaming with promises that their war would be even more glorious, more glamorous. Women sang songs, raised money, sewed flags, and rolled bandages; in some cases, they told their men to go to war or they no longer would be their men. Some women decided not to wait for *their* men. They went off to war on their own.

America's Civil War was a conflict unlike anything this nation had ever seen. After it was over, people hoped they'd never see anything like it again. It had more troops, fighting with more different kinds of weapons, killing more efficiently than any other American war ever had, to that time.

On one side stood the United States of America, a government less than a hundred years old. On the other struggled the government known as the Confederate States of America. There never officially was a nation called the "Confederate States of America." Those states seceding to form a new government never got around to officially approving that or any other name for itself; the name was just there, accepted by all, officially approved by none, a simple change in wording, taken from the name of the nation from which the Southerners were trying to divorce themselves. The older nation, of course, was a *union,* the younger one a *confederacy,* with the emphasis on greater states' rights and little central control. In the end, that difference proved to be one of the deciding factors in the coming conflict.

The Confederate Constitution also was much like that of its predecessor, but again it stressed states' rights. The Southern government had its seat first in Montgomery, Alabama, and then in Richmond, Virginia. Wherever the southern capital was, it had little real power, leaving to each state the responsibility to enact its own laws, even to print its own money, though one state's currency usually was honored by the others. The chief job of the Confederate government was to wage war.

The rebelling states were busy fighting, and even though their constitution called for one, they never got around to forming a supreme court. What legal action needed tending to, they tended to at a lower judicial level. A large portion of military officers in the Civil War had been peacetime lawyers. With so many attorneys in combat of a different nature, there was less need for them to wage legal battles. Apparently, no one ever missed the Confederacy's nonexistent supreme court.

Only 80 percent of the South's white population was literate, while 95 percent of New England's white adult population could read and write. In Richmond, the Confederacy's capital city, there were no public schools in the modern sense; its white students were sent to other cities, even to other countries. As in many other Southern cities, Richmond's black residents largely remained illiterate; in Virginia, it was illegal to teach them to read or write.

With war threatening to break out at any time, the regular army of the United States had about 16,000 men under arms. If prewar estimates are correct, more than 13,500 of them were stationed in forts locked within the newborn Confederacy. One such fort was on an island off Charleston, South Carolina.

Many Southerners, then and now, blame Abe Lincoln for starting the war. As with every other president before and after him, Lincoln inherited mistakes made by others before him. When his predecessor gave up the White House, he left things in such a pickle that war may well have been inevitable. James Buchanan, the nation's fif-

teenth president, tried to maintain a balance between slave states and
free. He favored individual sovereignty; that is, letting each state decide the issue for itself without the Federal government forcing any
area to outlaw slavery. While Buchanan was president, slaves were legal even in Washington, D.C. When it became obvious that war was
coming, Buchanan left the U.S. Army's garrison at Fort Sumter hanging out to dry, so to speak. He left it up to Lincoln to decide whether
to remove the Federal troops and give Fort Sumter to the Rebels; he
left it up to Lincoln to decide whether his troops would starve to
death on the island fort, would defend themselves and the fort, or
just what. Buchanan wasn't certain what to do, so he did nothing.

The Confederacy wanted Fort Sumter for its own; they certainly
didn't want a Union thorn wedged in their Southern backsides, but
the South didn't have a navy strong enough to take the fort. So the
army sent Gen. Pierre Gustave Toutant Beauregard to surround the
island from mainland posts, putting him in charge of the artillery
troops. On the other side, in the middle of Charleston's harbor, sat
his old artillery teacher from West Point, Union Maj. Robert Anderson, the same Robert Anderson who had enlisted young Abraham
Lincoln during the Black Hawk War.

Beauregard sent Anderson a note demanding the Union evacuate the fort. Anderson's reply was a wordy refusal, one typical of the
military and typical of the period.

> *I have the honor to acknowledge the receipt of your communication
> demanding the evacuation of this fort, and to say, in reply thereto,
> that it is a demand with which I regret that my sense of honor and
> of my obligation to my Government, prevent my compliance. Thank-
> ing you for the fair, manly, and courteous terms proposed, and for
> the high compliment paid me, I am, general, very respectfully, your
> obedient servant, Robert Anderson.*

This, of course, boiled down to Anderson saying "Thanks, but no
thanks, Beau." While the two sides waited for the two governments
to make up their minds, Beauregard acted on his own. Southern gentleman that he was, Beauregard sent Anderson and his men cigars
and wine to keep them occupied while their superiors decided on
the next step. Meanwhile, two military forces stared at each other
across the water of Charleston harbor.

Abraham Lincoln may have started the war in a philosophical sense, but it was a civilian who actually fired the first shot on Fort Sumter. Beauregard offered the honor to his aide, Roger Pryor, an ardent secessionist from Virginia who had resigned from the U.S. Congress the previous month to enter the Rebel army.

Pryor declined to open the war that April day, but another Virginia civilian gladly performed the job, sixty-seven-year-old Edmund Ruffin. It was 4:30 A.M. on the twelfth of April when the Civil War got under way.

Mary Boykin Chesnut, a confidant of Confederate First Lady Varina Davis's, was in Charleston when the war started.

> *I count four—St. Michael chimes. I begin to hope. At half-past four, the heaving booming of cannon.*
>
> *I sprang from my bed. And on my knees—prostrate—I prayed as never before.*
>
> *There was a sound of stir all over the house—pattering of feet in the corridor—all seemed hurrying one way. I put on my double gown and a shawl and went, too. It was to the housetop.*
>
> *The shells were bursting. In the dark I heard a man say "waste of ammunition."* . . .
>
> *The regular roar of the cannon—there it was. And who could tell what each volley accomplished of death and destruction. The women were wild, there on the housetop. Prayers from the women and imprecations from the men, and then a shell would light up the scene. . . .*[2]

Fort Sumter was built to defend Charleston, not to bombard it, so all of its 140 guns originally faced out to sea. Anderson turned forty-eight of them around and fought back. The opening round of America's Civil War was like one big fraternity party gone berserk. Each time the Union batteries got off a shot, the Confederates on the shore let out a cheer.

Union Gen. Abner Doubleday was among the military personnel on the island. Someone—it wasn't Doubleday—later claimed the general invented the game of baseball, but baseball wasn't on Doubleday's mind that day in April. He was busy firing the first shot from the Union side. Neither he nor any of the other Federal troops on the island were hurt during the bombardment. Neither were any of the attackers on land.

There were 130 men on the island at the time, including forty-three noncombatant workmen doing repair work on the fort. They also weren't harmed.

On the second day of the bombardment, the Rebels loaded heated shells into their cannon to set fire to the fort, and that took effect. Still no injuries to men on either side.

Finally, after thirty-four hours of bombardment, after more than four thousand Rebel shells fell onto Fort Sumter, and with the fort crumbling around him, Anderson surrendered. He asked Beauregard to be allowed to fire a ceremonial salute while Union troops lowered the American flag. Beauregard agreed, and at noon, Sunday, April 14, Federal troops began evacuating Fort Sumter. The Union flag was lowered; troops began a 100-gun salute, but on the 50th round, there was an accident. A Union soldier was killed, the only death during the firing on and capture of Fort Sumter.

That ended the ceremonial salute. Large crowds lined Charleston's Battery, as the waterside area is still known, watching the Federals leave Fort Sumter on boats taking them north.

Of the ten Union officers at Fort Sumter, six went on to become major generals in the Federal army. Three others resigned after the surrender, and one of those three joined the Confederacy, later dying in battle.

The day after Anderson surrendered Fort Sumter, Abraham Lincoln called for 75,000 volunteers to serve for three months to put down the insurrection.

One who already was in the Union army, but who was ambivalent about going or staying, was a West Point graduate and career army officer named Robert E. Lee. Lieutenant Colonel Lee was a man of deep integrity, a man whose ancestors helped found the United States. He was born, it was said, in the same room as two signers of the Declaration of Independence, his uncles Richard Henry Lee and Francis Lightfoot Lee. He opposed both slavery and secession. In January, months before the firing on Fort Sumter, Lee wrote to his son Custis.

Secession is nothing but revolution. The framers of our Constitution [would] never [have] exhausted so much labor, wisdom and forbearance in its formation, and surrounded it with so many guards and securities, if it was intended to be broken by every member of the

Confederacy at will. It was intended for "perpetual union," so expressed in the preamble, and for the establishment of government, not a compact, which can only be dissolved by revolution or the consent of all the people in convention assembled. It is idle to talk of secession.

He added, "If Virginia stands by the old Union, so will I. But if she secedes . . . then I will follow my native state with my sword, and if need be with my life."

In March, the War Department ordered Lee to report for duty in Washington City, as the nation's capital generally was called at the time. He was promoted to full colonel. At about the same time, the Confederacy offered him the rank of major general, an offer he ignored. He wanted to see what his home state of Virginia would do.

Three days after the fall of Fort Sumter, Virginia voted to secede. The following day, on behalf of President Abraham Lincoln, Francis Blair offered Lee the command of all Union forces. Lee did not immediately tell Blair whether he would accept or reject the offer. Instead, he took the time while riding back to Arlington, his home across the Potomac River, to think about the offer. There, sitting in an upstairs room, Robert E. Lee wrote the words he undoubtedly had hoped he would never have to; he resigned his U.S Army commission, later saying, "I could take no part in an invasion of the Southern states."

He told his wife, Mary, of his decision and wrote his older sister, Anne Lee Marshall. "Now we are in a state of war," he recorded, "which will yield to nothing." He told Anne he opposed the coming war, the revolution: "With all my devotion to the Union, and the feeling of loyalty and duty of an American citizen, I have not been able to make up my mind to raise my hand against my relatives, my children, my home."

He knew Anne would disapprove of his resignation, so he reminded her he loved her very much, adding, "I am now a private citizen and have no [other] ambition than to remain at home."

He didn't remain a private citizen for long, finally bowing to pleas that he join the Virginia militia. The Union almost immediately confiscated Arlington, the home Robert E. Lee and his family loved so much. His wife, Mary Anne Randolph Custis Lee, although crippled by arthritis, at first refused to leave, remaining there two weeks after the Federal government occupied Arlington.

The Lees and Abraham Lincoln had a mutual friend, Union Gen. Winfield Scott. Scott was Lincoln's military mentor and, according to the president, taught Lincoln much of what he learned about warfare.

Mary Lee told Scott, that, if it were not for the worry that her remaining at Arlington would cause her husband, she *would* stay there no matter what. But leave she finally did, regretfully abandoning generations of memorabilia from the Lee family as well as from Mary's family, the Custises, even items once owned by George Washington, since Mrs. Lee was Mrs. Washington's great-granddaughter. Occupying Federal troops stole most of what was there. The Lees never again saw their furnishings or lived in their home.

In the coming war, the Federal government turned the grounds into the nation's most famous graveyard, Arlington National Cemetery, knowing that the remains of so many lying so close by would prevent Robert E. Lee or anyone else from ever again residing in the mansion. Years later, long after Lee had passed on, his heirs finally were compensated for the government's seizure of Arlington. They were paid $150,000.

After the war Robert E. Lee became president of Washington College, as it was called then, in Lexington, Virginia. The school quickly became known as "General Lee's College." It's now Washington and Lee University, but still is "General Lee's College" at heart.

The man who led the Confederacy's Army of Northern Virginia through four long years died on October 12, 1870. It was just two days after the area had been hit by heavy rains and flooding. A small town, Lexington had only one funeral home, and the rains washed away all of the undertaker's coffins. It would take too long to have another shipped to Lexington, so members of the community spread out around the county, hoping to find one of the three that had been lost in the flood. Finally, they located one coffin several miles away, lodged on a downstream island. It was short, however, too short for Lee's near six-foot height, so they buried him without his shoes.

Robert E. Lee's worst defeats came in battles begun when he went looking for shoes for his nearly barefoot army. In death, he joined the many who had been barefoot at Antietam and Gettysburg.

It was not at his family home that Robert E. Lee was buried, not in Arlington National Cemetery. Rather, he was laid to rest beneath the chapel at Washington College. A recumbent statue of the general lies in the apse of the chapel, and Lee is buried in an underground vault. Beside him in the vault are the remains of several family members—wife, sons, and daughters.

The marble statue is separated from the chapel nave by steel gates, usually an open background to all services. Sometimes, in early June, when Washington and Lee University graduates celebrate the end of the school year with summertime marriages, they choose to leave the gates open and have General Robert E. Lee as a silent but ever present witness. At other times, a hushed silence surrounds the remains of the man who loved both state and nation and was caught between the two.

Outside the chapel there's another grave, with a plain granite slab often festooned by small Confederate flags. Beneath that granite slab lie the remains of Traveller, Lee's favorite horse.

Traveller was the horse's most famous name, but he had many others. Originally he was named "Jeff Davis," then "Greenbrier"; finally he was known as "Traveller." The big gray horse obviously was the general's favorite, but Lee had others during the war. One was named "Richmond," a bay stallion presented to the leader of the Army of Northern Virginia by the general's admirers. "Richmond," however, gave Lee a lot of trouble and could never be ridden near other horses he didn't know.

For several years after General Lee's death, Traveller had the freedom of Washington College, walking and running about the grounds at will, cared for by all. Now his grave is visited almost as often as his owner's.

Roger Pryor, the man who declined to fire the first shot of the war, went on to lead the 3rd Virginia Infantry at the Battle of Williamsburg, at Second Manassas, and at Antietam—or Sharpsburg, its name depending on which side you fought on or believed in. In a not uncommon occurance, he resigned his commission on August 18, 1863, because he had no brigade to command; he enlisted as a private in the cavalry under Fitzhugh Lee. The Union captured Pryor in late 1864 while he served as a special courier during an informal truce. Lincoln personally ordered him exchanged shortly before Lee's surrender at Appomattox. After the war Pryor went to New York, where he became a newspaper writer and lawyer. In yet another change of careers, he was appointed a lower court judge, then an associate justice of the New York Supreme Court.

As for Edmund Ruffin, who actually fired the first shot at Fort Sumter—he committed suicide in June of 1865. He left a note saying he was "unwilling to live under the U.S. government."

Robert Anderson, who defended Fort Sumter that fateful time in April 1861, was promoted to general. He was taken ill, however, and performed only limited service. He was back in uniform on Good Friday, April 14, 1865, about the same time President Lincoln was assassinated. It was four years to the day from when Major Anderson hauled down the American flag over a defeated Fort Sumter. This time General Anderson raised the Union flag over a recaptured fort, the same flag he had lowered when the war started in 1861.

And the Black Hawk War of 1832? Abraham Lincoln (he hated the nickname Abe, and even his wife called him "Father" or "Mr. Lincoln") never did get into action, but another young man did, Lt. Jefferson Davis, West Point class of 1828. In fact, young Jeff Davis captured Chief Black Hawk and took him to Washington to visit "The Great White Father," President Andrew Jackson. Didn't do Black Hawk any good, however; he lost his tribal lands despite pleas from Davis.

Davis was fairly well connected, and it was easy for him to plead for Chief Black Hawk. He graduated twenty-third out of thirty-three in his West Point class, and seven years later he eloped with his boss's daughter, Sarah Knox Taylor, the third daughter of Zachary Taylor. It was General Taylor who would lead the troops at Mexico City and later become the twelfth president of the United States. Zachary was the father of Richard Taylor, who, as a general in the Confederate army, served under his former brother-in-law, Confederate President Jefferson Davis.

This interrelationship was what is known down South as one's "family connections." The mid-1800s were a time when one's family connections or one's people (past generations) meant a lot, perhaps too much, to polite society. Even into the mid-twentieth century, Southern mothers often questioned their daughters as the younger generation prepared for a Saturday night date (movie, followed by hamburger, fries, and a Co-Cola, that beverage known more formally as Coca-Cola or simply Coke, to Yankees). "Who are his people?" Mama would ask. Even a hundred years after the war, the answer might determine whether the young man got to call on the young lady.

First South Carolina seceded from the Union on December 20, 1860, then Mississippi on January 9, 1861. Florida followed on the tenth, Alabama on the eleventh, and Georgia on January 19; Louisiana left on the twenty-sixth. On February 1 Texas voted to leave the Union. Then came Fort Sumter on April 14, 1861. Virginia seceded from the Union on April 17; Arkansas left on May 6, followed by North Carolina on May 20 and Tennessee on June 8.

The Confederacy had only one president, but he was inaugurated twice, once for each of its capitals. On February 18, 1861, on a platform in front of the Alabama state capital in Montgomery, Jefferson Davis was inaugurated as provisional president of the Confederacy. There was little doubt the new nation's capital would be moved to Richmond, and on February 22, 1862, while standing under the statue of George Washington on the grounds of Virginia's capital in Richmond, Jefferson Davis did it again, formally took the oath of office as president of the permanent Confederate government. It was George Washington's birthday, and the Confederacy hoped to tie the new nation to the first president of the old.

On Friday, April 25, 1861, the Richmond *Examiner* had carried the following article:

By the Grace of God, the work is done. Virginia is this day a State of the Southern Confederacy. Jefferson Davis is the President of this country—not Abraham Lincoln. Allegiance is due to the South, and not to the North. The path of duty and of feeling are now the same for all. "Our glorious Union" had a meaning to which we may all give the same signification.

Our brave troops have won a commander who knows what to do with them. The best military talent that the American continent af-

fords will take charge of their conduct. They will be soon parts of a complete organization, and be put to work worthy of their spirit and their intelligence.

The sister States of the Frontier must speedily follow the example of Virginia. The bubble of a Border State Conference is broken forever. Virginia stands in the center of the magic circle of the seven stars.

The "seven stars" was a reference to the First Confederate flag, the true "Stars and Bars." It consisted of three horizontal stripes—red, white, red—with seven white stars (one for each of the first seven states to secede from the Union) in a field of blue in the canton, the upper lanyard-side corner. Later, the number of stars changed to thirteen even though only eleven states seceded; the extra two stars represented Kentucky and Missouri, which, since they remained in the Union, also were represented by stars in the Union flag. Since the Union never officially recognized the secession, the eleven who seceded also remained represented in the Federal flag.

What some call the Stars and Bars is, in reality, the square Confederate Army battle flag. A three-foot by five-foot version was flown by Rebel ships. The battle flag was, in part, designed by General Beauregard. The second Confederate flag (also known as the Stainless Banner) consisted of an all-white banner with the square battle flag in the canton. In the closing days of the war, some believed this flag might be mistaken for a flag of truce, so a wide red top-to-bottom stripe was place opposite the canton. Yet another flag, the Bonnie Blue flag—a field of blue with a single white star in the middle—never became official even though it inspired a famous song.

Needless to say, there was much confusion over Confederate flags, with some units flying several different generations of the banner at the same time along with other emblems they devised themselves. It was the original Stars and Bars to which the *Examiner* referred.

A splendid train of kindred States will follow her to the Capital of a heroic Republic.

From the corrupting corpse of that Union of sin which lies on the ground arises the transfigured soul of its first life. The universe pursues the round of birth and death, and the artificial existences known as nations share the law of all other things.

Then, in a statement generally disregarded, the *Examiner*'s editor made clear where the capital of the new nation should be, and it wasn't Richmond.

> *It is desirable that Washington should be the capital of the Southern Confederacy. For such a measure there are very many good reasons. With that city as our capital, we should be looked upon by foreign nations as the victorious party—the real United States. Its public buildings and other public improvements have cost hundreds of millions, and several of them are equal to any in Europe. The Southern Confederacy would save much in convenience and money by adopting it as our capital. Not to do so, would be to sacrifice many hundred millions of private property, for real estate in Washington would be valueless were the capital removed. On the other hand, if it be made the seat of the Confederate Government, real estate would command higher prices than ever before, because mankind will feel confidence in the permanency of a Government, among whose people there will be no elements of discord. . . .*

> *No state probably will care to have the capital within its territory for fear that Federal mercenaries might be introduced into it to over-awe and oppress the people of the State. . . .*

> *The people of Washington are generally Virginians or Marylanders by birth or descent. Their manners, customs, feelings and attachments are naturally Southern, but have for a time seemingly diverted to the North, because their all was at stake, and they believed that that all could only be saved either by adhering to the North or becoming the capital of a Border Confederacy. . . .*

On May 20, 1861, the capital of the Confederacy was moved to Richmond. The Southern Confederacy never took Washington to use as a capital. Instead of Rebel troops in Washington, in less than four years, Federal troops marched into Richmond.

CHAPTER TWO

Sambo and Cuffee:
That "Peculiar Institution"

Slavery is a divine institution.
So is hell!

—Recorded by Ralph Waldo Emerson
October 1862

A lot of niggers in slavery time worked so hard, they said they hated to see the sun rise in the morning. Slavery was a bad thing, 'cause some white folks didn't treat their niggers right.

—Ria Sorrell, former slave [1]

The Civil War came as no surprise. Many believed war between the North and the South was unavoidable. It was as if the United States of America really was two nations; what, in today's psychological terms, might be called a bipolar nation. Six years to the day before the firing on Fort Sumter, the New York *Tribune* wrote, "We are two people. We are a people of freedom and a people of slavery. Between the two, conflict is inevitable."

The twenty-three states of the North counted some twenty-two million people. The South had a few more than nine million, and about three and a half million of those were black slaves. When the war started it is estimated that the South had just over one million white males between the ages of fifteen and forty, compared to the North's four million males eligible for military duty.

Slavery in America began in such a small, almost benign way, and developed into a major cancer on the nation's soul.[2] In August 1619, a ship captained by a Dutchman named Jope landed at Point Comfort, Virginia, downriver from England's twelve-year-old colony at Jamestown. Captain Jope carried twenty- or so blacks, and he sold them to the governor, Sir George Yeardley, and "cape merchant" Abraham Piersey. They paid the captain in food and water, provisions for his return trip to Holland.

Those first blacks arrived only a few days after the burgesses met at Jamestown, the first meeting of the first representative assembly in America. Strange that something so stamped with tyranny could begin at the same time as something so much a part of freedom.

Tradition, but not proof, says this first group of blacks were indentured servants, not slaves for life. That is, they were bought for a period of time (usually four to seven years or till the age of twenty-one), after which they would be freed. Like much else about blacks in America during the first quarter of the seventeenth century, this is uncertain, but may be an indication they were not perceived as essentially different from others brought to this country. It's also believed these first African-Americans not only were indentured servants, but like other such individuals they later were freed.

Selling an individual to pay for his or her transportation was not unusual. In that same year of 1619, a boatload of women were transported to the predominately all-male colony at Jamestown. In much the same way as indentured servants, these women were auctioned off to pay for their passage to Virginia.

Until 1624, when the Virginia Company of London lost its charter to the crown, most of the English colonists in the New World were indentured servants. Each colonist signed a voluntary contract with the company, stipulating that, in return for passage to Virginia, food, and clothing, he would serve the company as a colonist for an agreed-upon time. It was a voluntary contract. The company, in turn, sold the indenture contract to planters who agreed to feed, clothe, and house the servant. At the end of the agreed-upon time limit, the planter would provide the indentured individual with seed, tools, and whatever had been written into the individual's contract, and usually a parcel of land. This was the indentured servant's "freedom dues."

In 1638, nineteen years after the first blacks arrived in this country, Jamestown merchant George Menefie (he referred to himself as a lawyer) received a patent for three thousand acres of land for sixty people he had imported; twenty-three of these were described as "Negroes I brought out of England with me." Menefie was a dealer in white indentured servants, and he apparently dealt with the twenty-three blacks the same way he dealt with whites he had "brought out of England." That is, he sold their freedom for the price of bringing them over. Plus profit, of course; after all, he was a lawyer.

On the surface, being an indentured servant didn't seem to be such a bad deal. The individual usually was too poor to pay for transportation to America, much less set up a farm or store, operate a trade, or perform a service. Being an indentured servant was a way to get to the New World and to get started.

A lot depended upon the individual master. Not everyone treated his servants as well as he'd promised. Sometimes the master accused the servant of crimes whose penalty was serving more time. Thus, a seven-year indenture could become eight or nine, even ten years. Sometimes the master didn't give the freed servant everything promised. Sometimes the master would sell the servant to another master. It all depended on the individual, although there were laws on the books to protect servants.

In 1640, a white man was ordered by the Virginia court to "do penance for his offence at James City church in the time of divine service, according to the laws of England in that case provided." Doing penance in church was an old penalty. The crime in this case? The white man got his female black servant pregnant. The woman was whipped, just the way a white woman might have been under similar circumstance. The man, however, wasn't whipped, he just had to tell everybody he was sorry, probably whispering to himself he was sorry he got caught.

In Puritan New England it seems the difference between a servant and a slave was whether the individual was Christian. Since blacks at the time generally were *not* Christian, they fell, rather conveniently for would-be masters, into the slave category. Some Native Americans also were kept as slaves. In 1636 an Indian in Massachusetts was ordered to "bee kept as a slave for life to worke, unles wee see further cause." Some half dozen whites also were ordered "kept as slaves for life" as punishment for various crimes; however, most whites were released after less than a year. The court then said perpetual slavery would be only for "strangers," that is, anyone not of the prevailing religion.

In 1639, Samuel Maverick of Noddles Island caused a stir. As a visitor wrote:

Mr. Maverick was desirous to have a breed of Negroes, and therefore seeing [that his "Negro woman"] would not yield by persuasions to company with a Negro young man he had in his house; he commanded him will'd she nill'd she to go to bed . . . which was no sooner done but she kickt him out again, this she took in high destain beyond her slavery.

Over the next half century, blacks slowly trickled into America, North and South. By the 1640s some blacks in both Virginia and Maryland were serving for life, and some black children inherited their parents' obligation of lifelong slavery. Several blacks were kept as what was termed *perpetual servants* in Providence, Rhode Island. They were seventeenth-century black slaves living in an area which, during the nineteenth century, shouted abhorrence of slavery.

That old story about a Triangle Trade—Africa to the West Indies to New England, slaves traded for molasses turned into rum—essentially was fact. All three points of the triangle were guilty, all grew wealthy by selling and buying blacks.

It may have been economics, not morals, that prevented New England from becoming a major slave-holding area. Generally, New England farmers didn't grow labor-intensive crops. For the most part they were smallholders, working small farms each operated by one family with one or two indentured servants, then later with hired hands. Virginia, on the other hand, had deep tidal rivers, fertile soil, and a long growing season. By the time blacks were first sold into the colony, Virginia was well on its way to becoming an empire founded upon smoke. Tobacco was its chief crop, but it required cheap, ongoing labor. Labor which need not be skilled, simply strong and mobile. As time went on, the status of blacks progressively worsened.

The deterioration of blacks' conditions may have been caused by the Southern climate, as well as the economy. It was too hot and too muggy and fostered too many diseases new to outsiders. In the early years of the Virginia colony, six out of every seven settlers died within months of arrival. It took time, experts declared, for Englishmen and women to become "seasoned" to the New World's climate.

The economic argument has it this way. A planter might buy seven years service from a servant at a cost of £1,000. At the end of the seven years, the planter may have to put out another £1,000 (those freedom dues) to get the freed servant up and running on his own. With the high mortality rate, the planter more often than not never had to provide freedom dues. But once the situation settled down, once servants and everyone else were able to survive longer, more and more planters found themselves paying for the end-of-contract benefits.

Buying a slave-for-life, even if the initial price was higher, would be cheaper. No freedom dues settlement; longer periods of service; and—best of all, planters quickly learned—the new slaves contributed other new slaves without the master having to pay for them. Slaves gave birth to other slaves (sometimes with the master's help), increasing the investment.

By mid-century, living conditions in the Virginia colony were much improved. People could expect to live longer. The system of indentured servants was out; the system of slavery was in.

Slaves were the "strangers," as declared by the Puritans to the north. Somehow or other, Christianity had become linked with race. If they were not Christians when they were brought into America, they were counted as slaves.

Colonists first referred to them as *Negroes*, then, by the nineteenth century, as *blacks*. African-Americans of the late twentieth century would have been called *Africans* in the eighteenth. Their masters were first called *Englishmen*, then *free men*, and finally by that simple term, *white*.

In the mid-eighteenth century, Virginia continued putting a religious touch on its slave laws, but everyone was aware that religion had nothing to do with it. For generations slavery had been based on one thing: race. Masters were white. Slaves were black.

A few blacks were free, but their situation progressively worsened. Until 1691, whites and blacks could and did intermarry, as long as each was free, but in that year the legislature changed the law. Intermarriage between white and nonwhite peoples of Virginia became a crime punishable by banishment. This likely would have shocked many Virginia settlers, including John Rolfe, since he, a white man, married the Indian princess known as Pocahontas. When Rolfe got into trouble for marrying Pocahontas, it wasn't because he was white and she was Indian. It was because she was a princess and Rolfe was a commoner.

In general, Southern states were confused as to what constituted a "person of color." The term used in more polite Southern society many years ago fell into disuse in this country when South Africa used it during apartheid. Now the term is being used by some African-Americans in speaking not only of themselves but of Hispanics, Native Americans, and others.

North Carolina ruled that members of the Melungeon Indian tribe were white, believing them to be descendants of England's sixteenth-century "Lost Colony" of Roanoke Island. Yet, just across the border in Tennessee, those same Melungeon Indians were considered "persons of color," and therefore prohibited from marrying whites.

In the early eighteenth century, several families of free blacks lived on Virginia's eastern shore, in Accomack and Northampton counties. One (with the interesting name of Azaricum Drighouse) owned slaves. He did fairly well—good-size herds of cattle, a boat and a canoe, tools and raw materials. An estate valued at about £100. But Azaricum Drighouse couldn't mingle with most other free men; that is to say, with whites. By law, despite being free, he and his family were lumped with slaves and Native Americans.

Drighouse wasn't the only free black who owned slaves. Others were around New Orleans and Charleston. This fact—blacks owning blacks—often is used by those who would say, "See, blacks themselves believed in slavery." However, the "slaves" owned by many of those free blacks were members of their own families. They felt their wives and children, even their parents, were safer from bounty hunters if they owned them than if they were free and subject to random questioning by white authorities.

More than a hundred thousand free blacks lived in the pre–Civil War South, mainly in Virginia and Maryland. In the eighteenth and early nineteenth centuries, the cities of Jamestown and Williamsburg, successive capitals of Virginia before the government was shifted to Richmond, had free blacks among artisans. They worked side by side with white artisans and in most cases were not listed by race, but only by the job they performed. In these cases, no one cared too much whether the blacksmith or the cooper or the dressmaker was white or black. Varina Davis (she insisted her name be pronounced Va-reé-nah, not Va-rýe-nah) and Mary Lincoln apparently didn't care. Confederate President Davis's wife had a black dressmaker in Richmond; the same woman later became dressmaker to President Lincoln's wife in Washington.

Two hundred years after blacks first arrived in Virginia, as America's Civil War began, approximately one million white families lived in the South, and about 385,000 of them owned slaves, roughly 38 percent. Whites living below the Mason-Dixon line held nearly 4,000,000 slaves. That averages out to 10.26 slaves per family, but most of those who held slaves held only one or two. There were, however, many who held more than one hundred black slaves.

In 1860, slaves in the United States were valued at approximately two trillion dollars—that's a two with nine zeros. That put an average value of five hundred dollars on each man, woman, and child held in slavery.

Not everyone who fought for the South, or even stood up for the Confederacy, believed in slavery. Many officers in the Rebel army gave up their slaves years before the Emancipation Proclamation was written. Robert E. Lee called slavery "a moral and political evil," and he freed all of his slaves long before the war began.

Lee's Union counterpart, or at least his counterpart's wife, owned three slaves. During the war, Julia Dent Grant hired out two of them but kept one with her throughout the conflict. That slave, also named Julia, was with Mrs. Grant when the general's wife visited her husband in the trenches outside Petersburg during the final siege of Richmond. When Richmond fell, and while General Grant went traipsing off after General Lee and the remnants of the Army of Northern Virginia, Julia Grant toured fire-ravaged Richmond. She took her slave with her, which brings up an interesting problem involving the Emancipation Proclamation. Mrs. Grant's servant was at that moment perhaps the only slave in Richmond. All other blacks were free.

The Emancipation Proclamation was unusual and confusing. The opening paragraph reads:

> *[All] persons held as slaves within any State or designated part of a State that the people whereof shall then be in rebellion against the Unites States shall be then, thenceforward, and forever free. . . .*

The Emancipation Proclamation thus disallowed slavery in areas that were under rebellion but not controlled by the Federal government. Tricky. This allowed slavery in Gettysburg, Pennsylvania, say, but not in Richmond, Virginia. With the Proclamation taking effect on January 1, 1863, blacks living in Richmond were to be considered free; those living in other parts of Virginia might still be slaves. Norfolk and neighboring Portsmouth to the southeast were the only cities singled out for exclusion from powers of the Proclamation; they were not then "in rebellion against the United States." The two cities were abandoned to the Union in 1862.

The Union obviously controlled the area around Petersburg where Julia Dent Grant's husband worked in early 1865. Her owning slaves technically was legal, no matter how morally reprehensible. So, when Mrs. Dent and her black servant toured Richmond, perhaps the only slave in sight was the one owned by the Union commander's wife.

Blacks in Richmond might be considered "thenceforward, and forever free" by the United States government once the Proclamation took effect, but not so those living in Kentucky. Kentucky and three otherslave holding states, along with part of a fifth, did not secede from the Union. When the war ended, Kentucky still held sixty-five thousand slaves. The conservative government of Kentucky believed the Proclamation to be unconstitutional and refusing to abide by it, refused to recognize the liberty of any black "claiming or pretending to be free." Slavery remained legal in Kentucky until December 6, 1865, when the thirteenth amendment to the Constitution was ratified.

On rare occasions, Protestant ministers preached against slavery, but in more than 660,000 cases men of the cloth were slave owners themselves. That included at least 5,000 Methodist ministers owning 219,000 slaves and 6,500 Baptist ministers owning 125,000 slaves. In instances where ministers of the Gospel stood up in their pulpits on a Sunday morning and preached against slavery, it wasn't likely anyone in the congregation believed them.

More than 130 years after the war ended, many people still argue over what caused it: slavery, states' rights, economic reasons, the Puritan North against the gentry of the South, plain folk and factory workers against the aristocracy (or at least the aura of a superior class). Any or all of the above. Abraham Lincoln, in fact, managed to confuse an already confusing situation. It came during his first inaugural address. The dispute between North and South, Lincoln said, grew out of the fact that the Republican party was on record as opposing the expansion of the number of slaveholding states. At the same time, the new president said neither he nor the Republican party had any intention of interfering with "the property of the Southern people."

Earlier, we indicated plantation owners excused slavery on economic grounds. It was for financial reasons, some said, that they kept slaves. Only financial reasons. Economic truth is like beauty—all in the eye of the beholder. Plantation owners claimed they needed slaves to operate, but there is no evidence that slaves gave any plantation owner any advantage or disadvantage in large-scale farming. The same for urban manufacturers. During the Civil War, Richmond's Tredegar Iron Works operated with a mixture of free and slave labor, the slaves often rented out to the ironworks owners. Apparently, so far as the work was concerned, it didn't matter whether the employee was black and likely to be a slave or white and obviously free. At the time, Tredegar was the largest iron manufacturer in the South and the fourth largest in the nation.[3] It was forces of the labor market, not freedom or slavery, that determined who worked. If the cost of hiring slaves rose to a level equal to the free labor wages, fewer slaves were hired and more free workers were employed. If slave wages (*literally,* slave wages) fell, they were the ones hired.

After the war, freedmen preferred working the land on shares, rather than whole gangs getting together to work for the plantation owners, and sharecropping was, at best, *quasi-freedom.* Still, despite the hardships, most freed slaves chose freedom.

Among the few good things to come out of the Great Depression of the 1930s was the Works Progress Administration and the Civilian Conservation Corps. The C.C.C. helped build roads, state and federal parks, and even taught some job skills to many who had none. One W.P.A. project gave unemployed writers a chance to earn a living: It sent them out to gather oral histories, including histories of slavery as remembered by former slaves themselves.

Sarah Debro was interviewed as part of the W.P.A.'s oral history project. She'd been born a slave in Orange County, North Carolina, owned by Polly White Cain and her husband, Dr. (first name unknown) Cain. When Sarah Debro was interviewed in 1937, she was 90, living in Durham, North Carolina.

Marse Cain owned so many niggers that he didn't know his own slaves when he met them in the road. Sometimes he would stop them and say, "Whose niggers are you?" They'd say, "I's Marse Cain's niggers." Then he would say, "I's Marse Cain," and drive on.

Sarah Debro, former slave

With the invention of the cotton gin, the market for King Cotton grew by leaps and bounds, and so did slavery. It's estimated that the work of one cotton field slave benefited hundreds of cotton consumers. The cotton mills in the North, and workers in those mills, greatly benefited from Southern slaves. Virtually every cotton garment woven by a New England mill, every cotton shirt worn by a Northern man, woman, or child, was soaked in the blood and sweat of slavery. Abolitionists in the North, however, never considered that, in this, they too contributed to slavery.

When war came, America's cotton industry lost ground and money. The South withheld cotton from the world market, hoping to pressure England into coming into the war on the side of the Confederacy. Queen Victoria chose not to bend to the pressure, and England pushed its colony in India (where conditions were only marginally better than in America's South) into growing more cotton. It took years after the war for the rejoined Southern states to regain the cotton market.

Marse Cain was good to his niggers. He didn't whip them like some owners did, but if they done mean, he sold them. They knew this so them minded him. One day Grandpappy sassed Miss Polly White, and she told him that if he didn't behave hisself that she would put him in her pocket. Grandpappy was a big man, and I ask him how Miss Polly could do that. He said she meant that she would sell him, then put the money in her pocket. He never did sass Miss Polly no more.

Sarah Debro, former slave

Sadly, we're all familiar with photographs taken of freed slaves, grim evidence of the extent to which slaves were whipped and whipped again. Not every Southerner owned slaves, and not every slave owner whipped his slaves, yet whipping was a widely accepted punishment, an integral part of the system. Southern law allowed owners to punish their slaves, and whipping served as the most common form of physical punishment.

When plantation owner Bennet H. Barrow died in 1854 he left a diary telling of an almost daily mistreatment of humans. This "Inventory of the Estate of Bennet H. Barrow" gives the names and dates on which Barrow whipped slaves. In 1840 he owned 129 slaves, and if his plantation was typical of the time, at least 89 were ten years old or older. Barrow regularly whipped between 19 and 39 of them. Historian Herbert G. Gutman estimates that "half of [Barrow's] slave children under ten were whipped at least once."[4]

1837

Sept. 4 . . . had a general Whipping frollick

Oct. 2 More Whipping to do this Fall than altogether in three years owing to my D[amn] mean Overseer

Dec. 31 ran two of Uncle Bats negroes off last night—for making a disturbance—no pass—broke my sword Cane over one of their skulls

1838

Jan. 23 my House Servants Jane Lavenia & E. Jim broke into my store room—and helped themselves verry (sic) liberally to every thing. I Whipped [them]. . . worse than I ever Whipped any one before

Sept. 28 Dennis and Tom "Beauf" ran off on Wednesday. . . . If I can see either of them and have a gun at the time will let them have the contents of it. . . .

Oct. 12 [Tom ran off again] will Whip him more than I ever Whip one. I think he deserves more—the second time he has done so this year.

Oct. 20 Whipped about half to day

Oct. 26 Whipped 8 or 10 for weight to day—those that pick least weights generally most trash. . . .

Oct. 27 Dennis ran off yesterday—& after I had Whipped him

> *Nov. 2 Dennis came in sick on Tuesday—ran off again yester-*
> *day— without my ever seeing him—will carry my Gun & small shot*
> *for him—I think I shall cure him of rascality*
>   *Nov. 7 Dennis came in last night—had him fasted—attempted*
> *to Escape. Ran as far as the creek but was caught—the Ds rascal on*
> *the place.*[5]

Over and over again Barrow whipped Dennis; Dennis continued to
run off, apparently, whenever the chance presented itself. Each
time, he either was caught by Barrow or returned on his own.

Over and over again, Barrow writes about having "a general Whipping frolick." He "whipped about half to day." He had a "general
Whipping yesterday." And "whipped all my grown cotten pickers to
day."

Barrow's diary records at least six collective whippings—once
each in 1837 and 1838, twice in 1839, and once each in 1840 and
1841. Barrow used chains and extra work, humiliation (forcing men
to wear women's clothing), and seemingly constant whippings.[6] He
locked slaves in jail; he staked them out under the sun; he ducked
them in the plantation pond; he even beat his slaves with a tooth-
edged handsaw; sometimes, he shot runaway slaves. Obviously, the
slave named Dennis and those held in bondage with him preferred
death to that "peculiar institution."

Masters, you see, often were slaves to their own passions.

The Old South and, to an extent, the New, often referred to blacks
as either "Cuffee" or "Sambo." Cuffee, while becoming a pejorative,
apparently came from the name of a black sea captain, something
of a role model to blacks who generally could not aspire to such an
exalted position. His name, however, later took on a meaning far
from anything like a role model.

Sambo was and is a race stereotype, and here we'll walk a fine line
in explaining the designation. Southern lore has Sambo as the typical plantation slave, docile and irresponsible, loyal and lazy, humble and "chronically given to lying and stealing; his behavior was full
of infantile silliness and his talk inflated with childish exaggeration."[7]
In 1959, Smith College Professor Stanley Elkins said Sambo's "relationship with his master was one of utter dependence and childlike

attachment; it was indeed this childlike quality that was the very key to his being." Elkins goes on to say that "although the merest hint of Sambo's 'manhood' might fill the Southern breast with scorn, the child, 'in his place,' could be both exasperating and lovable."

The question, however, is whether the slave actually *was* docile or whether he *pretended* to be in order to survive. Is Sambo, as Elkins asks, a product of the slave race itself or of prejudice? There is no easy answer. If these "characteristics" actually existed among African slaves, were they used in role playing? If they did not exist but were only perceived by whites, they almost certainly were prejudicial and used, if only among whites, to hold down blacks in both the nineteenth and twentieth centuries.

Over three centuries, several million people were ripped from a variety of cultural backgrounds in Africa. They came from an area that encompassed roughly 1,300,000 square miles, about one-fifth of the African continent, "various countries, inhabited by a great number of savage nations, differing widely from each other, in government, in language, manners, and superstitions."[8]

While blacks were stolen from a variety of tribes, most in Virginia and the Carolinas came from the Gold Coast, the Niger delta region, and Dahomey. Basically, they were agricultural regions; women did the cultivating, while the men did the heavy labor. It was no Garden of Eden, and those who lived there had to work for everything they got. They had close-knit families and legal, political, and economic institutions. And they fought.

Around 1700, one of the rulers of the Ashanti tribe convinced his fellow chiefs to recognize him as the Asantehene, the king of all the Ashantis. They had an unwritten constitution, a tax and revenue system, and a military system that utilized armies of from thirty to forty thousand warriors. Some historians argue that it wasn't disease and heat that kept rapacious Europeans out of Africa, giving rise to the name "Black Continent" for a place they didn't know. Rather, it was the native armies that kept away the English, Dutch, French, and Germans.

None of this gives any indication of a dumb and lovable, foot-shuffling "Sambo."

Just coming to America wasn't easy. A heavy proportion of slaves came from the most warlike of tribes, much like the Ashanti, and many were taken in war or caught in surprise attacks upon their villages. Some were captured by other natives and then sold as slaves. So, the first shock was being taken captive. The next was a long march to the sea, which often took many weeks and just as often left many dead along the way, their bleached bones marking the trail. They were driven like beasts under the steaming jungle sun, tied together by their necks. For eight or more hours a day they staggered barefoot over thorny underbrush, dried reeds, and stones. Obviously, only the strongest survived the march.

Next came the shock of being crowded into pens and then sold to European slavers. Those rejected by slavers would be left to starve. Those bought were branded, marked with lead tags, and herded onto ships.

What followed was the dreaded Middle Passage and cannot simply be called a shock to the system. They were packed into ships' holds, a squirming, suffocating, pitiful mass of humanity, where they lived with disease, filth, and pestilence for as long as two months.

There were two schools of thought on how to pack a slave ship. One said that fewer slaves onboard assured a higher percentage of survival. That is, pack only one hundred in the ship and sixty-five might survive. The other slave-packing theory was much in the line of today's "risk management." While packing more into a ship's hold meant a larger percentage of deaths, enough would survive to make up the difference. Pack two hundred into the same space and, even if one hundred died—50 percent—you'd have one hundred left. Since their initial cost was low, the thirty-five additional survivors would give the slaver more of a profit.

Those who survived through the Middle Passage faced their next shock when they arrived in the West Indies. Would-be buyers scrambled onto the ships, manhandling, checking, and fondling the new slaves. These shipboard inspections got so bad, the Jamaica legislature finally ordered all sales be held on land.

At least one-third of those first taken prisoner died before they reached the trading stations and slave ships. Another one-third died before they even left the West Indies for mainland America. That means of an estimated fifteen million taken in Africa in war, or were bought or stolen, only five million survived to reach America. The majority of all African-born slaves came through this Middle Passage route, going first to the West Indies, then to the mainland. Few came directly from, say, the Gold Coast of Africa to the slave market of Charleston.

The question, then, is what kind of individual survived those continuing shocks; what was the individual like, the one out of three forcibly removed from Africa to become a slave in America? It seems highly unlikely that he or she would be docile and irresponsible, loyal and lazy, humble and "chronically given to lying and stealing; his behavior . . . full of infantile silliness and his talk inflated with childish" behavior. Not Sambo. Not one who really was as described. If Sambo existed, it was either to fool a master and get by or it was the product of a prejudiced mind. The newly arrived slave, no matter the shock he lived through, would not have forgotten his family, his kinfolk; would not have forgotten his language, taboos, the name he had been born with; would not have forgotten how he had fought great battles as a member of a society that was not unlike Anglo-Saxon England or the Hellene of Greece.

Sambo-ism was not inborn, not a characteristic of race. Even though those who went to Latin America went through the same series of shocks, there was no Sambo of Latin America. A similar word exists, *Zambo*, a Spanish term for "bandy-legged." It usually meant a cross between a black and a South American Indian, a mulatto. "Zambo" is not "Sambo."

Some historians have likened the theft of blacks from Africa and their subsequent slavery to the mistreatment of Jews by the Nazis before and during World War II: arrest, mistreatment, transportation away from home, encampment during which all previous culture was deprived, then death. Both are sometimes spoken of as a sort of perverted patriarchy. Both systems—slavery and concentration camps—depended upon terror for success. In both cases it was generally agreed that if one survived the first three months of captivity, one could also survive the next three years. Or, in the case of slaves in America, often thirty years or more. The Jews in Nazi concentration camps learned that the way to survive was to be inconspicuous. Do not call attention to yourself; those who did—even by such trivial means as wearing eyeglasses—risked death. As Stanley Elkins points out, in slavery "there were no rewards for martyrdom." To be inconspicuous "required a special kind of alertness—almost an animal instinct. . . ."

Just as with slavery, older inmates of Nazi concentration camps often exhibited a quality "characteristic of infancy or early youth."[9] The SS guard was all-powerful in camp, a father symbol to the prisoners. To prevent this cruel father from punishing the "child," even killing the "child," the prisoner performed just as expected. Even after being set free by the Allies, prisoners of Buchenwald and other German concentration camps—death camps—often leaned on Allied commanders as "fathers." Just as with African slaves, there were few suicides among Jews held in concentration camps, and most of those that did occur came in the early months of captivity or slavery.

Both Nazi-held Jews and African slaves wanted to survive, and whatever it took to survive, they did. Like the children of concentration camp victims, today's grandchildren of African slaves say "Never again."

So, was there a Sambo? In all probability, yes, but he was perceived in two different ways. First, it was a means to survive until the slave could escape. Second, and regretfully, the slaveholder and those who followed began to look on him or her as a happy, foot-shuffling, not-too-bright childlike individual. It was a picture that suited the slaveholder, a picture that suited those who would like to hold slaves.

Elias Thomas was eighty-four years old and living in Raleigh, North Carolina, when he was interviewed by the W.P.A. writers.

> We worked from sun to sun, with one hour and a half to rest at noon or dinner time. I was so small I did not do much heavy work. I chopped corn and cotton mostly. The old slaves had patches they tended, and sold what they made and had the money it brought. . . .
>
> My marster only had two children, both boys, Fred and John. John was about my age, and Fred was about two years older. They are both dead. My marster never had any overseers; he made boss men out of his oldest slaves. . . .
>
> I never saw a jail for slaves, but I have seen slaves whipped. I

saw Crayton Abernathy, a overseer, whip a woman in the cotton patch on Doc Smith's farm, a mile from our plantation. I also saw old man William Crump, a owner, whip a man and some children. He waited till Sunday morning to whip his slaves. He would get ready to go to church, have his horse hitched up to the buggy, then call his slaves out and whip them before he left for church. He generally whipped about five children every Sunday morning.

Elias Thomas, former slave

Southerners tended to fear freed slaves and regarded them as dangerous and detestable. After the war, some former slaveholders wanted all blacks shipped to West Texas or New Mexico.

At the time he was interviewed as part of the W.P.A. Project in 1937, Ben Horry was eighty-seven and living in Murrells Inlet, South Carolina.

I the oldest liver left on Waccamaw Neck, that belong to Brookgreen, Prospect, Longwood, Alderly plantations. I been here! I seen things! I tell you. . . .

Father dead just before my mother. They stayed right to Brookgreen Plantation and dead there after they free. And all they chillun do the same, till the old colonel sell the plantation out. Where we going to? Ain't we got house and rations there?

Ben Horry, former slave

The South fought to preserve its political, social, and economic heritage from the previous generation. The Rebels, if they were forced to give a reason for the Civil War, likely as not said it was to maintain the status quo and to be left alone. Not that most had much real knowledge of the constitutional issues. What they did understand was the abolitionists' philosophical attack on slavery. Yet, the average Southern soldier was not fighting for slavery; he was a farmer or laborer who fought to defend his home.

We's come a long way since them times. I's lived near about ninety years and heard much. My folks don't want me to talk about slavery, they's shame niggers ever was slaves. But, while for most colored folks freedom is the best, they's still some niggers that ought to be slaves now. These niggers that's done clean forgot the Lord; those that's always cutting and fighting and going in white folks' houses at night, they ought to be slaves. They ought to have an old marse with a whip

*to make them come when he say come and go when he say go, till
they learn to live right.*

I looks back and thinks. I ain't never forgot them slavery days.

Sarah Debro, former slave

Former slaves interviewed by the W.P.A. were survivors. Something
about them had to be different, and that difference may have been
their ability to live through the horrors of slavery and, sixty or so years
later, look back on that period of their lives as sometimes pleasant.

Ria Sorrell was twenty-one years old when America's Civil War began. She was ninety-seven when she was interviewed in 1937. Like
many others, she retained something of a filial devotion to her former master, with her former mistress as more of a villain.

*I just lack three years of being one hundred years old. I belonged to
Jacob Sorrell. His wife was named Elizabeth. . . .*

*Our houses was good houses, 'cause Marster seed to it they was
fixed right. We had good beds and plenty of cover. The houses was
called the nigger houses. They was about two hundred yards from
the big houses. Our houses had two rooms, and Marster's had seven
rooms.*

*We didn't have any overseers. Marster said he didn't believe in
them and he didn't want any. The oldest slave on the place woke us
up in the morning and acted as foreman. Marster hardly ever went
to the field. . . . I worked at the house as nurse and housegirl most
of the time. . . .*

*We worked from sunup till sunset with a rest spell at twelve o'-
clock of two hours. He give us holidays to rest in. That was Christmas, a week off then, then a day every month, and all Sundays. He
said he was a Christian and he believed in giving us a chance. . . .*

*There was about twenty-five slaves on the place, and Marster just
wouldn't sell a slave. When he whupped one, he didn't whup much;
he was a good man. He seemed to be sorry every time he had to whup
any of the slaves. His wife was a pure devil, she just joyed whupping Negroes. She was tall and spare-made with black hair and
eyes. . . .*

*When Marster come to town, she raised old scratch with the slaves.
She whupped all she could while Marster was gone. She tried to boss*

*Marster, but he wouldn't allow that. He kept her from whupping
many a slave. She just wouldn't feed a slave, and when she had her
way, our food was bad. She said underleaves of collards was good
enough for slaves. . . .*

*There was one thing they wouldn't allow, that was books and pa-
pers. I can't read and write.*

*I heard talk of Abraham Lincoln coming through when talk of
the war came about. They met, him and Jeff Davis, in South Caroline (sic). Lincoln said, "Jeff Davis, let them niggers go free." Jeff
Davis told him, "You can't make us give up our property." Then the
war started. . . .*

Ria Sorrell, former slave

The "meeting" between Lincoln and Davis, of course, never happened. In the same light, former slaves frequently told of Abraham
Lincoln visiting them individually. The stories generally held to the
same line. Slaves would be working in the fields, and a tall man would
walk by in the nearby dusty road; though they had never seen the
Union president before and never asked the man his name, they instantly knew it was Lincoln. The president would ask for a drink of
water, and they would give it to him. The vision would drink, thank
the gathered slaves, and then walk away.

The Visiting Lincoln Story is much like what today are known as
"Urban Myths," stories sworn to by person after person, but never
actually witnessed by the teller. One common urban myth is of a
young child being kidnapped from a shopping mall. First knowledge
of the attempt comes when someone walks into a rest room and dis-
covers a strange man (or woman) either dyeing or cutting a child's
hair, the child crying for his mother or father. The discoverer has arrived just in time to prevent the kidnapping. Like the Visiting Lincoln Story, the teller of the Urban Myth does not personally witness
the event but knows someone who got the story directly from someone who heard about it when it happened.

On the other hand, tales about the Ku Klux Klan were all too real.
W. L. Bost was eighty-seven, living in Asheville, North Carolina,
when he was interviewed. His postwar memories remained vivid.

They were terrible dangerous. They wear long gowns, touch the ground. They ride horses through the town at night, and if they find a Negro that tries to get nervy or have a little bit for himself, they lash him nearly to death and gag him and leave him to do the best he can. Sometime they put sticks in the top of that tall thing they wear (their hoods) and then put an extra head up there with scary eyes and great big mouth, then they stick it clear up in the air to scare the poor Negroes to death.

W. L. Bost, former slave

General Nathan Bedford Forrest, was a slave trader before the war, opposed abolition during the conflict, and after the war, joined the Klan.

Brawley Gilmore didn't know how old he was when the W.P.A. interviewed him in 1934, but he knew about the K.K.K.

John Good, a darky blacksmith, used to shoe the horses for the Ku Klux. He would mark the horseshoes with a bent nail or something like that; then after a raid, he could go out in the road and see if a certain horse had been rode. So he began to tell on the Ku Klux.

As soon as the Ku Klux found out they was being give away, they suspicioned John. They went to him and made him tell how he knew who they was. They kept him in hiding; and when he told his tricks, they killed him.

When I was a boy on the Gilmore place, the Ku Klux would come along at night a-riding the niggers like they were goats. Yes, sir, they had them down on all-fours a-crawling, and they would be on their backs. They would carry the niggers to Turk Creek bridge and make them set up on the banisters of the bridge. Then they would shoot them offen the banisters into the water. I declare them was the awfulest days I ever seed. . . .

The Ku Klux and the niggers fit at New Hope Church. A big rock marks the spot today. The church, it done burnt down. . . . The darkies killed some of the Ku Klux and they took their dead and put them in Pilgrims' church. Then, they set fire to that church and it burnt everything up to the very bones of the white folks. And ever since then, that spot has been known as Burnt Pilgrim. The darkies left most of the folks there for the buzzards and other wild things to eat up. . . .

[The former slaves] had a hiding place not far from Burnt Pil-

grim. A darky name Austin Sanders, he was carrying some victuals to his son. The Ku Klux catch him and they asked him where he was a-going. He allowed that he was a-setting some bait for coons. The Ku Klux took and shot him and left him lying right in the middle of the road with a biscuit in his dead mouth.

Brawley Gilmore, former slave

CHAPTER THREE

All the Presidents' Men:
The Best and Not So Bright

I am out of money, we are all out of money, but we don't need money down here— don't need anything but men, muskets, ammunition, hard tack, bacon, and letters from home.

—Lt. Col. James Austin Connolly
June 20, 1864[1]

It wasn't close, not even from the beginning, and if the South had looked at the realities instead of being led by its emotions, America's Civil War may never have happened.

The South had fewer fighting-age men than the North, and 39 percent of the population of the seceding states were black slaves. All legal and moral considerations aside, the South faced the very real possibility of those slaves rising up at the very time the Confederacy faced a larger and better equipped enemy from the North.

The South was in short supply of nearly everything needed to fight a war. Some of its artillery pieces were British-made three-, six-, and eight-pound howitzers captured in the War of 1812.

Only three percent of all the firearms made in the United States before the war were produced in the South. Most of the Confederacy's larger weapons came from three sources: ironworks in Richmond, ironworks in Atlanta, and those recovered from defeated Northern armies.

However, as one economist put it, "the South was richer than the North in all the necessities of life." It produced more corn and more livestock per person than did the North, and it had the decided advantage of producing cotton that both the North and the world at large wanted.

While it's true the South could produce enough food, it's equally true it had difficulty getting the food where it was needed, especially if it had to be moved by railroad. Before the war, railroads were not considered a major military factor, North or South. But as the fighting progressed—beginning, in fact, with the Battle of Manassas—railroads grew in importance. The South was way behind in railroading. At the beginning of the war, the Union had thirty thouand miles of railroad track, by far the largest amount in the world. The South had less than half that, and in four years of war, the North laid an additional four thousand miles of track. The Confederacy produced only four percent of all locomotives made in the United States prior to the firing on Fort Sumter. In 1860, of 470 locomotives built in the United States, only nineteen were built in the Confederacy.

Building railroads called for iron, and Northern states produced 93 percent of the nation's pig iron. In addition, the Union states produced 94 percent of America's cloth, and more than 90 percent of its boots and shoes. By the end of the war the South was producing enough weapons, but it didn't have enough men to use them.

If statistics were on the side of the North, on the side of the South was the very real fact that it was fighting for a cause it believed in, fighting to keep Northern invaders out. The South, then, should have won, no matter how unequally matched it was in men and materials of war.

On May 3, 1861, the Congress of the United States of America declared war on the Confederate States of America, and after that statistics and emotions no longer meant anything. All hell broke lose.

You get a group of historians together, even those of us who don't claim that name, and you get almost as many reasons for the South's loss as there are members of the group. The industrial might of the North. The North's larger population. The way the North stuck by Lincoln, stuck by the idea of winning the war.

The South had many reasons to win the war, perhaps too many. Everybody had his own reason, and frequently what one state wanted hurt the Confederacy as a whole, and the state in question might not even care.

Issues involving two Confederate state governors quickly come to mind, one from Georgia and the other from North Carolina. The

Georgia governor withheld resources from the Rebel army, claiming it was more important to protect his own state. North Carolina's governor kept thousands of uniforms for his own troops rather than supply other Confederate army units that might have needed them more.

Many people, especially in today's South, claim the Confederacy had better generals. Not so; it had only one: Robert E. Lee. Albert Sydney Johnson and Braxton Bragg were, at best, only competent, not great. P. G. T. Beauregard's victory at Fort Sumter doesn't count; the Union had no chance there. Beauregard was the hero at First Manassas, but who did he face on the other side? Irvin McDowell and a bunch of ill-trained Yankees who got going *backward* when the going got tough. McDowell's Yankee troops didn't stop until they ran back to Washington to hide under Abe Lincoln's long coattails.

When Second Manassas came along Robert E. Lee and Stonewall Jackson together faced the unfortunate John Pope, a general who did a lot to defeat himself. When Lincoln appointed Pope head of the Army of Virginia, the Yankee general alienated his own troops. In his infamous "Pope's Address" of July 14, 1862, he said,

> *I have come to you from the West, where we have always seen the backs of our enemy; from an army whose business it has been to seek the adversary, and to beat him where he was found. . . . Let us study the probable lines of retreat of our opponents, and leave our own to take care of themselves. Let us look before us and not behind. . . .*

Pope also made an enemy of Robert E. Lee, by calling for harsh treatment of all Southerners left in Union-occupied territory. He didn't help himself, either, when he said his headquarters would be "in the saddle," to which someone replied Pope had his headquarters where his hindquarters should be.

Other Rebel officers? The Confederacy's John Bell Hood, the Valiant Hood, he was often called? Well, Hood may have been good (and that's questionable), but he certainly was too ill to fight, part of the time; certainly too incapacitated to defend Atlanta from Sherman. James Longstreet? Not first-rate, and many questioned his loyalty. He was best man for his friend Ulysses S. Grant when Grant married Julia Dent. After the war he shunned his former Rebel companions, and many shunned him.

There's even the suggestion that the South's desire to win wasn't as strong as the North's. The South, after all, just wanted the North to leave them alone and go away.

Perhaps the chief reason the South lost was that the North had Abraham Lincoln. The South had Jefferson Davis.

Jefferson Davis graduated twenty-third in his class of thirty-three cadets. He had a wealth of experience in both the military and political worlds. He served valiantly in the Mexican War, and for seven years as a lieutenant in the northwest territory, where he fought in the Black Hawk War.

Davis was an experienced politician who knew his way around the House of Representatives, the U.S. Senate, and the White House; he'd been a member of President Franklin Pierce's cabinet. He'd sat on the Military Affairs committees of both the House and Senate. His years in and around the military left him well-acquainted with many high-ranking officers of both armies. To say the least, he felt at ease in the military world.

When the war of words turned into a war of bullets and cannonballs, Davis, as president of the Confederacy, adopted a strategy of defense. That is, if the Union didn't bother the seceding states, those states would not bother the nation they were leaving. Meanwhile, just to be safe, Davis would set up a military shield as close to the borders as possible, thus protecting the homes and businesses and farms of the new nation's citizens.

The problem was the new Confederate military lacked the resources—material, men, and money—to do the job Davis called for. The South's borders were enormous: 3,549 miles of coastline with 189 ports, harbors, and other navigable rivers and inlets.

So Davis positioned his armies along logical routes of invasion, and he created large military departments under single leaders. He expected the North to invade the Confederacy and hoped he could counter any large-scale offensive by aiming two or more smaller armies at the attacker. This meant several small pinchers, if you will, instead of one single blunt instrument. There was a major weakness in this. What to do if the Union sent not just one large blunt instrument against the small Southern pinchers, but several large blunt instrument armies at once?

Jefferson Davis was an extremely talented man with one major drawback: his personality. He was honest, a man of unswerving integrity, and he truly saw himself as acting in the best interest of his new nation. But he was a brusque man, with this brusqueness often compounded by a variety of physical ailments that added to his stress and discomfort and, in turn, exacerbated his temperament.

As a former soldier, he saw himself as *the* military man of the Confederacy. Too often, he sent his commanding officers minutely detailed orders. In short, he butted in when butting out was the way to go.

General Joseph E. Johnston was his commander in the East. At first they got along well, but Johnston began to chafe at Davis's detailed orders. Davis thought Johnston was spending too much money on the very defenses Davis had ordered. When Johnston was wounded—seriously but not gravely—in the Battle of Seven Pines outside Richmond, Davis took the opportunity to replace him. It could have been a major stumble by the Confederate president, but the man chosen to replace Johnston saved Davis: Gen. Robert E. Lee.

Lee had the ability to utilize the strengths and weaknesses of those around him, to overcome the faults possessed by some of his subordinates. He may not have thought of it in precise psychological terms, but Robert E. Lee understood that to get ahead in the military—any military, in any age—an individual had to have a tremendous ego. Lee was able to cope with the large and growing egos of his officers. And with that of his commander in chief, Jefferson Davis. Davis sometimes tried, but generally he did not fiddle around with Lee's plans. Not so with others.

To the west, Jefferson Davis gave his good friend Gen. Albert Sydney Johnston great latitude in handling the war beyond the Allegheny Mountains. After Johnston was killed at the Battle of Shiloh, Davis alienated the new commander, Gen. P. G. T. Beauregard, early on: Davis proceeded to break up Beauregard's western command. He split it between the prickly Gen. Braxton Bragg and the Northern-born Gen. John C. Pemberton. Pemberton, of course, went down to defeat at Vicksburg.

Braxton Bragg's officers frequently argued among themselves. General Nathan Bedford Forrest even took his cavalry command out of Bragg's control and rode off.

Davis stepped into the argument but made things worse, not better. Instead of telling them to settle down and get back to fighting the real enemy from up North, he tried shifting several generals to other fields of action. Among them, Gen. James "Old Pete" Longstreet, who had been sent west to help out. Davis ordered Longstreet to recapture Knoxville, a move that left Bragg with fewer than 30,000 men under his command just at a time when he needed them most.

Ulysses Grant was ready to break out of Chattanooga and was looking for a fight. He found that fight; he found the weakened Braxton Bragg "above the clouds" near Lookout Mountain: the Battle of Chattanooga. By himself, Bragg had defeated the Union army at Chickamauga. With the help of Jefferson Davis, the South suffered a disastrous defeat at Chattanooga.

Bragg took the blame for that defeat and resigned his commission. Jefferson Davis returned Bragg to Richmond and made him his military advisor.

In his place, Davis put the recovered Joseph E. Johnston in charge of the Army of Tennessee, even though the president still disliked the general. Johnston knew that he faced a vastly larger army now under command of Gen. William Tecumseh Sherman. Grant, by this time, had been given command of the Army of the Potomac and was facing Robert E. Lee back East in the final months of the war.

The U.S. presidential election of 1864 was coming up, and Abe Lincoln wasn't doing well in the polls, as it were. Johnston thought that if he could avoid a major battle with Sherman, avoid a major defeat, the North, which had grown tired of the war, might not reelect Lincoln. Whoever beat Lincoln might sue for peace. So Johnston struck lightly here, pulled back there. Struck again, pulled back again. Sherman was frustrated, and so was Jefferson Davis; Davis thought Johnston was a coward who avoided fights.

There wasn't much Sherman could do except follow Johnston down the road to Atlanta. There was a lot Davis could do, and he did it. He fired Johnston, replacing him with a man so ill—only one leg and one useful arm—that he had to be tied to his saddle, Gen. John Bell Hood. Hood did just what Davis wanted, just what Sherman wanted. He came out to fight. Sherman won easily, then burned Atlanta.

Riding on the heels of the fall of Atlanta, the North reelected Lincoln to a second term, just as Joseph E. Johnston had hoped would *not* happen.

Abraham Lincoln, as every schoolchild knows, never went to school; he learned everything he knew on his own. As it turned out, he learned a lot.

Lincoln was a small-time state politician; after one term in the U.S. House of Representatives he failed to get reelected. The famous Lincoln-Douglas debates of 1858 originally were called the "Douglas-Lincoln Debates," considering how the voting turned out. They ended with Stephen Douglas being elected to the Senate and Abe Lincoln going back to Springfield, Illinois, to practice law.

Abraham Lincoln had very limited military experience, nothing more than a short stint in the Illinois militia during the short-lived Black Hawk War. When his first enlistment ran out without any action, Lincoln reenlisted—"re-upped," we would say today. The second time, however, it was as a private. Again, no action, but as he and his fellow militia troops marched through they woods they came upon a group of four other soldiers recently killed by the enemy. And scalped. The sight of freshly scalped men turned Abraham Lincoln against a military career, and he apparently never regretted it.

In 1860 he was elected president of a nation badly split along emotional and state lines. In that election, the North cast a quarter of a million more votes *against* Lincoln than did the South. When election time came in 1864, Lincoln squeaked by in the popular vote, 54 percent for Lincoln against 46 percent for former general George McClellan. In the electoral college, however, it wasn't even close—212 to 21, with Lincoln losing only the electoral votes of New Jersey, Kentucky, and Delaware.

As a military strategist, Lincoln's genius lay in his vision. He never admitted the South had seceded, and he never once referred to them as the "enemy."

Despite constant carping, criticism, and disasters, Lincoln remained firm in his commitments to restore the Union and to end slavery. At the beginning of the war he knew practically nothing about the military or the military establishment. But he learned quickly. He may have been self-educated, but he absorbed books, sucking in information about everything military he could find. He picked the brains of those officers he respected, even some he didn't; it was all grist for his information mill. By the end of the war, Abraham Lincoln may have been the most insightful military man in America, North or South.

He was a gregarious, self-deprecating man with the appeal of a small-town lawyer. He developed a personal rapport with those around him. In the beginning, he venerated the ancient Winfield Scott, the head of the Union army, and took everything he could from a man who, while he was too old for the physical job at hand, had knowledge enough to go around.

Abraham Lincoln very seldom interfered with his field commanders. He did, however, make too many appointments based purely on political grounds. In the beginning, at least, he yielded to public demands to recall unsuccessful generals. If one of his generals failed, Lincoln seldom gave him a second chance. Some of his officers were more afraid of the president in their rear than of the enemy in front of them.

After the disastrous First Battle of Manassas, Lincoln searched for a general to command his army. He found George B. McClellan, and that was his biggest mistake. McClellan was a man of obvious intelligence. When he entered West Point he was only fifteen years old and needed special permission to get in.

The first thing McClellan did after taking command was to rename his force the Army of the Potomac. And then, the "Little Napoleon," as McClellan sometimes was called, proceeded to recruit, train, and march his new Army of the Potomac around Washington. McClellan himself sat around Washington's Willard Hotel. Meanwhile, recruits for McClellan's army were falling over themselves. There were so many new recruits in Washington that some had to be bedded down in the House of Representatives, which wasn't the first nor probably the last time anyone ever slept there.

McClellan's strong point was training an army; his weak point was using it. Lincoln had to poke, prod, and plead with George McClellan to move. One time, during a White House war council, Lincoln commented, "If General McClellan does not want to use the army, I would like to borrow it, provided I could see how it could be made to do something."[2]

When McClellan finally did move, it was a brilliant but overdue campaign up the Virginia peninsula. Then he decided to wait for more troops. And to delay. And to hesitate. McClellan wired Lincoln that he couldn't move because his horses were too tired; Lincoln wired back, asking what in the world they had done to get so tired.

Lincoln fumed in Washington, and George McClellan slowly trudged up the peninsula during Virginia's rainy season. Finally within sight of Richmond, literally so close that the Union soldiers set their watches by the chiming of Richmond's church bells, Mc-Clellan gave up. He retreated back down the peninsula and returned his army to the recruiting grounds around Washington.

McClellan might easily have beaten Robert E. Lee at Antietam. Thanks to the famous "lost orders," McClellan had Lee's plan of action: knew every move the Confederate general was going to make for several days. Yet, despite outnumbering the South three to two at Antietam, McClellan barely won. As it was, it was one of the bloodiest days in military history: the Confederacy suffered a casualty rate of more than 26 percent, while only 16 percent of the Union's forces were lost. The Battle of Antietam (or Sharpsburg; call it what you will) was virtually a draw.

Lincoln's mistake was not in appointing McClellan to head the army but in sticking with McClellan too long. Finally, he tried other generals.

He brought in Henry Halleck from the West, but no one, including Halleck, had faith in that bug-eyed former newspaper reporter turned lawyer turned soldier.

Lincoln went on to try Gen. Ambrose Burnside, but even Burnside didn't think he deserved the command. He was right; Burnside was almost wiped out at Fredericksburg three months after Antietam.

Brigadier General Edward Porter Alexander of Georgia was in charge of Rebel artillery at Fredericksburg. Before the battle on December 13, 1862, General Longstreet asked Alexander if the artillery was ready. Alexander replied, "A chicken could not live in that field when we open on it." Don't know about any chickens, but a lot of Union soldiers died.

Union Gen. Ambrose Burnside unwisely pushed his army across the river early in the morning. They drove head-on, time and time again. Just as General Alexander had predicted, Lee's artillery slaughtered them. As Lee stood watching his Confederate troops drive Federal forces back, he said to Longstreet, "It is well that war is so terrible, or we should grow too fond of it."

Of an estimated 120,000 Union troops, 12,630 were killed or wounded. Of 79,000 Rebel troops, only 5,300 were lost.

After December's disaster came January's miserable Mud March. What remained of Burnside's army was demoralized and almost totally lacking in confidence as a fighting unit. The general, however, wanted to make another try at crossing the Rappahannock. He led his troops downstream in an effort to avoid Lee's much stronger force, hoping to strike "a great and mortal blow to the rebellion." He planned to set out on December 26, but some of Burnside's subordinates didn't like the idea and sent word to President Lincoln. Lincoln didn't like it either and vetoed the plan.

Burnside was undaunted by either Lee or Lincoln, and on January 20 he moved his troops toward Bank's Ford. Just as he got under way, it began to rain. After two straight days of rain, the roads looked more like swamps, and small streams looked more like raging rivers. Burnside's maneuver soon came to be called the "Mud March." One officer blamed it on "Virginia mud," saying it was "a clay of reddish color and sticky consistency which does not appear to soak water, or mingle with it, but simply to hold it, becoming softer and softer." Elisha Hunt Rhodes agreed, confiding to his journal that "the wagons began to turn over and mules actually drowned in the mud and water. . . ." On the opposite side of the river, Rhodes added, Confederate troops mocked the Union army, putting up a sign "marked 'Burnside stuck in the mud.'"[3] He added, "We can fight the rebels but not in mud." After three days, Burnside called off the Mud March.

The rain may have been an "act of God," as some have pointed out, but the thought probably never crossed Lincoln's mind. To him, the Mud March was just another example of Ambrose Burnside's failure to lead, so Lincoln fired him. Only Burnside's haircut was left as a reminder.

Lincoln tried again with Joe Hooker, and Hooker was decimated at Chancellorsville. Hooker's force more than doubled Lee's troops at Chancellorsville, but still the North lost.

The North won at Gettysburg under George Meade, but it may have been more Robert E. Lee's mistake (or Jeb Stuart's, who showed up too late to help) than Meade's success. Critics agree that Lee never should have sent George Pickett's fifteen thousand–man division charging across that one-mile open field. Glorious charges don't always win wars.

And still Abe Lincoln searched for a general who understood at least as much about war as he did. Finally he found the man who fulfilled all his expectations, one original enough to employ Lincoln's strategy: Ulysses S. Grant. When a jealous Henry Halleck tried to sack Grant, Lincoln refused. "I cannot spare this man," Lincoln said. "He fights."

Lincoln had faith in Grant and promoted him to lieutenant general and chief of the armies. While Grant fought the war, Lincoln concentrated on the political aspects. Together, they won.

Abraham Lincoln looked around until he found the right man for the job. By the end of the war he had a cohesive strategy that worked.

Jefferson Davis interfered too often and usually in the wrong manner. As they say these days, he never got his act together, and he failed. Davis tried to defend his fledgling nation against invasion.

Lincoln, using Grant and Sherman, ignored the idea of invasion and raided the South, rolled over the South, destroyed the South.

Jefferson Davis had one thing Abraham Lincoln did not, and it may have been a deciding factor in the North's victory. As a man who had faced war, Davis had looked into the eyes of those he fought.

Lincoln lacked that experience. Except for the time he saw a few scalped troops, he never witnessed the horror, the fear, the terror of war. Never saw the terror the people of the South endured. He did not see the atrocities of war first-hand. Lincoln never was forced to see close-up the faces of those he defeated. Davis lived in the middle of those faces.

Lincoln usually is seen as a very compassionate man, while Davis is perceived as cold and indifferent to what was happening to his peo-

ple. Perhaps it was just the opposite. Perhaps Davis's experience—
actually seeing war—close up and personal—made him too shy, too
hesitant to quit. Perhaps the fact that Lincoln lacked combat experience allowed him to watch from an intellectual distance while Sherman made Georgia howl, while Grant sent regiment after regiment
of men into the Wilderness, and when that didn't work, sent them
to Cold Harbor. Sent men to die, seven thousand in the first seven
minutes at Cold Harbor.

Perhaps while this happened, while death after death piled up in
front of him, it became obvious to Lincoln that he must end the war
as soon as possible, not let it drag on as Jefferson Davis did. . . . End
the war. Get on with the healing.

Jefferson Davis was a trained military man. Abraham Lincoln was
not. Perhaps being a military man was exactly what the country did
not need in time of war.

CHAPTER FOUR

Hurry Up and Wait:
Fun, Games, and Mail Call

There is some of the most onerest men here that I ever saw and the most swearing and card playing and fitin and drunkenness that I ever saw at any place.
—Adam S. Rader
May 7, 1862[1]

I'm just enjoying myself because the days of men are few and I want to be as merry as long as I can, and when we get home again I [will] make it all up.
—Louis Merz[2]

Troops quickly gathered; squads, regiments, and battalions were formed in the North and South. For most troops in America's Civil War, it was the great adventure of their lives, the first time they'd been away from home, and they took advantage of it. Many were like Louis Merz and unknowingly acted out a song that came along in the 1950s: "Live fast, love hard, leave a beautiful memory." In Merz's case, it didn't last long. He wrote these words in early 1861; he died in the fall of 1862 at the Battle of Antietam.

As in any other war, the story of America's Civil War was "hurry up and wait." An estimated 95 percent of a soldier's time was spent in camp (and, of course, we're speaking of sailors as well; substitute *ship* for *camp*); only five percent was spent in actually fighting. They had to do something to fill the hours.

They drank hard; they played hard; they fooled around with wild, wild women. They swam in nearby ponds and rivers; they fought among themselves when the enemy wasn't at hand. In the winter they held snowball fights. In the summer they held foot races, boxing, and wrestling matches. They did just about anything else to ease the tedium, even played cricket, which if nothing else certainly lets a person wile away the many long hours between death and destruction.

They also played another game, one growing increasingly popular. It had at least two parents, one the rambunctious children's game first played in England in 1744 and called rounders. The other parent was that far more sedate game of cricket. When America got hold of this new game, we changed its pace, changed its rules, adopted it for our own, and renamed it baseball.

Less than a decade after the American Revolution began, students at Princeton College wrote home about playing "base," as it was called then. By the 1860s, Walt Whitman was writing about a game he referred to as "ball." A leisurely event in which, unlike other games, the defense held on to the ball.

Legend has it that in 1839, in Cooperstown, New York, a group of locals were playing what they called "townball." Its advocates associated townball more with local taverns than universities, and it was, to say the least, unruly. They played townball on a square field, with as many as fifteen players to a side. Every hit was fair and a batter flailed away at the ball until he managed to make contact with it. The pitcher was known as the "feeder," and his primary job was to gently lob the soft ball toward the batter referred to as the "striker." To put a player out, a fielder either caught the ball in mid-air or was able to hit the base runner with the ball as he ran from base to base; to protect players, the balls were soft.

That legend? Supposedly one Mr. Abner Doubleday sat watching this game of townball and decided to set down rules, then and there. The problem with the legend is that Doubleday wasn't in Cooperstown. When he supposedly sat watching townball and writing down his new game rules, he was a student at West Point. But give Doubleday credit for one thing: He never claimed to have anything to do with any part of the game. Others did it for him.

By the turn of the nineteenth century, baseball, as it began to be called, was everywhere. In 1840 a diverse group founded the New York Knickerbocker Baseball Club. When New York City became too urban, the Knickerbockers took their game across the river to Hoboken, New Jersey, to a grassy area known as Elysian Fields.

Then came more changes. The square-shaped field became a diamond; a base runner was out if he was tagged or thrown out trying to reach base. With players no longer regularly hit by balls, the ball itself was changed from soft to hard, and that really opened up the game.

Civil War–style baseball was anything but a pitchers' duel; one game between the 13th Massachusetts and the 104th New York ended with the score 66–20. Massachusetts won.[3] Games also tended toward the vicious side, with one Union soldier admitting after a game in Tennessee, "We get lamed badly."

Northern soldiers frequently wrote home about playing baseball while held captive in Southern prisons. The two activities, baseball and war, shared a goal—get home as fast as possible.

With baseball and wrestling matches as physical outlets and letter writing and cardplaying for more mental remedies, troops in America's Civil War did just what soldiers of any war, of any age, did and probably will do in any future war—which includes visiting bawdy houses.[4]

The Old South of Margaret Mitchell's *Gone with the Wind* was Bible country—moreover, evangelical Bible country. The Good Book was taken to be just that, Good. And taken literally. This is not to say Confederate soldiers didn't gamble (they did) or drink (bourbon whiskey was invented by a seventeenth-century Anglican priest at a James River, Virginia, plantation) or fool around with those wild, wild women (soldiers on both sides wrote so many tales of sexual exploits, *some* of them must be true). They did all these things, confessed their sins to the nearest priest or pastor, and did them again.

There was so much betting going on in the Confederate army, General Lee issued an order complaining that he was "pained to learn that the vice of gambling exists, and is becoming common in this army."[5] Lee issued the order; the troops ignored it.

A soldier's life, then as now, is often synonymous with degradation and immorality. Same for sailors, Marines, and the Coast Guard or their predecessors, the Revenue Marines. The Union listed two hundred Revenue Marines at the start of the war; sixty of them resigned to join the Confederacy.

Decks of playing cards often carried pictures of high-ranking political and military officials from both sides. Others pictured scantily dressed (if dressed at all) young ladies. Northern soldiers had better access to playing cards, which made them a hot trade item during informal truces. Confederates would trade tobacco (or nearly anything else they had) for a deck of cards. If they couldn't get them through trade, the Rebels often made their own.

Preachers loudly proclaimed the sinfulness of playing cards. Soldiers listened and went on with the game. Usually. Just before a battle they'd toss away their instruments of sin. If the men survived the fighting, they'd round up the cards and start sinning all over again.

They shot craps with dice, and while the game grew more popular with time, it didn't really come into its own until other wars. Soldiers held cockfights, with the loser winding up in the cooking pot. The cavalry, of course, held horse races. Lacking cards or dice or horses, the troops found something else on which to wager. Remember those little wooden boats with paper sails kids used to make? Johnny Reb and Billy Yank also made them, then bet on races held in nearby streams.

Perhaps the most inventive way troops found to gamble was with lice. They held lice races; since the camps and the men themselves were infested with such vermin, there never was a lack of some louse to bet on. Troops even staged battles between head lice, though visualizing such is both hilarious and difficult.

Traveling preachers and ministers of the Gospel tried hard to hold down the men's urge to gamble; usually their efforts failed. An Alabama soldier wrote:

Yesterday was Sunday, and I sat at my fire and saw the preachers holding forth about thirty steps off, and between them and me were two games of poker. . . . Chuck-a-luck and faro banks are running night and day, with eager and excited crowds standing around with their hands full of money. Open gambling has been prohibited, but that amounts to nothing.[6]

During lulls in the war troops sometimes built churches, competing in doctrine and architecture, the latter of which frequently went to elaborate degrees.

Just as in every other war, books and periodicals were written specifically for the troops. *A Mother's Parting Words to her Soldier Son*, by Richmond minister Jeremiah B. Jeter, was distributed to more than 250,000 Confederate troops. It dealt in a direct, nonsentimental way with the realities of life, upholding liberty, freedom, and Christian values. *How Do You Bear Your Troubles?* carried the advice to seek God's help. *The Gambler's Balance Sheet* and *The Eventful Twelve Hours,* or the *Destitution and Wretchedness of the Drunkard* weren't so popular, perhaps because they did more preaching than helping out the troops. One pamphlet, *The Silly Fish,* took on the issue of swearing. One who swears, the writer preached, is much like a fish that bites an empty hook; neither fish nor swearer gains anything from the event.

One obviously dangerous game, one undoubtedly frowned upon by the officers, involved filling empty canteens with gunpowder, corking them tightly, and tossing them into the campfire. They made, it was said, "considerable noise." Once, in a western-based Union cavalry division, the boys began playing this "pop goes the canteen" game, and their sleeping general mistakenly thought they were under attack. He called for his horse; he called for his scouts; he called for his infantry. When he found out what really happened, he called for the guard and ordered the troops to stop all the racket, then he returned to his quarters, mad as hell.

CHAPTER FIVE

❀

Homesick Times:
Readin', Ritin', and Loved-Starved Troops

*I must tell you a secret, down on the Jeems (sic) River the other day I saw a—a—
gal, that is a lady. Ef I could get that gal, I'd give anything that I've got. Yes! I'd even
part with my new red cotton Handkerchief.*

—Andy Crockett
May 22, 1862 [1]

As in all other wars, those who actually fought the Civil War were young. It was the old who ordered the war, leaving it to the young to fight. Away from home for the first time, both Johnny Reb and Billy Yank were, in a word, homesick, and that called for letter writing. Life away from their loved ones evolved from an acute pain into a chronic ache. Time after time, letter after sad letter, we read of how they wanted to be home. "I never knew what pleasure home afforded to a man before," an Alabama soldier wrote in a letter to loved ones in that home he missed so much.

Samuel Beardsley was forty-five when he joined the 24th New York Volunteer Infantry. He rose to the rank of lieutenant colonel, but that was long after this letter to his son.

> *I wrote your mother quite a long letter on Friday last and a short one on Saturday enclosing a draft for $100, which I trust came safely to hand. On Sunday, I left camp with five companies (about three hundred men) for Bailey's Cross Roads, about which place you will see a good deal said in the papers, as it is in close proximity to the rebels, and a skirmish takes place in that vicinity about every day.*

Beardsley was stationed near Washington, D.C. At the time, Bailey's Cross Roads was just what its named implied, nothing more than a crossroads. It remained so until the 1980s when it became one of the largest shopping centers in the country, housing stores and shops where Beardsley's "draft for $100" wouldn't go far.

His men ran into a small group of Rebel troops building a fortification nearby. The two sides skirmished—efforts that Beardsley said were intended "to draw us outside our entrenchments, and have a big battle, but this we cannot do until General McClellan gives the word." In this instance, his greatest problem wasn't the Confederates, but food supplied him by his own brother.

[After] I got back, I was seized by my old enemy, Mr. Diarrhea, and on Tuesday was very sick. Dr. Murdock gave me about half a tea cup of castor oil, which has done me some good, and I have today commenced taking tincture of iron, three times a day, and quinine twice a day. It is to give me strength, I believe. Dr. M. says I ought to go home for about three weeks and recruit (?) up, but I don't suppose this would be possible. He attributed my sickness in a great measure to sleeping in a damp tent, but I am today going to have a floor laid, whicn will obviate this difficulty. I attribute this last attack to eating a large quantity of pickled oysters while we were at Bailey's Cross Roads. (Your) Uncle Levi gave me a can of them and, being hungry, I ate freely of them, together with a goodly quantity of cheese, ginger cakes and sweet biscuit. It was imprudent, but it is so seldom that I have anything so tempting that, being quite hungry, I pitched in.

Dr. Murdock found wood for Beardsley's floor, and for a while he was "quite comfortable and it really begins to look like housekeeping." But things changed.

Last night we had a pouring rain and I got up to tighten the curtains of my tent when I stepped, splash, into a puddle of water which had run in. I have tried for more than a week to get lumber for a floor, but everything that would answer, board fences and all, are snapped up the minute a regiment locates itself, and our present camp has been occupied by three or four regiments before us. To show how difficult it is to obtain lumber, one of our officers had to pay $5.00 the other day for enough to floor a small tent about a third as large as mine.

You ought to see some of my furniture; for instance my outdoor washstand consists of a stake driven in the ground with a barrel head nailed on top. I also have a one-legged stool made of a small barrel head nailed onto a short stake. My writing desk is made of a large dry goods box in which I have made a shelf, where I keep my writing materials, candle sticks and candles, books, tumbler, matches, brushes, soap, a paper of nails and tacks, bottles of medicines, etc.— one of the most capacious as well as convenient shelves you ever saw.

Our eating arrangements are very poor but the best we can get.

Two of the soldiers have established a sort of boarding tent where we get most vile coffee, butter strong enough to walk alone, and some meat of some sort generally for breakfast or dinner. . . .

Give my love to Grandma and tell her I congratulate her on her seventy-first birthday and trust she will see many more. Tell Mary, with my love, that I will write her before long.

From your affectionate father[2]

It's interesting that one could be conscripted into a "volunteer" regiment, but that wasn't unusual in America's Civil War. Constantine Hege was one such unwilling recruit, conscripted into the 48th North Carolina Volunteer Infantry.

Dear Father:

I now have the opportunity of writing to you this afternoon stating that I am well at present, hoping that you enjoy the same blessings.

I want you to try to hire a substitute. If you do hire one, get a competent man to bring him to Captain Meikels'. . . .

It is said that the Yankees are about twelve miles from here now. I saw about three hundred Yankees from Salisbury [Prison] on their way home at Weldon [North Carolina]. I talked with several of them. They seem to be a fine set of men as are anywhere. . . .[3]

Later that year, Private Hege wrote home following the Battle of Fredericksburg, Virginia.

I now once more have . . . the opportunity of writing a few lines to you to let you know how affairs are here. . . . I was taken with a chill and then a pain on my side night before last, but I now feel right better this morning. I think it was just a bad cold, which I had taken because I had nothing but old pieces of shoe on my feet. My toes are naked, and my clothing are getting ragged.

There has been a very hard battle fought here at Fredericksburg Saturday. Our regiment was in the heart of the fight. I did not have to go into the battle because I am so near barefooted the colonel gave

orders that all barefooted men should stay at the camp. I can tell you
that I was glad then that my shoes did not come, because I would
rather lose a hundred dollars than to go in a battle. . . .
    I must close by giving you all the best wishes and respects and if
we never meet on earth I hope to meet you in a better world. [4]

Constantine Hege's father never hired a substitute to replace his son.
Instead, the younger Hege was captured by Union troops in the fall
of 1863. Constantine decided he'd had enough, swore allegiance to
the Union, and returned to civilian life as a steelworker in Bethle-
hem, Pennsylvania.

Letter writing, it seems, was so compelling to some soldiers they even
wrote home explaining how and when they wrote home. J. H. Puckett described the setting around him.

I am seated in a beautiful grove of "black Jack" with my back lean-
ing against one, flat in the dust, short pencil, no board, nothing but
my knee and finger to keep my paper straight, my face Southward,
fires and smoke all around me, boys cooking dinner, crowds in talk-
ing distance discussing [the war] . . .[5]

Robert Gill of North Carolina apparently was more concerned about
letter writing than about the surrounding fighting, until it got too
close. "The Yankees keep Shooting," he wrote, "so I am afraid they
will knock over my ink so I will close."[6]

    Another North Carolina soldier was worried about his mother's
apparent illiteracy, something she must have inherited from him.

Mother when you wright to me get somebody to wright that can wright
a plain hand to read I Cold not read your leter to make sence of it
wrote so bad I have lurned to do my own reading and writing and
it is a grate help to me.[7]

The Emory University archives now holds a letter written on February 12, 1862, by a rather confused soldier named W. C. Simmons.
While other writers used such phrases as "I seat myself to write you"
or "I take pen in hand," Simmons tried to use both clichés at the same
time: "[It] is with pleasure this morning that I take my Seat and pen
in hand to drop you a few lines."

    Frank Moss of Texas more or less took pen in hand to correspond
with his sister: "I am writing with a corn Stalk pen whien [sic] it wont

write on one Side I turn over on the other. Pen points are worth a dollar a peace Scarce at that."[8]

Writing home and receiving letters from friends and loved ones probably was the most important nonmilitary activity among the troops North and South, although a shortage of paper often precluded modern-style envelopes for their letters. They got around it by using the paper itself. As one historian explains the procedure, "[The] writing sheet simply [was] folded, sealed with wax and addressed on the outside." Only when secrecy or privacy were concerned did the average soldier resort to envelopes.[9]

Many of us today complain about the uncertainty of the mails. Obviously, it was even worse during the Civil War, especially for Southerners who wrote to friends in the Union. Many people placed messages in Southern newspapers, hoping Northern newspapers would print the notices, and their friends in the Union would see them.

PERSONALS
United States Papers Requested to Copy
John Wentworth Philadelphia, Pa:

Have just seen your personal of October 29th. Are very well and delighted to hear from you. Write at once by flag of truce, and let us have your address so that we can write you through same channel.
All send their love.
Emma Elliott

Despite the war, despite having, in the case of some Vicksburg, Mississippi, printers, to use wallpaper instead of newsprint, newspapers throughout the South continued to publish. Richmond, for example, had half a dozen newspapers that published throughout the war. They continued up to the day the city fell and was almost destroyed when the retreating Rebels set fire to tobacco warehouses. Even then the *Whig* managed to put out an edition the following day, albeit no longer espousing states' rights on its masthead.

At least two of Richmond's wartime newspapers were religious in nature, and another, the *Anzeiger,* was "printed in German [and offered] great advantages as an advertising sheet, being the only German newspaper now published in the Confederacy."[10] Several news-papers were offered not only in daily editions but in monthly and semi-weekly editions as well. Personal letters always were a vital part of their coverage.

> *To Mrs. Kate Hooper, Alexandria, Va.:*
>
> *I received a letter from your brother on the 1st inst. He is stationed at Monroe, Walton County, Ga. on detached service, being unfit for field duty in consequence of wounds received at the Battle of Chicka-mauga. He is very well and doing well and anxious to hear from you. Give my love to my uncle and Adeline. I will write by the next flag of truce. Pap is well and sends his love to all.*
>
> *Yours Truly,*
> *Jimmy*

Through the nineteenth century, "inst." or "instant" was used to in-dicate "the time now present." In other words, this month. In the case of this particular letter, November 1862. "Ult." or "ulto." was the ab-breviation for *ultimo,* meaning "of last month."

From Richmond to Portsmouth, Virginia, is less than a hundred miles (about an hour and twenty minutes, as the author has often driven it hastily if somewhat illegally), but by early 1862, the two cities were cities in different nations. Portsmouth and Norfolk across the Elizabeth River were abandoned to the North shortly after the bat-tle of the ironclads, the *Monitor* and the *Virginia.* Richmond, though under siege, was still in Confederate hands, and communicating over those hundred miles often was difficult.

> *Ossie, Portsmouth, Va.*
>
> *K cannot come home without a permit from the Federal authori-ties. Try to get one for her and child, and send as soon as possible. J. G. and N were all well when last heard from. Cousin M lost her youngest a few weeks ago. . . .*
>
> *Love to all at home,*
> *Nat*

The Vietnam War brought a call for a U.S. government accounting of MIAs, troops missing in action, but Vietnam was not unique. There are MIAs in all wars. Many of the troops who fought in the Ameri-can Revolution are still missing two hundred years later. Many who marched away from home to fight in America's Civil War never were heard from again.

Just as now, their loved ones held out hope, often using newspapers to gain word of missing soldiers.

Information desired of Madison F. Hawthorn, Sergeant of Company F, 12th S O V, missing since 30th September.

(Unsigned)

Those who crossed the lines between Johnny Reb and Billy Yank might use newspaper to let everyone know they'd made it safely.

Mrs. Mary E. T., Baltimore, Md.

Arrived safe. All right. O is well. Heard from Joe—Do not know yet.

Bob

Today's personal columns vary from love wanted to love for sale, from prayers for peace to children wanted for adoption. In the mid-1800s, columns often were used to transmit bad news.

F A F Jones, New Orleans, La.

Laura, myself and baby are well. Have not heard from you for some time. Poor Justament died 12th August. . . . Answer through New York News; Richmond Enquirer to copy.

Doctor

Sometimes individuals passed letters through the lines by flag of truce, a practice dependent upon the goodwill of the initial recipient to send the letter on.

Mrs. S. B. Deale, Gurkeysville, Baltimore county, Md.

Have written by flag of truce, but have not received a line since my return. Am anxious to hear in regard to your health; mine has been uninterruptedly good. Not heard from Mame since August. Love to J. J., children and all friends. . . .

Bob

Both North and South, friends and loved ones asked those on the other side of the war to help out.

To H. O. Hardy, Esq. New York city:

My son, Thomas A., a private in Company G, 4th regiment Virginia infantry, was taken prisoner by the enemy near Petersburg on the 27th October, ult. Please ascertain to what prison he was sent and supply his wants I heard he was not wounded. We are all well as usual.

Thomas A. Hardy

During the war, personal ads usually cost about two dollars per insertion. The Richmond *Enquirer* suggested "all notices should be

inserted five times as making it more certain of reaching the party."
Such personal notices, the *Enquirer* added, "are copied into the
columns of the *New York Daily News*." All "personals: intended for parties in the *Confederate States* and published in the *New York Daily News*
are regularly transferred to the columns of the *Enquirer* and the parties to whom they are addressed are supplied with a copy of the paper containing the same."

> *Mrs. O. L., New York:*
>
> *Your personal in Richmond* Enquirer *noticed. Your children are
> well. Have written three times since August 18th. . . . L. has her
> music. No school since July. Everything as usual. L. writes you to-
> day. Anxious to see you.*
>
> A. U. W.

Sometimes, the request for aid reached far beyond the borders of
either Confederate or United States.

> *Miss Elizabeth Shepherd, care Rev. Robert Shepherd, Jr.,*
> *6 Ashfield, West Terrace, New Castle upon Tyne, England:*
>
> *My Dear Daughter—Your poor father died on the 17th of Septem-
> ber, and your sister Isabella on the 19th of October. I am now left
> with no one but little Mary and am very feeble. Do try to come or to
> send for us soon; can't come alone.*
>
> *Your affectionate mother,*
> *Mary James* [11]

It is impossible to determine how many of these personals actually
reached the intended reader. Regular mail itself often went unde-
livered. When Richmond was evacuated and burned in April 1865,
the Confederate Post Office was destroyed, and with it thousands
of letters waiting for their owners, a disaster as much to historians
as to the intended recipients. Historians look on letters the way ar-
chaeologists look on middens (garbage heaps of past generations).
They tell, in unwashed detail, stories often lost in more formal sur-
roundings.

A private from Georgia wrote, in the convention of the times, to
one we assume was his girl back home. "Dear Miss Bettie," John Holloway wrote. "Don't you think that I will know how to appreciate a
comfortable home with its luxuries after my enlistment is out? I think

I will at any rate." He told about the battle he'd just been in, of the typhoid fever going around camp, and about his hopes that it all would soon end. "I will now bid you farewell for the present," Holloway added, "hoping you all the happiness that this cold world can give and at last a happy one beyond the skies, where the wicked cease from troubling and weary are at rest. Yours most affectionately, John Holloway."

Even before the war, the South was way behind the North in education, a point especially obvious when reading letters written home by the troops. That is, if the soldier could write. Many could not and relied on friends to do the job for them. Frequently, those friends couldn't spell, apparently believing in the old adage that it's a poor soul who can think of only one way to write a word. We don't condemn them for their poor spelling; some of the world's greatest writers sit in the poor spellers section of class. William Shakespeare, for instance. Only six authenticated examples of Shakespeare's autograph exist, and all six are spelled differently. That puts Civil War soldier-writers in good company.

While we don't condemn them for poor spelling, it is interesting to list some of the more unusual examples found in letters of the period.

accitment	meaning excitement
afeard	meaning afraid
agetent	meaning adjutant
carey	meaning carry
ceep	meaning keep
A brim ham lillkern	meaning Abraham Lincoln
Chic a har mana	meaning Chickahominy
dyereaer	meaning diarrhea
Fluriday	meaning Florida
regislatury	meaning legislature [12]

When Company A of the 11 North Carolina Infantry was organized, twenty-seven out of the hundred men enrolled had to make their marks rather than sign the roll. The same for another North Carolina unit: thirty-six privates out of seventy-two signed with an *X*.

They could always look up to Nathan Bedford Forrest. He was uneducated and wealthy. Some of the more educated enlisted men didn't like serving under such a nonaristocratic officer, but that never bothered Forrest.

The 1800s had many words and phrases peculiar to the times: *absquatulate* or *almighty* or *chirk*. Phrases such as to have a "brick in your hat" and be "cold as a wagon tire" and "plug-ugly."

To *absquatulate* meant to disappear or leave, as in "in the heat of battle, he absquatulated." *Almighty* didn't necessarily mean God but huge, as in "I was almighty sad when they conscripted me into the army." *Chirk* meant cheerful, and if you had a brick in your hat, you were drunk. Being cold as a wagon tire means to be deceased, dead, passed on. And plug-ugly originally referred to a member of a particular Baltimore gang but later came to mean just about any rowdy or boisterous individual. Most of us know that to skedaddle meant to run away, as in the Great Skedaddle by the Yankees at the Battle of Manassas.

Victorian Age individuals, of which those living during America's Civil War most certainly were included, generally avoided referring to legs as legs in polite company; they were "limbs." A similar substitute is still around today, "bosom" for breast. In really delicate mixed company, as silly as it sounds to us, Civil War ladies referred to a chicken breast as a "chicken bosom." Those same delicate and discreet individuals would never think of using the words *pants* or *trousers;* they called them "inexpressibles."[13]

Not all Rebel soldiers were uneducated, of course. The South had units comprised of cadets from the Virginia Military Institute. Washington College (like VMI, it's in Lexington, Virginia) also sent many of its students to war, mainly to the First Company of Rockbridge Artillery. That unit had on its rolls four individuals with master of arts degrees, twenty holding bachelor of arts degrees, and at least forty others who were currently students at Washington College, the University of Virginia, or other colleges at the time war broke out. Another unit, Company E of the 11 Virginia had as its captain a professor at Lynchburg College, as well as many of his students. Some other units, in fact, had more college-educated soldiers than they had noneducated men. Not all of those with college educations were officers, either. To some, it was preferable to be a private in the Richmond Howitzer Battalion (the unit organized by Thomas Jefferson's grandson, George Wythe Randolph) or the Hampton Legion than to be an officer in any other regiment.

Among individuals who could read and write, there was a high incidence of desertion, especially when they saw some educated sons of plantation owners avoiding combat. One private from North Carolina wrote home that he had no intention of sticking with the war. "All of the gentel men has got out of it," he wrote his wife, "and i don't intend to put my Life between them and their propty."

The Union side had its share of college students and graduates. According to the *Official Records,* the 2d Massachusetts Regiment had many graduates of Harvard College. Unfortunately, the 2d Massachusetts also had the doubtful honor of having one of the highest casualty rates among officers of either side of the war. Sixteen of the 2d Massachusetts' officers were killed or died of wounds or disease; thirteen of them were Harvard graduates.

CHAPTER SIX

Seven Days Do Not an Army Make:
Or Do They?

I prefer Lee to Johnston—the former is too cautious & weak under grave responsibility—personally brave & energetic to a fault, he yet is wanting in moral firmness when pressed by heavy responsibility & is likely to be timid & irresolute in action.
—Gen. George B. McClellan
Letter to President Lincoln, April 20, 1862

Here lay the wounded, the dying, and the dead, hundreds upon hundreds in every conceivable position; some with contorted features showing the agony of death, others as if quietly sleeping. Hundreds of letters from mothers, sisters, and friends were found upon them....
—Unidentified Confederate soldier
Written July 19, 1862

At the beginning of the war George McClellan was known as the "Little Napoleon." Later he was called "Little Mac." He was a brilliant organizer and administrator. He just didn't known when to stop organizing and start fighting. As a leading expert on America's Civil War puts it, George McClellan was "totally lacking in the essential qualities of successful command of large forces in battle."[1]

As the new commander of Union forces, George McClellan helped recruit an army. Then he trained it. Then he trained it some more. What he didn't do was take it off to war. He ignored questions from the president, but that didn't bother Lincoln too much. "I will hold McClellan's horse," Lincoln told his assistant private secretary, John Hay, "if it will only bring us success."

By early January of 1862, however, Abraham Lincoln had had enough. McClellan had trained his men, sat around Washington's Willard Hotel, then trained his men some more. During a White House war conference, Lincoln reportedly said, "If General McClellan does not want to use the army, I would like to borrow it, provided I could see how it could be made to do something."

A special House and Senate Committee on the Conduct of the War had been formed after the Union's loss at the Bull Run Battle.

With the Union army sitting around on its haversacks, the committee, in the best Congressional tradition, held a hearing and invited
General McClellan to testify. What, they wanted to know, was he going to do with his new Army? Instead of meeting with the committee, McClellan got sick: typhoid fever, one of the great scourges of
the war.

The president asked QMG Montgomery C. Meigs, "What shall I
do? The people are impatient; [Treasury Secretary Salmon] Chase
has no money and tells me he can raise no more; the General of the
Army has typhoid fever. The bottom is out of the tub." Lincoln believed George McClellan had spent too much time recruiting and
training an army and too little time fighting.

The president called a meeting of his cabinet. Several members
wanted to charge head on into the Confederates encamped around
Manassas. Others wanted to make a flanking movement by water.

McClellan, meanwhile, was working on a similar plan. The Little
Napoleon wanted to make an end run around the Confederate army:
transport his army down the Chesapeake Bay, then up the Rappahannock River to Urbanna, Virginia, landing behind Rebel lines. Lincoln had fought the idea. He believed it would leave the way open
for the Rebels to rush in and capture the Union capital.

Lincoln held a second meeting. This time his military men agreed:
push overland to Manassas.

McClellan heard about it and miraculously recovered from his attack of typhoid. He convinced the president to give him one more
chance, so Lincoln approved McClellan's end-around plan. "I don't
care what plan you have," he said, "all I ask is for you to pitch in."

George McClellan agreed to an alternate plan. He would leave a
forty thousand–man army outside Washington, then take the majority of his force down the Chesapeake and march up the Virginia
peninsula. He believed he could take the Confederate capital at Richmond with ease. On March 14 he sent a message to his men.

*For a long time I have kept you inactive, but not without a purpose:
you were to be disciplined, armed and instructed. . . . I shall demand
of you great, heroic exertions, rapid and long marches, desperate com-
bats, privations, perhaps. We will share all these together; and when*

*this sad war is over we will all return to our homes, and feel that we
can ask no higher honor than the proud consciousness that we belonged to the Army of the Potomac.*

A very rousing message, especially considering it came from a man
who hadn't done much since being given their command.

From the beginning of this end-around movement, things went
wrong for the Union army. McClellan wanted two hundred thousand
men but got about half that many. He had to fight to take control of
the Potomac away from Rebel forces, so in late February he sent a
force to break through the Confederate stranglehold. It didn't work;
the boats carrying the Federal troops were the wrong size, six
inches too wide to sail through a lock on the Chesapeake and Ohio
Canal. That set off Union Secretary of War Edwin Stanton. Boats too
large to get through the canal, Stanton said, "means that [McClel-
lan] doesn't intend to do anything." Lincoln, in his usually homey
fashion, agreed: "I am no engineer, but it seems to me that if I wished
to know whether a boat would go through a hole . . . common sense
would teach me to go and measure it."

In November of 1861 he'd made McClellan general in chief of
the Union army, but on March 11, 1862, President Lincoln relieved
McClellan of that title; Lincoln wanted his general in chief to defend Washington, not go sailing off to Richmond. George McClellan wasn't pleased with this demotion.

In April of 1862 he landed at Fort Monroe, at the tip of the peninsula between the James and York Rivers. With him were more than
a hundred thousand men, fifty-nine batteries of artillery, twenty-
five thousand animals, eleven hundred supply wagons, and tons of
equipment.

McClellan apparently believed his spies, chief of whom was Allan
Pinkerton, the Chicago private detective, who said that the Confederacy had from 180,000 to 200,000 men facing him along the peninsula. In truth, about all the South had were 15,000 men, the flashy
but temperamental Gen. "Prince John" Bankhead Magruder and a
bunch of Quaker guns, wooden cannon made of trees to look like
the real thing.

The Rebels also used Quaker guns at Centreville, near Manassas.
After Confederate troops left Centreville, a Union soldier discovered

the fake cannon and said, "We have been humbugged by the rebels." Well, the Rebels humbugged them again on the peninsula.

McClellan also fought the rain; he lost that battle also. When he was pushing for his peninsula invasion, the Little Napoleon claimed Virginia roads were in good condition year-round. They weren't. Those primitive things that Virginians of 1862 called roads were so muddy, they led to the story of a mule that sank so deep all you could see were his ears.

Rebel General Johnston and his army had been in winter quarters around Manassas. On paper he had a growing army, troops coming in almost daily from several states. Trouble was, he now had so many men, he had to reorganize his army into new regiments, brigades, and divisions. He also had to promote new officers to lead them. Half of his men had never been in battle; but that was all right, because more than half of his officers had never commanded their divisions in battle.

He also had to contend with frequent outbreaks of diseases. Among other illnesses, his new troops were racked with measles and typhoid.[2] Epidemics swept Joe Johnston's troops, taking hundreds of lives and sickening many more.

They also had another "disease." They tended to go home or to run off at the most inopportune time. General D. H. Hill once wrote that "several thousand soldiers . . . have fled to Richmond under pretext of sickness. They have even thrown away their arms that their flight might not be impeded."

When the Confederate Congress passed the "Furlough and Bounty Act," the Rebel army lost even more men. The law promised new recruits a fifty-dollar bounty and a sixty-day furlough. Just about the time McClellan set sail for Fort Monroe, Johnston's men began demanding their promised furloughs. One ten thousand–man Confederate division was down to less than six thousand men.

As the peninsula campaign progressed, there was McClellan (with a king-size ego and faulty intelligence from chief spy Allan Pinkerton) facing Prince John Magruder with an even larger ego (and his Quaker guns) near Yorktown, the site of Lord Cornwallis's surrender to George Washington in 1781. A week earlier the USS *Monitor* met the CSS *Virginia* within sight of Fort Monroe. The Union navy was there protecting McClellan's rear and blockading the rivers to keep the Confederates from resupplying its troops by water. They needn't have worried; the South didn't have enough ships to do much fighting or blockade-running.

Magruder was something of an amateur actor. While he was in the Union army, he served alongside then Lt. Ulysses S. Grant during the Mexican War. Magruder staged a performance of Shakespeare's *Othello* with himself in the lead role. Costarring in the role of Othello's wife, Desdemona was five-foot-seven, 150-pound Lieutenant Grant. In drag. Dressed in wig and crinolines, surely a sight to see.

Now, however, Magruder played another role: a general commanding a large, formidable army. Considering how few men he had, it took all of his acting skills and then some to pull it off. He moved troops here, moved them back, aimed those Quaker guns at the Yankees, moved them to another location, and he even ran a railroad back and forth all night long. Anything to make McClellan believe the South's fifteen thousand troops numbered more like a hu..dred and fifty thousand. McClellan wrote his wife, saying, "It seems clear that I shall have the whole force of the enemy on my hands."

A Confederate corporal from Alabama knew differently; he'd been marching around in circles to fool McClellan. "I am pretty tired," he wrote home. They'd been "travelling most of the day, seeming with no other view than to show ourselves to the enemy at as many different points of the line as possible."

Lincoln pushed McClellan to move forward, telegraphing his general, "You must act" to break the enemy's lines. McClellan wanted more men and wrote his wife, "I was very much tempted to reply [to President Lincoln] that he had better come and do it himself."

The *New York Times* in June 1861, ran a headline: FORWARD TO RICHMOND! It quickly was shortened to ON TO RICHMOND! The South, of course, had its own version: FORWARD TO WASHINGTON! It took four years for the first campaign to succeed, and then it wasn't under George McClellan. The FORWARD TO WASHINGTON! campaign never really got started.

McClellan's peers of 1862 and his critics of 1996 argued that, should the general have gone all out in his peninsula campaign, he most likely could have beaten the Confederates separating him from Richmond. All it would have taken, they believed, was for McClellan to stop gathering men and material and start fighting his way to Richmond. The irony is that McClellan believed he was doing just what he *should* have been doing: digging in. "Not a day, not an hour, has been lost," he wrote: "Works have been constructed that may almost be called gigantic." It's a wonder the end of the Virginia peninsula didn't fall off into the ocean; here was McClellan digging trenches for all he was worth, facing Magruder (and later Johnston and Lee) with the Rebels busy digging their own trenches.

While McClellan dug in, Johnston succeeded in getting his own army out of Manassas and down to the peninsula. "No one but McClellan," the Rebel believed, "could have hesitated to attack." McClellan slowly felt his way toward Richmond; Johnston wasn't about to wait, and launched a massive assault on Union troops about seven miles from the Confederate capital, at Seven Pines. It was May 31. The North called it the Battle of Fair Oaks; they were more successful in that part of the engagement. The South called it the Battle of Seven Pines, because that's where *they* were successful. Federal morale soared as they pushed the Rebels back. Confederate morale took an even more severe blow late in the day.

It was coming on to night when General Johnston rode out close to the front. He was hit twice by Union fire, a bullet in the shoulder and shrapnel in the chest; it looked as if he might not survive. Major General Gustavus W. Smith temporarily took over.

The following day, Confederate President Davis turned to his chief military advisor and appointed him the new commander. It was Davis's best appointment of the war. General Robert E. Lee took over.

He renamed the Confederate force the Army of Northern Virginia, and from then until the end of the war it was Lee's army, and he was proud of it.

The Battle of Seven Pines saw 54,000 troops engaged, divided almost evenly between North and South. The Federals lost 5,031 in the battle, which is another reason the North claims to have won the battle. The Confederacy's losses were higher, totaling 6,134.

Forget the fact that the South's losses at Seven Pines were greater than the North's. You can forget it, because George McClellan himself seemed not to remember it. The North in general may have claimed victory, but General McClellan lost confidence and became even more cautious.

As the Confederacy's new commander, Robert E. Lee immediately began rebuilding his force. He reassigned officers and called Jackson in from the Shenandoah Valley. Lee then turned to reinforcing the defenses around Richmond, which game him the nickname "King of Spades." He ordered his men to dig trenches around the capital city.

At the same time President Jefferson Davis and the men in the ranks noticed a change in the way the Rebel army was run, others did also. In Richmond, diarist J. B. Jones commented, "What a change!" "No one," he wrote on June 15, 1862, "now dreams of the loss of the capital."

On the night of June 11–12, the vainglorious Brig. Gen. James Ewell Brown "Jeb" Stuart began his now famous "Ride Around McClellan."

Lee had instructed Stuart to make a reconnaissance of the Federal right flank, around Mechanicsville; he was to scout the area between the Chickahominy River and Totopotomoy Creek. Well, Stuart did that, and then some. His ride around McClellan's army was more of a raid on the whole Union force on the Virginia peninsula.

Colonel John Singleton Mosby, soon to be called the "Gray Ghost" of the 1st Virginia, told Stuart his men had found only a few Union patrols in the area, information that greatly encouraged Stuart. Taking about twelve hundred men, many of them locals who knew the area well, Stuart hit the trail. It was about 2:00 A.M. on the twelfth when he left Hanover Courthouse, north-northeast of Richmond. There's a tavern nearby, once owned by Patrick Henry, of "give me liberty or give me death" fame. The tavern is still there, now used as a dinner theater.

Stuart wasn't satisfied with merely carrying out Lee's orders to check McClellan's lines; he marched and rode nearly 150 miles, destroyed a significant amount of property (some of it arguably Confederate property), captured many prisoners, even destroyed two boats on the Pamunkey river. In the course of it all, he made a fool of McClellan and embarrassed the whole Union Army of the Potomac. That included his father-in-law, Philip St. George Cooke. Stuart rode all around them, leaving his father-in-law in the dust, chasing son-in-law Jeb.

Cooke declined to send his five hundred horsemen forward without infantry support, because he erroneously believed Stuart had foot soldiers accompanying the Rebel raid. It was a scheme Stuart (and Jackson) often used: infantry troops riding behind cavalrymen, on the same horse, sitting on a pad behind the cavalry rider's saddle. Once near the area of battle, the infantry would dismount and go into combat as foot soldiers.

Stuart's ride did several things. It greatly lifted the South's morale; it greatly increased Stuart's own self-importance; and it gave Lee the information he needed to drive McClellan off the peninsula. That information was welcome, because the next several days were among the most important in the war: the Seven Days' Battles: Oak Grove, June 25, 1862; Mechanicsville, June 26; Gaines's Mill, June 27–28; Garnett's and Golding's Farms, June 27–28; Savage's Station and Allen's Farm, June 29; White Oak Swamp, June 30; Malvern Hill, July 1. Together, the Seven Days' Battles saw more than 105,000 Union troops fighting 90,000 Rebels.

The Seven Days' Battles were bloody, vicious brawls. In some cases it's not certain which side won. The North lost nearly 16,000 troops, while the South suffered more than 20,000 casualties. The Rebels also captured 52 cannon (which they later lost back to the Union) and more than 30,000 small arms.

The Seven Days' Battles changed the face of both armies. When the fighting was over, both sides were made up of veterans, no longer green troops gazing on the elephant of battle for the first time.

In the end, it was the Confederacy that held the peninsula and pushed the Federals away from Richmond. In doing this, Robert E. Lee altered the complexion of the war. It may be argued that by saving Richmond in the spring and summer of 1862, Lee led the South on a course which took it to even more severe devastation. If, this argument goes, McClellan had won the campaign and captured

Richmond, America's Civil War would have ended then. Every other battle that followed, every other death in years to come, might not have occurred.

President Lincoln paid George McClellan a visit during the Peninsula Campaign. Most of the general's officers believed they should make another try at taking Richmond, and Lincoln was willing to approve the plan. Not McClellan, not with the army he had. He wanted more men, a demand the president thought unrealistic.

Finally, Lincoln lost patience and told General Halleck at the War Department in Washington to order McClellan to quit the peninsula. McClellan claimed the order "caused me the greatest pain I have ever experienced." He left anyway. McClellan's first units pulled out on August 14; the last left twelve days later. The Peninsula Campaign was over; the "On to Richmond" movement was put on hold.

The South had a new hero in Robert E. Lee. The North now doubted the ability and field effectiveness of George B. McClellan. though Richmond was momentarily saved, it remained under siege until the end of the war.

What of "Prince John" Magruder, the man who so thoroughly convinced McClellan that his fifteen thousand men actually were a hundred and fifty thousand? That action was the highlight of an otherwise mediocre career. After that he became cautious and bumbling; as in many cases of those not quite up to military staff standards, he tried to do everything himself, in person. He grew overexcited and overzealous and confused. At one point during the Seven Days' Battles he mistakenly marched three of his units *away* from the scene at Malvern Hill. James Longstreet had to convince Magruder of his mistake, and it took nearly three hours to straighten out the mess.

In October the Confederacy sent Magruder to command the District of Texas, which later included New Mexico—obviously, far from the center of fighting. He captured Galveston on January 1, 1863, but was himself captured later in the war. He refused parole, and after the war he refused to swear allegiance to the United States. He became a major general for Emperor Maximilian of Mexico. Like so many others, Magruder eventually returned to the United States to lecture about his war experiences.

Outside Williamsburg, there's a historical marker alongside U.S. Route 60, telling about Prince John Magruder and the Battle of Williamsburg; not many people stop to read it. There's also the Fort Magruder Inn and Conference Center; it does pretty good business.

CHAPTER SEVEN

Jackson and McClellan:
Disparate Classmates

McClellan is an intelligent engineer and officer, but not a commander to head a great army in the field.... [He] wishes to outgeneral the Rebels, but not to kill and destroy them.

—Gideon Welles, U.S. Secretary of the Navy,
1861–1869–September 3, 1862

I do believe Jackson had genius and in that respect stands alone in the annals of this most stupid and uninspired of struggles.... To have fought against him is next to having fought under him.

—Charles Francis Adams, Jr.
Grandson of former president
John Quincy Adams, July 23, 1863

Two of the most interesting and possibly misunderstood men in the Civil War were Thomas Jonathan Jackson and George Brinton Mc-Clellan. They both graduated from West Point in 1846, but that's about the only way in which they were alike.

Thomas J. Jackson often is pictured as a semicrazed but brilliant tactician who went into battle holding one hand in the air while constantly sucking on lemons; he's seen as a man whose religious views colored his actions during the war, a dour college teacher who never laughed.

It's hard to pin down the legend about Jackson and lemons, but it's doubtful. After all, it would be difficult to obtain a supply of lemons in the South of 1861. Besides, Jackson liked other fruit as well, especially peaches. Then, too, he had dyspepsia, and he refused to eat the very foods he enjoyed most. That is, if he liked something, he refused to eat it; if he didn't like it, it was the food he chose to indulge in. When he realized he liked bread thickly slathered with butter he avoided butter and stuck with dry bread. This could mean that if he liked lemons, he would deny himself their comfort. Or, of course, maybe he hated lemons and therefore *did* suck on them during battle.

Biographer G. F. R. Henderson says Jackson "never smoked, he was a strict teetotaler, and he never touched a card," adding, "His diet . . . was of a most sparing kind."[1]

True, he often held up his right hand, index finger pointing skyward. He claimed it balanced his body's flow of blood.

True, again, he definitely was a character, possibly the biggest character of the war and with apparently little sense of humor. He never quite got the jokes that sent his aides off laughing.

Jackson was shy, introverted, had poor eyesight, and was partially deaf. He was almost six feet tall and weighed about 175 pounds; he had piercing blue eyes, a brown beard, and in general an unsophisticated appearance. He'd been orphaned at age seven and raised by kinfolk in Virginia's backcountry, receiving only the briefest of educations between bouts as a field hand. He was awkward, as homespun as the clothes he wore when he rode up to West Point in 1842; he carried all of his belongings in his horse's saddlebags. He was ill prepared for the Academy, but rose to be number seventeen in his class of fifty-nine students. A classmate said, "If we had to stay here another year, Ol' Jack would be at the top of his class." While at the Academy, he received no demerits for poor behavior, not one in four years. At night, before taps would signal lights out, Jackson would pile coals up in his room's fireplace, giving him light to study late into the early morning hours. That way, he caught up.

Douglas Southall Freeman describes Jackson as "a man . . . of contrasts so complex that he appears one day a Presbyterian deacon who delights in theological discussion and, the next, a reincarnated Joshua."[2]

Like others in the class of 1846, Jackson served in the Mexican War. He came out as perhaps the most celebrated member of his graduating class. He also came out committed to the military.

In 1851 he was offered a job at the Virginia Military Institute (VMI), teaching natural and experimental philosophy, a subject he knew little about. Frankly, he was a lousy teacher of natural and experimental philosophy. Each afternoon, after classes, he'd study and outline what he'd teach the next day. In class he'd run through what he'd read, teaching it by rote. If a student asked for more information, Jackson would reverse his mind's tape, and replay the entire lecture. If the student asked again, Jackson would take it as insubordination. He was, however, an exceptional artillery instructor, and students who feared him in class said that if they ever went into battle they wanted to go with Professor Jackson.

It was while he was at VMI that he fell in love and married. Fourteen months later his wife died while giving birth. In 1857 he married for the second time. Like his first wife, his new wife, Mary Ana Morrison—Ana, she was known—was a minister's daughter.

Fellow Confederate Gen. Richard Ewell thought Jackson was crazy, at first referring to him as "this old fool," predicting that if Jackson had his way the North would march right in and take over Richmond. Ewell also thought Jackson's subordinates were afraid of him. "I never saw one of Jackson's couriers approach," Ewell said, "without expecting an order to assault the North Pole."

General A. P. Hill called Jackson a "slumbering volcano" and a "crazy old Presbyterian fool." Jackson joined the church while in Mexico, but it wasn't until he reached VMI that he really took to organized religion. To say he was a Presbyterian isn't saying quite enough. He was a strict Calvinist, going far beyond the Presbyterian church itself.

But there was genius in Jackson's madness, and both Generals Hill and Ewell, as did a lot of others, soon realized this. Despite a frequent lack of supplies, Jackson's men were in superb condition. They had to be, if they were to march as often, and as fast, and as far as their commander demanded of them. He trained them rigorously, drilled them, made them march and march again, made them run, climb ropes, and shout as loudly as they could to expand their lungs. Then he pounded into them the confidence that they could win. It was Jackson's singled-minded ability, along with his genius, that brought him victory after victory. Among the questions most frequently asked by those who play the "what if" game of history are, "What if Stonewall Jackson had not died when he did? What if he had been there with Robert E. Lee at Gettysburg?"

Jackson was ambitious, but he never really minded someone else getting all the credit. He once wrote Ana, "I am thankful to my ever-kind Heavenly Father that He makes me content to await His own good time and pleasure for commendation—knowing that all things work together for my good."

While a student at West Point, fellow cadets called him "Ol' Jack." While a teacher at the Virginia Military Institute, his cadet students called him "Tom Fool Jackson." At the start of America's Civil War, he was referred to as "Old Blue Light" Jackson, because of the fiery glow of his eyes. Within months he was known by all as "Stonewall."

Like Robert E. Lee, Thomas J. Jackson opposed the idea of secession, but he said he would go whichever way his home state of Virginia did. He was born in that western part of Virginia that, during America's Civil War, seceded from the seceded state and became West Virginia, but that didn't matter to him; he considered himself a Virginian.

When the war began Jackson resigned from VMI; four days after Virginia seceded from the Union, he led the school's battalion of cadets to Richmond where they were wanted as drillmasters. He entered the Virginia militia as a colonel and was ordered to Harpers Ferry, where he organized what later became the famous "Stonewall Brigade." Two months later he was commissioned brigadier general in the Confederate army. His first action came outside the town of Manassas Junction, Virginia, near the little stream called Bull Run.

At Manassas, Jackson served alongside another new brigadier general, South Carolina's Barnard E. Bee. Teachers teach, and students dutifully learn, that Bee was looking at the flow of Rebel troops, most of whom were flowing backward, and couldn't help noting Jackson and his troops standing firm atop Henry House Hill. Those same teachers teach and those same students remember General Bee shouting, "Yonder stands Jackson like a stone wall." In one version of the teachers' tale, Bee adds, "Rally round the Virginians."

There are two ways to look at this. One would have it that General Bee saw Jackson refusing to be driven back. A second view has it that, while Jackson wasn't retreating, he wasn't moving forward, either. This version has Bee referring to him as a stone wall, because Jackson wouldn't charge while the charging was good. This version has Bee saying, "Look at Jackson standing there like a damned stone wall! Let's go to his assistance!" The version of Bee calling on his South Carolina troops to go to the assistance of the Virginians, however, is not a very popular view of things if you are in Virginia or are from Virginia. Beyond localism, it seems likely that whatever Bee said, he meant it as a challenge to his own troops.

Union brigades are known by numbers—the XVI Corps, the 12th Illinois Infantry. Confederate troops are known by their commander, and after that day at Bull Run, Jackson's men were known as the Stonewall Brigade.

The man had a deep and abiding faith in God. It's been said Jackson was fighting for *God,* not *man,* and he asked a lot of his men in the name of God. It was certainly part of his strict Calvinist-Presbyterian belief to avoid alcohol. Jackson, however, claimed it wasn't religion that prevented him from drinking alcoholic beverages. Rather, he claimed, "I like the taste of them, and when I discovered that to be the case I made up my mind at once to do without them altogether." Sometimes he gave in, such as one cold day in 1862 when Jackson took a glass of wine to warm himself. Or he thought it was wine; actually, it was straight whiskey. It warmed him up, all right. So much Jackson had to open his coat. It loosened his tongue, and aides claimed it was the only time Stonewall Jackson talked freely in their presence.

Generally, he objected to fighting on Sunday. Once, after conducting such a battle in early 1862, Jackson wrote his wife, Ana, "You appear much concerned at my attacking on Sunday. I was greatly concerned too; but I felt it my duty to do it, in consideration of the ruinous effects that might result from postponing the battle until the morning." In other words, Jackson was a pragmatist; he didn't want to fight on Sunday, but if he felt it a necessity, he'd do his damndest.

Not that he'd have put it that way; he also hated cursing. Shortly before the above letter to his wife, Jackson was appalled when a fellow officer, Gen. Richard Taylor, cursed in his presence during the heat of battle. Said Jackson to the son of President Zachary Taylor, "I am afraid you are a wicked fellow."

Then there was the time a Rebel soldier saw a particularly ill-dressed soldier swaying on his horse and demanded a share of the whiskey the seemingly drunk horseman had been drinking. The ill-dressed man was Jackson, one of the most careless dressers in the Confederate army. He wasn't drunk, either, just possibly the worst horseman in the Rebel army.

While part of the Federal army pushed its way up the Virginia peninsula in 1862, another part of the Union army set out to control Confederate forces in the Shenandoah Valley. They would take the valley away from the Rebels, they vowed, and deny the Confederacy the much-needed foodstuffs. That done, the Union army would move eastward to support George McClellan's actions against Richmond.

What the army brass in Washington hadn't considered in laying this plan was Thomas J. Jackson. He was unpredictable, and that, probably more than anything else, is what made him a military success. In the 1862 battle (more correctly, multiple battles) of Virginia's Shenandoah Valley, he practiced almost perfect Napoleonic theories of war. He fought, ran, attacked again, and moved off; he struck the enemy, turned away, then reversed directions. The Union army couldn't keep up with him, and everyone thought Jackson had many more troops than he did. The Shenandoah Valley campaign became a virtual textbook study in how an outnumbered force, with a brilliant leader using rapid maneuvers, can defeat a larger force.

That's when his fast-marching infantry became known as the "foot cavalry." They marched 679 miles over 48 days, averaging 14 miles a day. The Stonewall Brigade fought six battles between March 23 and June 9, 1862—Kernstown (3,000 Rebels against 9,000 Federals), McDowell (6,000 with Jackson facing 15,000 Union troops), Front Royal (where he captured $300,000 worth of Union supplies), Winchester (the North lost 3,000 men while Jackson's casualties numbered only 400), Cross Keys (Jackson was almost captured himself while fighting on two fronts), and Port Republic (after which Jackson telegraphed his wife, "God has been our shield"). In between these six major battles, Jackson's men took part in almost half a dozen other serious skirmishes. At the end of the campaign he had about 15,000 troops; at one point he had faced and beaten Federal troops numbering more than 80,000.

Folks in the Union plainly were afraid of him, and they built dirt forts around Washington, D.C., terrified that Ol' Jack was headed their way. Northern mothers used him to keep their children in line, saying "Stonewall will get you if you aren't good!"

If he was hard on the enemy, he was sometimes just as hard on his subordinates. Troops in the field loved him, but members of his officer corps were, as A. P. Hill said, likely to be afraid of him.

Jackson's specialty was the flank attack. It was, however, following one such flank attack that he was killed by his own men. Together, he and Robert E. Lee had devised one of the most ingenious battle plans of the war, some say of *any* war. At one time, Jackson so out-flanked the enemy, he wound up behind them.

A lot of former Virginia Military Institute cadets served in the Stonewall Brigade, and their former professor called out to them, "The Institute will be heard from today." It led to the greatest Con-federate victory of the war, the Battle of Chancellorsville, and it led to Stonewall Jackson's death.

The incident occurred about nine, the night of May 1, 1863, among a cluster of pine trees about a mile south of the mansion and tavern that gave the battle its name. As was his custom, that night Jackson rode out on a personal reconnaissance of the situation. Ear-lier, Jackson himself had ordered his men to pass on the word that Union soldiers were hiding among the trees.

He and several members of his staff were heading east on the Or-ange Plank Road when nervous men from his own command, troops from North Carolina, began firing. General A. P. Hill was with Jack-son and shouted out, "Cease firing," but the firing did not stop. The leader of the Carolina troops yelled back, "It's a lie; pour it into them, boys!"

Jackson's horse, Little Sorrel, bolted into the woods. By the time the shooting stopped, two of Jackson's staff members had been killed. Hill found Stonewall lying on the ground. He'd been hit in several places and his left arm hung limp. It was "very painful," he told Hill. "My left arm is broken."

It took a while to find a litter, and just as they headed for the rear, the Union artillery, after hearing the Rebel firing, opened up. One of the litter bearers was killed; another ran off. They found an am-bulance and Jackson's chief surgeon, Dr. Hunter Holmes McGuire, who had been with Jackson since First Manassas.

McGuire administered a shot of morphine to Jackson, and the am-bulance rumbled off with Stonewall rolling around inside. There fol-lowed a four-mile bumpy road, with Dr. McGuire holding a finger to the general's artery. Back at a field hospital near Wilderness Tavern, McGuire saw that Jackson's left arm was shattered. He amputated the arm about two inches below the shoulder.

A biography of Dr. McGuire, written for the American Medical Association by Dr. Morris Fishbein, incorrectly states, "Dr. McGuire amputated his (Jackson's) right arm. . . ."[3] Ironically, Jackson had been referred to as Lee's strong *right* arm.

On Monday, the general was taken to the Guinea's Station plantation of a friend, Thomas Chandler, where Dr. McGuire had Jackson placed on a bed in Chandler's three-room office building next to the main house. For the first few days, Jackson seemed to recover well.

As soon as he learned of Jackson's wounds, General Lee sent Jackson a letter. "Could I have directed events," Lee wrote, "I should have chosen for the good of the country to have been disabled in your stead." Lee went on to congratulate Jackson on what he presumed was a victory at Chancellorsville; it was a victory, but it came at a severe cost. Not only Jackson, but 13,000 other casualties—22 percent of the Confederate force was lost.

Jackson received Lee's note and replied, "General Lee is very kind, but he should give the praise to God."

By Sunday, May 10, his wife was at his side. It was obvious Jackson was gravely ill. Ana shared her husband's strong religious beliefs, and asked him if he was ready to die on a Sunday. His reply: "I prefer it." He repeated the comment to a friend, Alexander S. Pendleton: "It is the Lord's Day. My wish is fulfilled. I have always desired to die on Sunday."

Dr. McGuire tried to ease his pain with brandy, but as usual, Jackson refused to drink alcoholic beverages. "It will only delay my departure," he said, "and do no good. I want to preserve my mind, if possible, to the last." In that, he apparently did not get his wish. Jackson ran a fever and was delirious. His last words were "Order A. P. Hill to prepare for action! Pass the infantry to the front!"

It was 3:15 P.M., on May 10, when Lt. Gen. Thomas Jonathan "Stonewall" Jackson died. He died not of the wound itself, not even directly because of the amputation; rather, he died of a complication common enough for the time: pneumonia.[4]

Pneumonia is common enough for our time, as well. According to Dr. Lin J. Drury of Chicago, pneumonia may occur in postoperative cases caused by either bacteria or viruses, and may be either primary or secondary (that is, a complication of another disease). The microorganisms that give rise to pneumonia are always present in our upper respiratory tract but, generally, cause no harm unless the patient's resistance is severely lowered by some other factor.

In Jackson's case, of course, the "other factor" consisted of several gunshot wounds to various parts of his body and the need to amputate his left arm. Age may also have been a factor; Jackson was only thirty-nine when he died, certainly not elderly by today's standards, but not especially young by the standards of the mid-1800s, not when you consider the life of a Civil War soldier. Jackson had received several severe wounds; he was bounced around for miles in a horse-drawn ambulance over washboard roads. Amputation (with unclean hands, instruments, and bandages) and sepsis followed. No antibiotics were available.

He was allowed, as was common practice in 1863, to lie in bed; the less you moved a patient, it was felt then, the quicker he would recover. It's now known such nonmovement can cause pleurisy—in this case, a complication of the pneumonia. Pleurisy can cause the patient's lungs to fill with pus, a condition known as empyema. Death may result. In effect, the patient drowns in his own fluids.

Unbeknownst to Robert E. Lee, Jackson no longer was alive when Lee asked the Rev. Beverly T. Lacy to speak to his good friend and cavalry leader. "Give him my affectionate regards," Lee said, "and tell him to make haste and get well, and come back to me as soon as he can. He has lost his left arm, but I have lost my right." When he learned of Jackson's death, Lee said, "I know not how to replace him."

After Stonewall's death, all other would-be generals would be measured against him. All failed. "Oh, for another Jackson," was the frequent cry from both the military and the civilian South. As Thomas J. "Stonewall" Jackson ended his mortal life, he began a new one as a myth.

George Brinton McClellan finished second in their West Point class of 1846. In the early days of the war, he was the hope of the Union. It was believed he would lead them to victory. In many ways, he led the North to disaster.

If Stonewall Jackson was *un*predictable, McClellan was *too* predictable, so much so that everyone knew he would not take a chance. In failing to take that chance he lost what he most wanted, to be known as the best soldier around.

McClellan was brevetted for bravery twice during the Mexican War and spent a year in Europe observing military operations there. He resigned his commission in 1857 when he was just thirty years old and became a vice president of the Illinois Central Railroad. He was very successful, and perhaps should have stuck with running trains and not reverted to soldiering. Abraham Lincoln had been one of the Illinois Central's attorneys, and he and McClellan got to know each other. When war came, McClellan joined as a major general of the Ohio Volunteers. Lincoln made him a major general of the regular army.

Ten days before the Great Skedaddle at Manassas, McClellan had a minor success at the Battle of Rich Mountain, in what is now West Virginia. That got him noticed and he was given command of the Division of the Potomac, the Union army protecting Washington, D.C. You might say his success brought on his failure. It also brought on conceit. On July 27, he wrote his wife, Ellen Marcy McClellan.

> I find myself in a new & strange position here—Presdt, Cabinet, Genl Scott & all deferring to me—by some strange operation of magic I seem to have become the power of the land. I almost think that were I to win some small success now I could become Dictator or anything else that might please me—but nothing of that kind would please me—therefore I won't be Dictator. Admirable self denial!

Three days later he reaffirmed his own self-belief.

> Who would have thought when we married, that I should so soon be called upon to save my country?

Ellen Marcy, known as Nelly, had received several proposals of marriage, including one from George McClellan's roommate, Ambrose Powell Hill. Her decline of Hill's offer was a tale of unfulfilled love known by many on both sides of the war. Perhaps apocryphal but interesting is the story told of Hill's troops storming McClellan's command during the Peninsula Campaign. The fighting was fierce, and one Federal officer was heard to grumble, "God's sake, Nelly, why didn't you marry him?" Hill, who graduated one year after McClellan, later married the sister of fellow Confederate John H. Morgan.

For years George McClellan struggled with authority figures, an odd problem considering his chosen career. He was distrustful, it seems, of everyone but himself and his wife. Many of his letters to Ellen were released to the public in 1887 in *McClellan's Own Story*, but he had greatly censored those letters, bending events and, he believed, public opinion his way. He may have tried to camouflage his own inadequacies. If so, he also failed in that.

While sounding supremely self-confident, McClellan often exaggerated his enemy's strength and didn't believe in his own. It is easy perhaps to look back at history 130 years ago and join those who claim McClellan had "a paranoid personality disorder with narcissistic tendencies."[5] Such a disorder, Joseph T. Glatthaar says,

> *causes its sufferers to become extremely secretive. They hesitate to confide in others for fear the information will be used to their detriment. A lack of sufficient trust induces them to doubt the reliability of others. Seldom if ever do they delegate responsibility, instead overseeing the minutest details personally.*[6]

McClellan *was* extremely cautious and always demanded more men, more material, more of everything, including more time before going into battle. Lincoln once said, "Sending reinforcements to McClellan is like shoveling flies across a barn."

After the Peninsula Campaign and the Seven Days' Battles, as he awaited Confederate forces near Sharpsburg, Maryland, he wrote Ellen on September 5, 1862, "Again I have been called upon to save the country."

He came close, but a good portion of that success was due to several events over which McClellan coincidentally had jurisdiction. First, two Union army privates were sitting out in an open field. Second, both of these nineteenth-century G.I.s were addicted to nicotine. Third, at least one of them was blessed with curiosity. And fourth, that curious individual chose not to litter the countryside that day but to do a bit of reading.

It was September 12, and Pvt. B. W. Mitchell of Company F, 27th Indiana Infantry, was lounging with a friend in a field near Frederick, Maryland. Not long before then, the field had been used by a member of Lee's staff as a campsite. Private Mitchell found three cigars wrapped in a piece of paper and was so happy he almost threw away the wrapper. Mitchell was curious, and, instead of throwing away the paper, he read the paper. It was a copy of Robert E. Lee's Special Order No. 191.

First thing George McClellan knew, he was holding in his hands Lee's plans for the coming battle. McClellan couldn't have been more confident. "Here is a paper," he said, "with which if I cannot whip Bobbie Lee, I will be willing to go home."

McClellan didn't whip Bobbie Lee; the best they could do was fight to a draw, with both sides whipping hell out of each other. The Battle of Antietam was the single most deadly day of America's Civil War. Moreover, it was the single most deadly day of any other American war.[7] McClellan's Army of the Potomac lost 12,401—2,108 dead, 9,540 wounded, and 753 missing—twenty-five percent of the Federal troops who went into action at Antietam.

As usual, we can't be precise about Confederate losses; they were too busy just trying to keep up and didn't have time to keep accurate records. By best reports, Lee's Army of Northern Virginia counted 1,546 dead, 7,752 wounded, and 1,018 missing—10,318, or 31 percent of *his* army. The combined total for twelve hours of battle at Sharpsburg, the fighting along Antietam Creek, came to 22,719 casualties. Lee and his lieutenants met that night west of Sharpsburg. General James Longstreet finally rode into camp after a trip to town, where he'd helped a family whose house had been set on fire by the artillery shelling. Lee was relieved to see him. "Ah," he said, "here is Longstreet; here is my old warhorse." They talked about many things, but what they didn't talk about was giving up the fight. Lee had decided to stay and wait for McClellan's actions.

Nearby, where Rebel troops tried to rest from the day's battle, an old slave woman approached a tired and worn-out Confederate soldier. "Did you have a hard fight today?" she asked. "Yes, Auntie," the soldier replied, "the Yankees gave us the devil, and they'll give us hell next."

Robert E. Lee stood on a hill that next day, looking with field glasses at the field in front of him. He expected to see McClellan and the Union army charging the Rebel lines. They were "still too weak to assume the offensive," Lee said, adding, "we awaited without apprehension the renewal of the attack." The renewal never came. Lee shook his head and turned around, uncertain of McClellan's tactics. Apparently, the Union's great little hope was also uncertain. "The day passed," Lee later reported, "without any demonstration on the part of the enemy . . ." So, knowing his troops were too weak to attack, Lee headed home, headed back down south.

The uncertain George McClellan made no attempt to resume the fight; he may have believed he'd done enough. Some experts argued then and argue now that a second day of fighting could have ended America's Civil War right then and there, with the Union victorious.

George McClellan saw Abraham Lincoln as his inferior. He even called the president a "great gorilla."

Lincoln visited McClellan and, with an old friend from Illinois, stood on a hill, overlooking the "Little Napoleon's" encampment, a broad expanse of tents arrayed below him. "Do you know," Lincoln asked his friend, "what this is?"

The friend answered, "It is the Army of the Potomac."

"So it is called," the president said, "but that is a mistake; it is only McClellan's bodyguard." In a parody of what Lincoln reportedly said about Gen. Ulysses S. Grant, the president reportedly said of McClellan, "I *can* spare this man; he won't fight."

The rail-splitter from Illinois was finished with the man who once thought he could have been the nation's dictator.

The Army of Northern Virginia's drive into the North in the late summer of 1862 was over. As the Rebels headed south, the 18th Mississippi Regimental Band began playing the same song they'd played when the army marched out of Virginia ten days earlier: "Maryland, My Maryland." But troops along the way shouted it down. Instead, the band had to play another song, "Carry Me Back to Old Virginny."

They left behind thousands who fought valiantly. Soldiers from both North and South now filled the Maryland air with death. "No tongue can tell," a member of the 9th Pennsylvania wrote, "no mind conceive, no pen portray the horrible sights I witnessed this morning."

They left other thousands in hospitals. Soldiers from both North and South now filled the air with moans and screams and cries for help; the wounded "filled every building and overflowed into the country round," a witness said, "into farmhouses, barns, corn-cribs, cabins . . . wherever four walls and a roof were found together."

Antietam may have been the worst, but there was more to come.

CHAPTER EIGHT

✂

Great Raids; Meager Results

There is always hazard in military movements, but we must decide between the positive loss of inactivity and the risk of action.

—Gen. Robert E. Lee, C.S.A.
June 8, 1863

The American Civil War lasted approximately 1,395 days. There were a dozen or so major battles and more than 10,000 skirmishes, "military events" some historians call them. It was the first modern war and the last "romantic" war. It was human drama at its worst and, in some cases, its most humorous.

On October 19, 1864, the Civil War came to the small village of St. Albans, Vermont. St. Albans was flush with money; why only the day before, the U.S. Army had been in town, buying nearly seven hundred horses.

The local horse traders were busy congratulating themselves on the sale, and their wives were busy stocking up on everything from needles to new hats, making the shopkeepers as happy as the horse traders. At least forty of the local men were in the capital city of Montpelier where the Vermont legislature was about to open. The town's lawyers were in Burlington, where the supreme court was in session.

And while the local dignitaries were either out of town or drinking to the good health of the horse trading business, while bank officials were busy counting the money just deposited from the horse sale, a small band of Confederate soldiers rode into town. What came about was something not normally seen in far upstate Vermont. Something, for the most part, not even noticed in St. Albans. After all, the village was on the shores of Lake Champlain, far from Richmond where Johnny Reb and Billy Yank stared at each other across the trenches. Far from Atlanta, where William Tecumseh Sherman was preparing for his March to the Sea. It was, after all, only a small group, about twenty young men, strangers to St. Albans.

They were young, their average age only twenty-three, courteous, friendly, a bit taller than most local boys and, all in all, fairly handsome. The first of the group had drifted in nine days before and settled in at the Tremont House Hotel; he claimed he was from St. Johns, Canada, on a sporting vacation. That might have explained his strange Southern accent and why he wasn't in the army, off fighting the Rebels. Over the next few days, others arrived by ones and twos. They all expressed interest in firearms—after all, they were hunters—and they looked for horses. Vermont was the home of Justin Morgan, and the breed of horse named for him, the only American-made breed of horse, the Morgan. It was considered the lightest, toughest, and the best cavalry horse available, which is why the Union army bought so many.

Five of the Rebels walked into the St. Albans Bank on Main Street just before the 3:00 P.M. closing. They pulled revolvers and seized the tellers by the throats, announcing they were Confederate soldiers and that they were taking the town and its money. Over the next few minutes they made off with about sixty thousand dollars but left behind more than twice that amount.

Down the street, another group of five Rebels was looting the Franklin County Bank, but they were even less successful: They got only about twenty-five thousand dollars and again left at least twice that amount behind. The robbers were pleasant enough and courteous, but obviously amateurs in the holdup game.

The First National Bank was also robbed, and all together the Rebels stole about two hundred and eight thousand dollars without firing a shot, without causing or suffering a casualty.

Now came the problem of getting out of town. They tossed around bottles of "Greek Fire"—a concoction that was supposed to burst into flames when exposed to air—but it didn't work, not even in the American Hotel's watercloset, which one raider, for reasons unknown, tried to burn.

They had not, however, arranged for enough horses, but they cleaned out Bedart's Saddle Shop of saddles, bridles, and blankets, enough for the few horses they had managed to beg, borrow, or steal. As they rode out of town, one local citizen reportedly fired a shot at the robbers. It was never confirmed whether he hit anyone.

The Confederate raiders rode on to Canada, known for its sympathy to the Southern cause. But thirteen of the bank robbers were arrested in Montreal, and approximately $80,000 of the loot was recovered. Later, however, the court ruled it had no jurisdiction over the matter, freed the men, and returned the money to them. Five other raiders were arrested, but they, too, were released.

The leader of the gang claimed the entire $208,000 was turned over to Confederate Commissioners near Niagara Falls, Canada. The Canadian government said it repaid the banks the equivalent of $88,000.

In 1911, the leader of the Confederate raiders visited St. Albans, taking his wife and daughter on a trip down memory lane. It was, according to newspaper accounts, truly friendly on both sides.

On April 6, 1862, near Shelbyville, Tennessee, about a hundred miles from where the Battle of Shiloh was just getting under way, the Great Locomotive Chase also was about to begin. Shiloh was one of America's bloodiest days ever. The Great Locomotive Chase, arguably, was one of the most bizarre. Two dozen Union soldiers, mainly from Ohio, set off on a raid, or more accurately, an adventure. They set off to steal a Confederate railroad.

A civilian who claimed his name was James J. Andrews was spying for the Union army, mainly around railroads. Smuggling medicine into the Confederacy, smuggling information back to the Union. Now he wanted to take over one of the few railroads in the South, the Western and Atlantic. The State of Georgia owned the line, which snaked 138 miles northward from Atlanta to Chattanooga, where it tied into one line to Lynchburg, Virginia, and another to Memphis.

By the evening of the seventh, Andrews and his band of volunteers were ready to go. They would make their way to Marietta, Georgia, board the first northbound train they found, and steal it, burning bridges behind them as they rode the Western and Atlantic rails. If successful, the raid would cut Chattanooga off from reinforcements and material, civilian and military.

The group planned to walk to Marietta, but a handful of them got tired of that and hitched a ride on a Confederate troop train. They weren't noticed.

On Saturday, April 12, they boarded the train they'd chosen to steal, careful to book stops along the way so as not to arouse suspicion. The locomotive was the powerful wood-burning *General*. At the town of Big Shanty (later called Kennesaw for the nearby mountain), while fellow passengers got off the train to have breakfast at Lacy's Hotel, Andrews and his raiders commandeered the *General*, its tender, three empty boxcars, a string of passenger cars, and some of the passengers themselves.

Nearby, Confederate guards at a training camp watched but took no action. The train foreman, however, did. He shouted to the conductor that somebody was moving the train. As the train crew ran shouting onto the platform, the Rebel guards woke up and took a few ineffectual potshots at the *General* as it rumbled away. The Western and Atlantic crew took off after their train, running along the tracks.

As the *General* steamed along, the raiders stopped now and then to tear up the tracks behind them, hoping to frustrate their pursuers. The *General's* conductor, who had been among those having breakfast at Lacy's, was now among those chasing after the stolen train. He'd run, hop aboard any train he could commandeer, and ride it until he hit torn-up track. Then he'd jump down and run some more on foot, find another train, and ride it to the next patch of torn-up track. The conductor was on his third commandeered train when he saw the *Texas*, a southbound locomotive heading his way. Flagging down the *Texas*, the conductor explained the situation, and they took off after the stolen *General*. Full steam ahead. Or full steam backward; the *Texas* was running in reverse. It was also catching up. Twice the Federals onboard the *General* unhitched box cars to delay pursuit, but by the time they emerged from a tunnel north of Dalton, the *Texas* was just a quarter mile away from the *General*. Time was running out for the Union raiders and so was wood. The two locomotives thundered on, at times reaching speeds approaching the then unheard-of one mile-per-minute.

Just short of the Georgia-Tennessee border, the raiders were in real trouble: Not only were they short of firewood, they were short of water for the boiler as well. They had traveled nearly a hundred miles from Big Shanty but could go no farther. The steam locomotive didn't have so much as a puff left in it. Andrews told them it was all over. Abandon ship—or train—and every man for himself. Off they ran into the nearby woods.

Six hours after it began, the great locomotive chase was over. Almost as quickly as the adventure ended, the raiders were captured, all of them, and given swift trials—not as prisoners of war, since they had been disguised as civilians, but as spies. James Andrews and seven others were given death sentences. Eight other raiders escaped, only to be recaptured and taken to Castle Thunder Prison in Richmond. Finally they were exchanged, and nearly a year after taking part in one of the most dramatic raids of the war, they were back in Washington.

A few weeks earlier, Congress had authorized a new medal to be given for conspicuous heroism. And, in the first ceremony of its kind, the survivors of the raid on the *General* received the Congressional Medal of Honor—even James Andrews, their leader. But for him the award came posthumously; he'd already been hanged.

The Great Locomotive Chase and the Raid on St. Albans, Vermont, didn't amount to much, not over the four years of war, not when you consider the toll the war took. They are, however, part of the fabric of that strange period of time, nineteenth-century America, America's Civil War.

CHAPTER NINE

Discovery and Design:
The New Ways of War

War is progressive, because all the instruments of war are progressive.
—Gen. Ulysses S. Grant, U.S.A.

One of the problems with being a soldier in time of war is there's a chance you'll be killed, which, from the military standpoint, is sort of what war is all about. And the more ways of performing this task successfully, the better military folk feel about their jobs.

America in the mid-1800s contributed much to the way wars were fought and the way warriors died. Trench warfare was one of the ways—both armies dug in on the Virginia peninsula, at Petersburg, and at Atlanta—but it wasn't the only new "weapon" in America's Civil War.

In May 1862, Rebel troops slowly retreated toward Richmond. George McClellan and his Union army pursued them even more slowly, slogging their way up the muddy Virginia peninsula. The Federal cavalry loped along, positive they had Johnny Reb on the run. Suddenly the world exploded in their faces, shocking the Union troops and outraging their officers. No sounds of artillery screamed overhead. Somehow, from somewhere, the troops were under attack. All the Union officers saw were their own dead and dying. An invisible Rebel army had attacked them.

McClellan's men stumbled across the first land mines used in battle, one of the latest inventions born of America's Civil War. They were the controversial work of Confederate Gen. Gabriel James Rains.

Like so many other Confederate officers, Gabriel Rains graduated from West Point and served the Union army in both the Seminole and Mexican Wars. He was a lieutenant colonel in July 1861, when he resigned his Federal commission to join the South.

The next year, as brigadier general, he commanded the Rebel post at Yorktown, Virginia. As Confederate troops retreated up the peninsula, Rains tried to delay Union forces by leaving land mines, primed mortar shells buried in roads and near watering places. He may also have set booby traps—shells wired up to door handles, for instance—but he denied that. Certainly, someone set booby traps for the Yankees, and it probably was Gabriel Rains.

Both sides were indignant over the idea of hiding bombs under dirt and twigs, bombs just waiting for unwary soldiers or their horses to set them off. Members of both armies considered land mines a devious, and therefore ungentlemanly, way of fighting war. Lieutenant General James Longstreet ordered his troops not to use land mines. Longstreet wrote to Rains, "It is the desire of the major general commanding that you put no shells or torpedoes behind you, as he [Longstreet] does not recognize it as a proper or effective method of war."[1] Using mines, Old Pete Longstreet believed, was a barbarous way of fighting war, and he wanted nothing to do with them. Rains disagreed and took his argument to Confederate Secretary of War George Wythe Randolph.

America's Civil War saw the birth of many new weapons of war and witnessed the final vestiges of chivalry in battle. Secretary Randolph's ruling waffled decisively, if somewhat on the chivalrous side of the issue. "It is admissible," this grandson of Thomas Jefferson wrote, "to plant shells in a parapet to repel assault, or in a road to check pursuit [but] it is not admissible to plant shells merely to destroy life and without other design than that of depriving the enemy of a few men." He seemed to be saying, whatever you do, don't deprive your enemy of only "a few men."

Secretary Randolph solved one part of the problem by removing Rains from the army and installing him in the War Department to serve as an explosives expert. While he was there, Rains also built torpedoes, the first such weapons to be used in naval warfare. Not torpedoes as we know them, not the twentieth century's self-propelled bombs, shot underwater by submarines and surface vessels or dropped from the air. Rains's Civil War version really was a floating land mine, resembling a tin can full of gunpowder, floating just under the water, waiting to be struck. It was such torpedoes that Union Rear Adm. David Glasgow Farragut saw in Mobile Bay and shouted, "Damn the torpedoes! Full steam ahead." Better, we suppose, than "Damn the tin cans!"

During the Peninsula campaign Rains mined the waters of the nearby York River to keep Federal ships from landing at Yorktown. That's when he set those land mines (and probably booby traps as well) to delay McClellan's unsuccessful push to Richmond.

Gabriel Rains was fifty-nine years old at the time and commanded a brigade under Gen. D. H. Hill. He turned his hobby of working with explosives into a career. Until then he'd never dealt professionally with ordnance, but when he got the chance, he went at it wholeheartedly. His contraptions ranged upward in size to using nearly a ton of black powder.

By the end of the war, Confederate torpedoes accounted for the sinking of dozens of Union ships. More ships were lost to torpedoes than from all other causes combined. Rains claimed his torpedoes sank fifty-eight Federal ships.

He didn't have an easy time of it either. In addition to working against his own people, such as Longstreet, who thought land mines and such were sheer barbarity, he lacked two major items: money and electrical wire. He was first given twenty thousand dollars to build his torpedoes. Eventually the Confederate government appropriated more, but it was always too little and too late.

Many of Rains's torpedoes were exploded by wires leading from the shore to the underwater tin cans. That meant finding electrical wire, and the Confederacy had very little of that commodity waiting for Gabriel Rains. He partially solved the problem by sending women spies behind enemy lines to steal wire for the Rebel cause. And he looked for other sources. He dredged up abandoned Union cables from the bottom of the Chesapeake Bay, shredded them into wire, and used them for his bombs. Through these various means, Rains succeeded in finding enough wire to do the job.

Eventually, he even convinced desperate Confederate officials to let him fill the James River with torpedoes to keep Federal ships away from Richmond. That idea worked well, as did his next scheme, scattering thirteen hundred land mines in the roads around the Rebel capital. When the Confederate lines finally broke in April 1865, and Lee was forced to abandon Richmond, Federal troops had to use Rebel prisoners to guide them around Rains's land mines.

Not long after the war began, Gabriel was joined by his brother, soon to be Lt. Col. George Washington Rains. Together they developed something of a family explosives business. George manufactured gunpowder, and Gabriel built mines, torpedoes, and booby traps.

George Rains was fourteen years younger than brother Gabriel and did much better at West Point than did his older sibling. In 1842 he graduated third in his class of fifty-six. An engineer, George taught at the academy for a while but resigned his commission in 1856 to become president of an ironworks. Three months after the war broke out, he was commissioned a major in the Confederate army and was given command of munitions at Augusta, Georgia.

Like Gabriel, George Rains faced an urgent problem. When the war began, the South had no explosives factories. None. Like so much else, the South had depended on the North for gunpowder. In fact, the last time gunpowder had been manufactured in the South was during the Mexican War. The Confederacy even lacked a prime ingredient of gunpowder, potassium nitrate, better known as saltpeter.

The first thing George Rains had to do was find saltpeter. He located it in the limestone caves of Tennessee, Georgia, Alabama, and Virginia (where one of the last surviving Rebel soldiers dug saltpeter as a young boy), but it wasn't nearly enough for the South's needs. Just as brother Gabriel found alternative ways to obtain electrical wire, George developed other methods of obtaining potassium nitrate. And like Gabriel, he used spies, his agents smuggling in nearly three million pounds of the chemical from Europe. Still, it wasn't enough, so George put out a call for chamber pots and outhouses. His men dug up old privies and latrines and dumped the smelly but inevitable by-product of human nutrition into saltpeter ponds. Then they processed it into potassium nitrate. The outhouses-to-saltpeter scheme worked, and thanks to George Rains, the South eventually had plenty of gunpowder. He went on to build several gunpowder plants, factories in Richmond, Charleston, Wilmington, Mobile, and Savannah.

These mills not only supplied Confederate troops with much-needed gunpowder, they made a profit for the Southern cause. The large gunpowder plant Rains built along the Savannah at Augusta not only saved millions of dollars of Confederate money, it showed a $385,000 profit. In three years the Augusta plant produced 2,750,000 pounds of gunpowder.

After the war, the Union army took over the plant and used the Confederate produced gunpowder for artillery practice. It was, Federal troops said, the finest gunpowder they'd ever seen.

When America's Civil War ended, George Rains quit taking lives with gunpowder and began giving them back through medicine. He taught chemistry at the Medical College of Georgia.

His brother lived for a while in the ruins of Atlanta, moved on to Charleston, and joined the U.S. Army Quartermaster Department. Gabriel Rains never did admit using booby traps, but he proudly told how, on that spring day in 1862, he turned the world upside down with his land mines.

Another new "weapon" appeared on July 1, 1862, when the Union instituted the first income tax in American history. Nine months later, the Confederacy adopted one of its own, and life hasn't been the same since, North or South.

Both the Confederacy and the Union built rockets, but they didn't amount to much. The Union's rockets were designed by English inventor William Hale and weighed about six pounds each. Hale offered to build them for the Union, but they turned him down. In what now might be seen as an infringement of Hale's patents, Federal engineers used his plans to build a few rockets. They never got around to building enough to do any major damage during the four years of war.

The so-called minnie or minié ball wasn't, either. First, it was incorrectly pronounced. It was invented, more or less, by French army Capt. Claude Minié, who gave it his name, if not its French pronunciation. Unlike rockets, the minnie or minié ball *did* make a difference in the war. Second, it wasn't a ball, but rather what has been referred to as a "a cylindro-conoidal" projectile.[2] Simply put, bullet-shaped. In 1848, Minié perfected a bullet small enough to be easily rammed down a muzzle-loaded rifle. Before then, a lead ball would rattle around the barrel when it was fired, going everywhere except where it was intended. Minié's invention had a wooden plug base that expanded when fired. Even though it wasn't round enough to officially be a ball, it didn't matter. Round or not, it was a big improvement over the old poured-shot bullet.

The trouble with Claude Minié's new bullets was the cost; they were expensive. Leave it to an American to come up with a cheaper model. James H. Burton of the Harpers Ferry Armory designed an all-lead bullet with a deep cavity in its base. The cavity filled with gas that expanded when fired, and that improved things a lot. Soldiers were more likely to hit something with a minié ball. Or hit someone. Still, the new bullet carried Claude Minié's name, never to be called a Burton ball.

When the Civil War started, Virginia had a large stock of flintlock muskets left over from earlier wars. They were stored in the Richmond Armory, where workmen substituted a percussion lock for the flintlock, and grooved the barrel, making it a rifle, not a musket. They added a sight and the South wound up with modernized rifles, just waiting for the new improved minié balls. The improvement cost only $1.50 per weapon.

Cheaper bullets made for cheaper lives. The Union army realized this and, early in the war, issued "bulletproof vests" to some units. Generally, the soldiers regarded them with contempt, and very few of the vests were ever worn into battle. Rightly so. A sergeant in the 15th Iowa said that when they were tested, about half the allegedly bulletproof vests "were bored through by musket balls." Obviously, he didn't like them. "If the bullet did not go through it," he added, "it would knock a man into the middle of next week so that he might as well be killed first as last."

America's Civil War saw the first practical machine gun—actually two of them. Both were built by Southerners, one for the South, the other for the North.

The first was the Williams rapid-fire gun, invented by Confederate Capt. R. S. Williams. His was a one-pound steel breech-loader with a four-foot-long, two-inch bore. It operated by a lever attached to a revolving cam shaft, which rotated a cylinder. Each time the cylinder revolved, a cartridge from a hopper above it dropped in, and a sliding hammer struck the cartridge's percussion cap. It got off eighteen to twenty shots per minute, working so well in its initial test at the Battle of Seven Pines in May 1862, that the Confederate government ordered more of the Williams guns. Near the end of the war, Union troops captured a Williams rapid-fire gun. It's now on display at the West Point Military Academy Museum.

The problem was, the Williams gun fired so rapidly, the breech overheated and expanded. Then it wouldn't relock until it cooled down.

The machine gun everyone knows about was invented by a man whose primary job was healing, not causing death and injury—Dr. Richard J. Gatling of North Carolina. While Williams's gun had one barrel that revolved around a single shaft, Gatling's was a multiple-barrel weapon, a rapid-fire weapon that could sweep a field of hard-charging opponents, leveling them in seconds. It didn't have the Williams gun's drawback of overheating when fired, but the Union War Department distrusted the Southern inventor. The Gatling gun wasn't really put to a field test until Petersburg, and by then it was too late to do any good. Or harm. It's still used today in modified forms.

The war also saw the first repeating rifle used in combat. The rifle invented in 1860 by Christopher M. Spencer of Connecticut was more effective than the old muzzle-loading weapons. The Spencer repeating carbine was the first successful breech-loading repeating rifle ever manufactured. It carried seven cartridges at a time. The Rebels didn't have anything like it. They were so awed by the repeating rifles, they claimed a Union soldier could "load it on Sunday and fire it all week without stopping." The Confederates captured some Spencer rifles, but they couldn't use them; they didn't have the special cartridges needed to fire them and no metal to manufacture such cartridges.

The Spencer repeating rifle was a nineteenth-century weapon used against an army mired in the eighteenth century, and Federal troops would have been even more effective if it hadn't been for the

Union army's accountants. The U.S. Army was stuck in that mess we call "bureaucracy." The bean counters didn't like the new weapon. A soldier carrying a Spencer rifle could take along a hundred rounds of ammunition, not just the forty the muzzle-loaders carried. Carrying two and a half times as much ammunition would have aided the individual soldier, but it would have cost the government too much money, the accountants believed. They solved their (if not the soldiers') problem by ordering only 77,181 Spencer rifles. It is estimated that as many as 2.1 million men were enlisted in the Union army. That meant only one Spencer for every 27.2 Union soldiers.

Because the federal bookkeepers ordered so few repeating rifles, the war lasted longer than it might have; therefore, their decision cost many lives. It was a solution with which today's risk managers—those who bet lives against cost—probably would agree.

As for the Confederacy, it remained supremely confident, a confidence that percolated not only through the military and political leaders, but boiled within common folks as well. Many in the South voiced the feeling: "We can whip the Yankees with popguns." The author of a Raleigh, North Carolina, schoolbook agreed. Johnson's Elementary Arithmetic carried the following questions:

1) A Confederate soldier captured 8 Yankees each day for 9 successive days; how many did he capture in all?
2) If one Confederate soldier kill[s] 90 Yankees how many Yankees can 10 Confederate soldiers kill?
3) If one Confederate soldier can whip 7 Yankees, how many soldiers can whip 49 Yankees?[3]

This was, of course, for children. Coming as it did in the third year of war shows that the South's belief in its invincibility had not abated. For the adults who did the fighting, there was more to war than just claims that "factory- and shop-bred Yankees," as the Northern troops often were called, would fall down at the sight of a good, patriotic Southerner.

An item often mistakenly believed to have been invented during the Civil War actually had been around for years: the submarine. The first submarine used in warfare came not during the Civil War but in the American Revolution. The earlier version was called the *Turtle* and amounted to little more than a sealed barrel with propellers for propulsion and guidance. But it got the job done. Yale College student David Bushnell invented the *Turtle* and used it in 1776 to sink a British frigate in New York harbor.

Two other submarines, of sorts, made their debut in America's Civil War. The first was the CSS *David*, which may not have been so much a submarine as a semi-sub; it didn't completely submerge. It was fifty feet long and six feet in diameter amidships. It was given the name *David* because its inventor hoped to use its slingshot-torpedo to sink the Union navy's Goliath, the *New Ironsides.* It didn't, and it almost cost the four-man crew their lives.

The *David* carried a torpedo filled with 60 pounds of black powder at the end of a long spar, basically a pole, attached to the bow (that is, the front) of the little boat. A steam engine located aft powered the little vessel; a stubby smokestack located forward reached above water. The crew worked in a cubbyhole located between the engine and smokestack. The *David*'s captain, Lt. William T. Glassells, was also the inventor of this particular submarine.

On the night of October 5, 1863, Glassells and his mates aimed the *David* toward Goliath. During the trip across the Charleston harbor, Glassells had his head out, above water. He was prepared in case his torpedo device didn't work; he carried a double-barrelled shotgun. He needed it. When the *David* was a few yards from the *New Ironsides,* the Federal ship's officer of the deck, a young acting ensign, spotted the Confederate boat and let out a yell. Glassells let go with his shotgun. The next few minutes were rather colorfully described in a newspaper account nearly a hundred years later.

> The young officer slipped like a flung garment, blood-spattered, to the deck. A rattle of small arms followed. A moment's silence and the roar of a thousand cannon split the air. A salt water geyser shot skyward. The giant New Ironsides reared, plunged, righted herself, quivering from stem to stern.
>
> Under her starboard quarter, three men floundered. A fourth clung desperately to the wheel of a queer little craft, watching as the geyser broke, descended, poured itself down the vessel's stumpy smokestack. Almost with anguish, [the small boat's captain] saw the coals of his

fire swamped with water, sputter like himself, smoulder, fade out and
die, leaving him to drift, helpless in the midst of the Yankee fleet.[4]

Glassells and one other member of the Rebel boat's crew were taken
prisoner. A fourth crew member, the engineer, tried to surrender, but
Union riflemen continued shooting at him. Finally, the engineer
gave up trying to give up and swam back to the *David*. As he put it,
"Since no quarter was to be given, I thought I might as well save the
David."

He and the pilot crawled back into the semisub, relit the engine
and, with a bit of coaxing, steamed back into Charleston with thirteen bullet holes in the hull. The *New Ironsides* received minimal damage herself, and one Marine onboard suffered a broken leg. Other
Union sailors, including the officer of the deck, received even less
severe wounds.

A year later, a true submarine was launched against Union block-
aders off Charleston. The *H. L. Hunley* took on the U.S. Navy on
February 17, 1864, just over four months after the *David* incident.
Unlike the *Turtle* or the *David*, the *Hunley* was more in the shape of
a modern submarine, even if it was just a converted boiler. It can't,
however, be called a Confederate vessel. The *Hunley* was designed
and owned by a private group. It was built to make a profit for its owners by sinking Union ships; the owners had a letter of marque given
them for underwater privateering. It was dated 1861, signed by a New
Orleans customs agent.

The *Hunley* lost several crews when the boat sank before making
its first and only military or privateering venture. It carried a crew of
nine, all busy hand-cranking a single propeller. Like the *David*, the
Hunley, carried a black-powder torpedo, one hundred pounds this
time, on a bow-mounted spar. That February night its crew set its
sights on the USS *Housatonic*, a Federal sloop blockading Charleston.
The *Hunley* reached its target; the torpedo was placed and set off.
The *Housatonic* went down and so did the *Hunley*, probably when the
sub's own torpedo exploded.

The *Hunley* literally was lost, simply never returning from its mission. The sunken sub wasn't found for more than 130 years. It lay on
the bottom the ocean, off the coast of Charleston, when it was located
in 1995 by an organization headed by Clive Cussler, author of the

novel *Raise the Titanic.* Apparently Cussler not only intends to write about the *Hunley* but plans to raise the vessel. Others object, saying the *Hunley* should remain untouched, with the bodies of its Confederate crew still buried in the sands off Charleston.

The North had something like a submarine of its own. A Frenchman named Brutus de Villeroi offered to build one for the Federal navy. President Lincoln liked the idea and ordered the USS *Alligator* built at the Philadelphia Navy Yard. De Villeroi's original plans called for a propeller-driven craft, whose power came from a fresh-air breathing steam engine, but they didn't build that one. The Union version that was built, however, operated by oars. In June of 1862, the *Alligator* scuttled along the bottom of Hampton Roads, Virginia. But it never attacked anyone, and later, when it was being towed out to sea, it foundered off Cape Hatteras, North Carolina. Its grave is in the same general area as another, more famous vessel, the USS *Monitor,* which went down later that same year.

Lincoln wanted to continue the submarine project, and a Washington inventor came up with plans for a rocket-powered sub. No thanks, the government said, but the inventor went ahead with plans for a rocket-powered unmanned torpedo, which actually was tested and actually had some success. The first test torpedo blew up a mud bank at the Washington Navy Yard. Good shot. The second blew up a ship, the schooner *Diana.* Not so good. Of course, the *Diana* was a Union ship and the rocket-torpedo was a Union invention, but let it be duly noted: It was the first powered torpedo to sink a ship.

The third test came a month later and, but for the lack of imagination on the part of its Federal navy observers, might have driven warfare generations ahead of itself. Inventor Pascal Plant set off his rocket-powered torpedo in the Anacostia River, not far from where the Anacostia joins the Potomac. The torpedo bore through the water, *became airborne for about 300 feet,* then splashed back into the river. The Navy Department's witnesses gave up on the idea. This short-sighted group failed to realize what they had just seen, the first sea-to-land missile, perhaps even today's SLAAM, a submarine-launched anti-air missile. After all, the Civil War did see the first air force of sorts.

While animals and even humans were sent aloft in balloons in the late eighteenth century, America's Civil War saw the first manned balloons used for reconnaissance. It's not known if they did any good, and the first aerial reconnaissance, naturally, resulted in the first antiaircraft attack, as the Rebels tried to shoot down the Union's balloons.

With more Union forts and naval bases in the South than in the North at the start of the war, the Confederacy had a foot up in weaponry, which was good inasmuch as the South didn't produce nearly as many guns as the North. And, too, during the first two years, scores of Union cannon and hundreds of Union rifles fell into Rebel hands. There's the story of a North Carolina soldier who's been captured by Federal forces at the Battle of Antietam. He's being marched through the Northern camp when he sees the rows of Federal cannon lined up. He stops and his bluebelly guard asks him: "What now, Johnny Reb?"

"Mister," the Rebel says, "y'all got near 'bout as many of these U.S. guns as we'uns has."

Robert E. Lee's forces captured fifty-two field pieces during the Seven Days' Battles in Virginia. Braxton Bragg captured another eighty-one during the fighting in Kentucky and Tennessee. The South, however, lost artillery at Vicksburg and Chattanooga. By 1863, with things going downhill for the South, the Confederacy had to think more seriously about building their own weapons, not relying on what the Yankees left behind, such as in the Great Skedaddle at First Manassas, when some fresh Union troops left the battlefield and didn't stop running until they reached Washington. By now the Yankees had stopped running.

America's Civil War saw the first use of mobile siege artillery mounted on rail cars. It was also the first widespread use of railroads as mobile hospitals, as well as the use of the railroads themselves as a major means of transporting both troops and supplies into battle. The railroads were, of themselves, your typical good news–bad news. They were ideal for supplying the troops but were inflexible and, therefore, vulnerable to attack.

There was an organized signal service; the Federal army used flags in the day and torches at night. The first use of a portable telegraph on the battlefield came during America's Civil War, and that was significant. Another significant event was the first time spies in the field used portable telegraphs. They stole battle plans and transmitted erroneous information to the enemy.

America's Civil War saw the first draft; both sides used it. So many men in the army led to the first voting by troops in the field. And, in 1864, the overwhelming support of the troops in the field helped reelect President Abraham Lincoln.

The war saw the first instant coffee; the Union tried it, but the troops hated it. Hospital ships and the army ambulance corps were other "firsts." And the Union's first ironclad, the *Monitor*, had the first flush toilet onboard a warship.

The first photographs taken during combat came during America's Civil War, though, because of the available equipment, most photographs were taken before or after a battle, sometimes while the troops were sitting around camp or when they simply posed for the photographer.

James F. Gibson and Alexander Gardner worked under Mathew Brady after the Battle of Antietam. The pictures they took over the next several days were gruesome beyond the comprehension of America at mid-century. When the pictures were displayed in Brady's New York City gallery, people were appalled, as well they should have been. A reporter wrote about the pictures after seeing Brady's exhibit.

The dead of battle-field come up to us very rarely, even in dreams. We see the list in the morning paper at breakfast, but dismiss its recollection with the coffee.

There is a confused mass of names, but they are all strangers; we forget the horrible significance that dwells amid the jumble of type. . . .

We recognize the battle-field as a reality, but it stands as a remote one. It is like a funeral next door. It attracts your attention, but it does not enlist your sympathy. But it is very different when the hearse stops at your door and the corpse is carried over your threshold. . . .

Mr. Brady has done something to bring home to us the terrible reality and earnestness of war. If he has not brought bodies and laid them in our door-yards and along streets, he has done something very like it.[5]

The bodies, some bloated from lying in the September sun, were repulsive, "bloodstained relics of the stale battlefield," Oliver Wendell Holmes wrote. The future Supreme Court chief justice added:

> *It is so . . . like visiting the battlefields to look over these [photographic] views that all emotions . . . come back to us, and we [bury] them in the recess of our cabinet as we buried the mutilated remains of the dead they too vividly represent.*

Brady and/or Gardner and/or Gibson did the job together, and in the beginning of the war Brady took credit for all the work. They often altered the facts when taking post-battle photographs. Where there was no dead soldier, they placed one. Where there was no weapon, they gave the victim a musket. In fact, they carried a musket around with them and put it in different places, with different bodies. This altered the face of the battlefield. They cheated, if you will, by not telling the public the truth. In today's supercritical world, they would have been justly criticized—first, for showing the bodies, and second, for altering the truth.

During the Vietnam War, a television cameraman pictured in closeup an American soldier, lighter in hand, setting fire to a Vietnamese hut. It was a simple beginning to a confusing atrocity. American soldiers went on to shoot many of the old men and the women and the children who lived in that village, My Lai.

It could be said television that day changed the course of the Vietnam War. So, too, in its own way, did the photographs taken at the Antietam battlefield change the course of America's Civil War.

Undoubtedly, the greatest change in the way war was fought came when the Union first enlisted black troops. About a thousand free and slave Negro troops had served in the American Revolution, but the Civil War saw the first *specific* call for black troops. Almost from the beginning blacks served in the Union navy, albeit more often than not as coal stokers, but not on the ground, in the army.

At the beginning of the war, free Negroes tried to enlist in the Federal army but were refused. The first Negro foot soldiers (or colored, as they often were called) were organized in July 1862 by Gen. David

Hunter. They came not from the North but from the South, the 1st South Carolina Regiment, and they would have fought for the Union, but President Lincoln vetoed the idea. Later they were made part of the army, the 33rd Regiment, United States Colored Troops.

The 79th U.S. Colored Infantry was the first African-American regiment to go into combat, its initial combat coming at Island Mounds, Missouri, on October 28, 1862. The 79th's officers were white, a fact that was routine throughout America's Civil War—white officers over black troops. Only later did the army commission a black—Maj. J. R. Delany, the first black officer in an American army. By the end of the war, 15 percent of the men in Federal forces were black, and there were about 4,300 black casualties.

In September 1862, Confederate President Jefferson Davis called for a draft of blacks. He wanted 4,500 blacks, only he wanted them to build forts, not to fight, and even that idea was rejected by the Confederate Congress. Two years later, Davis tried to push through a bill to turn slaves into soldiers. He couldn't get Congress to approve that one, either; too many Southern leaders still held to the theory of master and slave. Davis commented, "If the Confederacy falls, there should be written on its tombstone, 'Died of a theory.'" It did, and somebody should.

Before the fall of Atlanta, Irish-born Confederate Gen. Patrick Ronayne Cleburne put forward a plan to free the slaves and use them as soldiers. His commander, Joseph E. Johnston, wouldn't even send the proposal on to Richmond, saying it was a political, not a military, matter.

Finally, in March 1865, at the urging of Robert E. Lee, the Confederacy actively recruited blacks to fight. They formed into companies and marched up and down Richmond streets. The Confederate government wondered how it would uniform their new black troops. Southern women vowed to give them a flag all their own, which a pessimist might see as a way to keep them from coming too near other Confederate flags. But these new troops, blacks who joined the Rebel army to fight for a Confederacy formed to keep them slaves, never got into action.

On April 1, 1865, two days before the fall of Richmond and eight days before Lee's surrender at Appomattox, Jefferson Davis wrote

Lee, "I have been laboring without much progress to advance the raising of negro troops."

There was another first in America's Civil War, one counterproductive to both North and South, abhorrent and heinous to both sides of the war. April 14,1865, marked the first assassination of a president of the United States.

CHAPTER TEN

Ships of Iron; Men of Steel

[As] gunpowder made armor useless on shore, so armor is having its revenge by baffling its old enemy at sea; and that, while gunpowder robbed land warfare of nearly all its picturesqueness to give even greater stateliness and sublimity to a sea-fight, armor bids fare to degrade the latter into a squabble between two iron-shelled turtles.

—James Russell Lowell
Observation on ironclads[1]

The USS *Monitor* never fought the USS *Merrimack*. The two ships that fought in Hampton Roads, Virginia, on March 8, 1862, were the USS *Monitor* and the CSS *Virginia*. And the *Virginia* wasn't built in Norfolk; it was rebuilt in Gosport. It wasn't the Norfolk Navy Yard then, but the Gosport Navy Yard. Most historians just can't seem to get these things straight, but we'll give it a try.

The Gosport Navy Yard went back to when the United States of America was first born. It sat on the south side of Virginia's Elizabeth River, adjacent to the small but thriving port city of Portsmouth. Across the river was the larger and even more thriving city of Norfolk. With the first stone drydock in the country, Gosport was the most important naval facility in America. But on April 20, 1861, the order went out: Gosport Navy Yard and all of the ships that couldn't move out were to be destroyed.

Undergoing repairs at Gosport at the time were nine of the U.S. Navy's major ships, including the propeller-driven frigate, the USS *Merrimack*. She'd been launched in 1855 and had been at the Gosport Navy Yard for over a year after a long cruise to Panama. She sat there, decommissioned and awaiting repairs, unable to steam off or even to be towed away. So, early on the morning of the 21st, sailors went about destroying the *Merrimack,* first with sledgehammers and then with torches. When they finished, not much was left of the ship down to the waterline; the *Merrimack* was a picture of charred timbers, twisted rigging, all covered with mud. To many who saw her, it seemed the *Merrimack* was lost forever.

Three weeks later, however, Stephen Mallory, the new Confederate Secretary of the Navy, wrote to the South's congressional naval committee. He regarded the building of "an iron-armored ship as a matter of the first necessity." Such a ship, he believed, "could traverse the entire coast of the United States, prevent all blockade and encounter, with a fair prospect of success, their entire navy."

With Mallory's note in hand, the new commandant of the Gosport Navy Yard, French Forrest, began salvaging the *Merrimack.* Two weeks later, he had the *Merrimack* sealed and out of the mud, pulling her into drydock. The best cost estimate for repairing the ship and adding iron to her was $172,523, amounting to a bit over two million dollars in modern terms. A bargain at the price, if the plan worked. They rechristened the ship the CSS *Virginia.*

Workmen at the Gosport Navy Yard built what might be called a teakwood penthouse on the *Virginia'*s deck, then bolted on the armor.

Meanwhile, Richmond's Tredegar Iron Works were working around the clock turning out the iron plate. One thousand tons of armor in one- and two-inch-thick layers of rolled railroad iron. Each plate to be eight inches wide, ten feet long. It was to cover a 172-foot portion of the *Virginia'*s 262-foot overall length. The iron shield would be thirty feet wide at its base and seven feet high, laid against the frigate's casement at a 35-degree angle.

At the *Virginia'*s bow they added something of a throwback to ancient times, a 1,500-pound, two and a half foot long iron ram extending two feet below the waterlevel. For weapons, the *Virginia* would carry two 7-inch pivot guns, one each at the bow and stern, and two 6.4-inch "Brooke" rifles along with six smoothbore 9-inch Dahlgren guns, leftovers from the *Merrimack* herself.

The fledgling Confederate navy was confident it could build the ship. What many weren't so confident of, however, was whether the ship would float. After all, it would weigh over four thousand tons. If it *did* float, how far upriver—any river, but principally the James

River if the *Virginia* were called on to defend the Confederate capital of Richmond—how far up river could the ironclad steam? In fact, at low tide the Elizabeth River between Norfolk and Portsmouth wasn't particularly deep. And not far away, in Hampton Roads, sandbars could be a hazard at low tide. Would the ironclad *Virginia* be effective under those conditions?

Good questions, but no one would know until the *Virginia* was completed and that was months away.

While the USS *Merrimack* was being converted and renamed into the CSS *Virginia,* Lt. John Taylor Wood was busy recruiting sailors for the ironclad. Wood was the grandson of U.S. President Zachary Taylor.

Lieutenant Wood was a recent graduate of the U.S. Naval Academy at Annapolis, but it was as a Confederate naval officer that he went looking for sailors. Not just among naval personnel, either, but among Gen. John Magruder's small band of infantry on the Virginia peninsula. Magruder needed all the troops he could get to face the coming battle with Gen. George McClellan, but he told Wood to recruit all he could. "I visited every camp," Wood later wrote, "and the commanding officers were ordered to parade their men, and I explained to them what I wanted. About two hundred volunteered, and of this number I selected eighty who had some experience as seamen or gunners." The Confederate navy was going all out to man its experimental ship, even if they had to use army recruits.

As the *Virginia* was being rebuilt, the partially converted ship was being described as something like a huge turtle with a chimney in the middle of its back. Up north, they were working on their own ironclad, one that looked even weirder.

It was no secret in Washington that the Rebels were doing something down in Virginia, building an ironclad ship of some kind. On November 17, 1861, the New York *Herald* carried a story: "The *Merrimack* is still in the dock and it is the opinion of intelligent men that she will never float. She is being encased with three inch boiler iron."

Three weeks before that article ran, the U.S. Navy laid the keel of the Union's own first ironclad warship, the USS *Monitor.* It was October 25, 1861, and the place was at Long Island, New York; at the time, the ship carried no name. Three months later, the ship's inventor claimed the Federal ironclad would serve as "a severe monitor" to pro-Confederate European leaders who might think about backing the Rebel cause. The new ship now had a name, approved by the U.S. Navy Department. Actually, approving the name came much more quickly than approving the ship's design. The Federal navy already had three ironclads underway or in final stages of blueprint, and they were considering another twenty proposals.

Not long after the Union army's loss at First Manassas, the Navy Department placed a notice in the Washington *Evening Star,* advertising for bids for ships, "either of iron or wood and iron combined." The deadline for presenting bids was September 3, 1861.

Sixty-year-old John Ericsson was ready with his bid. In fact, he had a pasteboard model of the ship he hoped to build. He'd built the model seven years earlier, but nobody wanted to hear about it then— a small, iron-plated ship, not much showing above water, with one revolving turret and a small forward-mounted pilot house.

On August 29, Ericsson sent Abraham Lincoln a letter, introducing himself and his design. The postal system of 1861 apparently was as erratic as that of today; Ericsson's letter got to its destination late, after the deadline, and was ignored. In early September, a New Haven, Connecticut, grocer-turned-shipbuilder was awarded a contract to construct the *Galena,* an ironclad that didn't look much different from existing steam frigates, except for the metal plating. The fact is, it looked very much like the *Virginia* being rebuilt in the South.

The *Galena*'s designer was Cornelius Bushnell. When someone suggested Bushnell talk with Ericsson, he agreed. The two men met and Ericsson showed Bushnell his seven-year-old model. Bushnell was so interested in Ericsson's plans, he asked President Lincoln to look at them. So at 11:00 A.M. on September 12, nine days after the deadline for submitting plans for an ironclad, Abraham Lincoln first met John Ericsson and his model for an extraordinary ship. This time, everyone agreed it was a novel plan. Lincoln, in his usual humorous manner, noted: "All I have to say is what the girl said when she stuck her foot into the stocking. It strikes me there's something in it!" Ericsson got a contract to build the USS *Monitor.*

In order to meet the 100-day deadline for building the ironclad, Ericsson had to farm out much of the work. The turret, for instance, was built by the "Novelty Iron Works" of New York. Still, the *Monitor* didn't make the deadline and came in one day later than the contract demanded. That same contract called for "the vessel to be rigged with two masts with wire rope standing rigging, to navigate at sea." Apparently, no one quite trusted steam to power the ironclad all the way to wherever it might go. The *Monitor,* however, didn't have the required masts, and when it left New York, no one knew if the *Monitor* could meet another contract clause, steam upriver at eight knots speed. When it first left port, it didn't steam at all; it had to be towed all the way from New York to Hampton Roads, Virginia, wallowing in the wake of the tugboat *Seth Low.*

Already, the CSS *Virginia* was playing havoc with Union ships in Hampton Roads. The *Virginia* had been completed on March 7, 1862, and immediately sent into action. Almost as incomplete as the *Monitor,* even the *Virginia*'s guns hadn't even been test fired or her engines started. But, on March 8, the Confederate ironclad went to work, heading straight for the Union's 24-gun sloop, *Cumberland,* guarding the Union's Fort Monroe and blockading the James and York Rivers. A sailor onboard the *Cumberland* commented that the Rebel ship "looked like a huge, half-submerged crocodile. Her side seemed of solid iron. At her prow I could see the iron ram projecting straight forward."

When the "half-submerged crocodile" came near, the *Cumberland* opened fire. The shots bounced harmlessly off the *Virginia*'s side, looking, as one Union officer put it, "like India rubber," not iron cannon balls. The *Virginia* fired point-blank at the *Cumberland* and then rammed her broadside. The ironclad's ram broke off, but otherwise her crew hardly noticed the collision. Not so the *Cumberland;* she heeled over, her crew continuing to fire even as her deck was awash and the ship clearly was headed for the bottom of Hampton Roads.

The *Virginia* turned to the USS *Congress* and, at two hundred yards, smashed the Federal ship to pieces, setting it on fire. About an hour later, the *Congress* hoisted a white flag. In the best maritime tradition, Rebel crew members tried to save the *Congress*'s crew, but in many cases they were unable to do so.

Next in line for the ironclad was the *Minnesota,* and the *Virginia* drove the Union ship aground. The problem was, the ironclad drew twenty-two feet of water, and she couldn't finish the job. The tide was on its way out, and the Rebel commander decided sinking the *Minnesota* could wait until the next day's high tide. It had been a good day for the first ironclad.

When he heard what happened in Virginia, U.S. Secretary of War Edwin Stanton agreed. He said, "The *Merrimack*," as the North still insisted on calling the *Virginia,* "will change the whole character of the war. She will destroy every naval vessel. She will lay all the cities on the seaboard under contribution."

The Rebel navy thought the same thing until the next day.

Thousands of picnickers lined the shore that Sunday, March 9. News of the success had thrilled Southern hearts, and local residents gathered to watch as the *Virginia* went back to work. She immediately headed for the helpless *Minnesota,* sitting all alone behind a sandbar.

Almost helpless, almost alone. Alongside the *Minnesota* lay a ship such as had never been seen before. A Rebel seaman called it "an immense shingle floating on the water, with a gigantic cheesebox rising from the center. No sails, no wheels, no smokestack, no guns." The strange vessel was, another sailor said, like "a pygmy compared with the lofty frigate which she guarded." Within hours, the U.S. Navy wished it had a whole patrol of pygmies.

The *Monitor* and the *Virginia* hammered away at each other—shot, shell, canister, and rifle balls. So close, they collided five times. Smoke half blinded the sailors, but nothing did any major damage to either ship. For four and a half hours the battle continued, the first battle between ironclads.

Both ships had major problems. The *Monitor*'s gun turret didn't work properly. The *Virginia* took so long to turn about—as much as a half hour—and required such deep water in which to operate, that none of what was left of its ram nor its remaining eight working guns did much damage. The *Monitor* backed off into shallow water, behind a sandbar, aware the *Virginia* drew too much water to come after her.

The *Virginia*'s crew thought the *Monitor* was giving up, so the Rebels cheered and steamed back to port, claiming victory. The crew of the *Monitor* saw the enemy withdraw, so they cheered, thinking *they* had won. In truth, neither side had won, but that relatively short sea battle changed history.

* * *

A few years later, the city of Portsmouth annexed the small town of Gosport and with it the navy yard, but for reasons known only to the federal bureaucracy, the Navy decided to drop the name "Gosport Navy Yard" and call it the "*Norfolk* Navy Yard," even though the yard itself was not in Norfolk but in Portsmouth, Virginia. However, the name "Portsmouth Navy Yard" was already taken by another government facility, one supposedly in Portsmouth, New Hampshire. Yet, the "Portsmouth Navy Yard" is not in Portsmouth, New Hampshire. It's in Kittery. And Kittery isn't even in New Hampshire, it's in Maine. This is all very confusing, and only the United States government can explain it; so far, it hasn't.

So, there never was a battle between the *Monitor* and the *Merrimack,* although, admittedly, the names roll together nicely, *Monitor* and *Merrimack.* To add to the problem, nearly everybody confuses the USS *Merrimack* (with a *K*) with the USS *Merrimac* (without a *K*). The *Merrimack* (which became the *Virginia*) was not the *Merrimac;* they were two different ships. The first battle of the ironclads, then, was fought in Hampton Roads, Virginia, by the *Monitor* and the *Virginia,* not the *Monitor* and the *Merrimack.* Certainly not the *Merrimac,* which was in another part of the war.

The ships, by whatever name, fought only once. Whatever she was called, it was the *Virginia's* only real fight. Two months later, when the Confederate navy evacuated Norfolk, Portsmouth, and the Gosport Navy Yard, the navy tried desperately to steam the *Virginia* up the James to protect her and the city of Richmond. But it was just as many had feared: even though the crew removed every piece of equipment it could, the ship couldn't make it up the shallow James River. Her captain felt he had no choice; he scuttled and burned the *Virginia* not far from where she was conceived, within sight of where she took part in her one and only battle. Off Craney Island, Virginia, her crew lowered the colors. They set fire to her and scuttled the CSS *Virginia.*

The public, however, didn't understand and didn't like the idea. The Confederacy court-martialed her captain. However, the court later declared, "The only alternative, in the opinion of the court, was to abandon and burn the ship then and there; which in the judgment of the court was deliberately and wisely done by order of the accused."

Fourteen years later, the United States Navy refloated the ironclad *Virginia* and towed it back to the Gosport Navy Yard, which once more was in Federal hands. There, the "turtle with a smokestack," the "huge, half-submerged crocodile" was scrapped. Only bits and pieces remain today, revered and tucked away—an iron plate in the Norfolk Navy Yard Museum in Portsmouth, another plate at the Museum of the Confederacy in Richmond; some few parts, however, remain mired in the mud at Craney Island. The site now is part of a U.S. Navy fuel depot and off-limits to would-be relic hunters.

The *Monitor* didn't fare much better. The Union navy tried towing it here and there—tried dragging it up the James River, where it might shell Richmond as part of George McClellan's Peninsula Campaign. But Confederate troops at Fort Darling, on Drewry's Bluff overlooking the James, fired on the ironclad and drove the *Monitor* off. The Union ship's turret guns couldn't be elevated enough to reach the fortifications above.

In mid-December the Union sent the *Monitor* south, hoping to capture Wilmington, North Carolina. Once again, she had to be towed. The *Monitor* wasn't the most stable of open-sea ships, and she ran into a storm off the area known as "the Graveyard of the Atlantic," Cape Hatteras. At about 3 o'clock on the morning of December 31, she sank in 220 feet of water.

For ninety-one years the Navy carried the *Monitor* as a ship of the fleet. Only in September of 1951 did Washington list her as "out of commission."

For 112 years the *Monitor* lay hidden from view at the bottom of the ocean, until a Duke University expedition found her in 1974, overturned in the silt and sand, her turret broken off. The wreck of the *Monitor* is protected from would-be relic hunters by the Federal government and the depth at which she lies, accessible to only the most experienced divers. Some say the *Monitor* is waiting for her next battle, hoping for a rematch with the *Virginia*.

Chapter Eleven

All in the Family:
More than Just a Brothers' War

I advise you, and as strongly as ever, to not come to war. I tell you you will repent of it if you do, I do believe. You have no idea of what it is to be a soldier.
—Pvt. Joseph Boyd, C.S.A.
April 12, 1862, letter to his brother[1]

Edward Ketcham was a second lieutenant with Company A, the 120th New York Volunteer Infantry. His brother, John, was also a lieutenant, serving with Company M, the 4th New York Cavalry. They were both Quakers, a religious group usually associated with pacifism—nonviolence. But they both joined up anyway. Sometimes they saw each other, sometimes they fought in the same battle. They were together at the Battle of Gettysburg, and John watched as enemy fire killed Edward. It was up to him to tell their mother. On July 8, 1863, he wrote her:

> *Don't let it kill thee, Mother. Thee and I are all that is left of us. As all the men lay on their faces, Edward was sitting up to look around. A sharpshooter's bullet struck him in the temple and went through his head. He put up his hand, and said, "oh!" and fell on his elbow, quite dead.*

Four months to the day after writing that letter, John also died, a prisoner in Richmond.

As America's Civil War struggled on, as deaths mounted, the story of John and Edward Ketcham became less and less unusual. Sometimes two members of the same family died, sometimes more. At Gettysburg, a North Carolina family lost all four of its sons. Another Confederate mother lost all seven of her sons during the four-year war.

In 1861, when the 55th Illinois was mustered into service, there were ninety-one pairs of brothers among the thousand or so men serving. By 1865, when the war ended, fifty-eight of those brothers had died in battle. Sometimes death came while fighting on opposite sides of the Brothers' War.

John Crittenden was a United States senator from Kentucky, an old line Whig who tried to hold the Union together by compromise. He hoped to prevent a war by having both sides in the issue bend just a little, not enough to make either side break. But he couldn't get Congress to agree with him. The House voted *for* his compromise. The Senate voted *against* it.

It seemed everywhere Senator Crittenden looked, the people were split on how they felt. Back home in Louisville, his home state of Kentucky had a governor who favored secession but a state legislature that wanted to stay in the Union. The city was almost literally divided down the middle. A group of Union volunteers marched up and down one side of a street while a group of Confederates drilled on the other.

The divided feelings were even closer for Senator Crittenden. Two of his sons were major generals: Maj. Gen. Thomas L. Crittenden wore the Union blue while Maj. Gen. George B. Crittenden wore Confederate gray. Their brother, Eugene W. Crittenden, was a colonel in the Rebel army.

They weren't all that unusual. The war ripped apart cities and states; it tore apart families and brought others together. At the First Battle of Manassas, Frederick Hubbard and his brother Henry saw each other for the first time in six years. Frederick was with a New Orleans artillery unit. His brother, Henry, was with the 1st Minnesota infantry. Henry was wounded and carried to a field hospital. The wounded man in the cot next to him was Frederick.

Mary Todd Lincoln's youngest brother joined the Confederate army, as did three of her half-brothers and three brothers-in-law.

In the backwoods of Kentucky, the story goes, a Union soldier questioned an old woman. "Are you Union or 'secesh'?" he asked. She said, "A Baptist, an' always have been."

At the Battle of Gettysburg, where John Ketcham watched his brother, Edward, die at Culp's Hill—among the most bitterly fought-over pieces of land—both of landowner John Culp's sons died. One was with the Union; the other was a Confederate.

During the Battle of Atlanta, former U.S. vice president, now Confederate Gen. John C. Breckinridge, was taken prisoner by his cousin, W. C. P. Breckinridge of the Union army. The former vice president's daughter also stayed with the Union. Margaret E. Breckinridge was a U.S. Sanitary Commission worker.

Commodore Franklin Buchanan commanded the Confederate ironclad *Virginia* while his brother was an officer aboard the Union ship *Congress*. The Rebel saw his Federalist brother, McKean Buchanan, die onboard that Union ship, killed by gunfire from the *Virginia*.

When war came, Albert M. Lea of Baltimore, Maryland, was a U.S. Army engineer. He resigned to join the Confederate cause. His son, Edward, was second in command aboard the USS *Harriet Lane,* a Federal warship named for former President James Buchanan's daughter.

The elder Lea was sent to build Rebel defenses, first in eastern Tennessee at the Cumberland Gap, then to the port of Galveston, Texas. In the fight for control of Gulf ports, the *Harriet Lane* was ordered to bombard Galveston, the city Lea's father defended. Two Rebel gunboats were sent to blast the Union ship out of the water. Confederate Albert Lea knew his Union son was onboard the Lane, but he also knew it was his duty to destroy the Federal fleet.

In the raging battle, the younger Lea was critically wounded. After the *Harriet Lane* struck her colors, Albert Lea was told his son had been injured and was dying. Quickly, the Rebel went to find his Union son. He found Edward lying on deck. He knelt beside him, taking his dying son in his arms.

It was brother against brother, neighbor against neighbor. We may call it the "Civil War," but there was nothing civil about it.

It was particularly distressing to families in the divided border states. At Gettysburg, the Union's 7th West Virginia was commanded by Lt. Col. Jonathan Lockwood. Opposite him that July day was the Confederate 7th Virginia, with Lockwood's cousin among the Rebels driven back and wounded.

Famed Confederate cavalryman Jeb Stuart also had family on the other side; his father-in-law, Philip St. George Cooke, was a general in the Federal cavalry. Another member of the Cooke family, St. George Cook's son, John Esten Cooke, helped persuade Stuart to ride with the Confederacy. He wrote Jeb saying he must not "remain with the Lincoln humbug." John Esten Cooke called Lincoln "a foreign despotism," one he would fight against and urged Jeb to do the same.

The fighting often pitted lifelong friends against each other. To a great extent, it was due to the small size of the prewar Union military. The size and the fact that, in the South more so than in the North, the military was often thought of as a good career for second sons. The first son would inherit the land, while the second son went into the military. As it grew more and more likely that war would come, many Southern officers resigned their Northern commissions and went home, back down South.

When the war began, 313 Union officers resigned their commissions and returned to the South. Such names as Robert E. Lee, Jeb Stuart, and Pierre Gustave Toutant Beauregard—all West Point trained, all Union officers—all resigned to become officers in the Confederacy. Most knew each other. They, truly, were a band of brothers.

In the Mexican War, Robert E. Lee commanded not only Stuart but Beauregard, McClellan, and Ulysses S. Grant. Lee once commended Grant for bravery. The commendation was delivered to Grant by John Pemberton, a Northern-born officer who later chose to join the Rebels. In 1863 Pemberton commanded Confederate forces guarding Vicksburg, Mississippi, and when Union troops finally defeated the Rebels at Vicksburg, it was Pemberton who surrendered to Grant.

In another battle, another Confederate officer was forced to surrender to Sam Grant. It was the Union victory at Fort Donelson and the general was Simon Bolivar Buckner. Buckner and Grant were friends at West Point, and when Grant went broke, Buckner loaned him money. Before he sent Buckner off as a prisoner of war, Grant repaid the favor. Over cigars and coffee, Grant told Buckner he realized Buckner might need money, so he offered to lend it to him.

On the night of July 3, 1863, Confederate Gen. George Pickett sat by the fire writing a poem to his wife, Mary. It was the night before the fatal third day of the Battle of Gettysburg. Lewis Armistead walked up to Pickett and stood looking around at their mutual friends and comrades. "Lo," his friends called him, short for Lothario. It was something the shy Virginian surely wasn't, a fact his friends knew very well. Armistead was tall, with steel-gray hair despite his young age. He handed Pickett a package and asked that it be sent to Mira—Almira Hancock—the wife of Armistead's closet friend, Winfield Scott Hancock. Hancock now stood on the opposite side of the battlefield, wearing a Union blue uniform with major general's insignia. Armistead had been booted out of West Point during his second year following a dining hall fracas in which he hit Jubal Early over the head with a plate. But he still proudly wore his West Point ring.

Lo Armistead removed that ring from his pinky finger—it was the customary finger on which to wear them at the time. Pressing the ring into Pickett's hand, Lewis Armistead told his fellow Virginian to give it to Pickett's wife as a remembrance.

Pickett himself was just thirty-eight at the time. He'd graduated fifty-ninth in his fifty-nine-man class at West Point in 1846, the same class as George McClellan and Stonewall Jackson. He'd fought in Mexico but resigned his Federal commission to become a Confederate brigadier general. He wore his hair long, in highly perfumed ringlets. Once, when some admiring women asked Gen. Robert E. Lee for a lock of his hair, Lee suggested they ask Pickett instead; he had more of it, Lee said.

When it came time to fight that July day, Pickett called, "Up, men, and to your posts. Don't forget you are from Old Virginia!" Pickett himself did not charge; he and his aides watched from a nearby farmhouse. It wasn't a pretty sight.

It was three o'clock that Friday when the Confederates stepped off perfectly dressed rank after rank, still pretending it was the Age of Napoleon. And they pretended the enemy had been leveled by an earlier artillery barrage. It hadn't.

Flags flying, 12,500 Confederate soldiers marched side by side. Another 2,500 waited in reserve.

A mile-wide spectacle for history to record. They charged in the open, no place to hide, just the knee-high grass and a few stone walls. The line of Rebels had covered about three hundred yards when the Union cannon opened fire. The Confederate line wavered but marched on.

Union troops knelt at the top of the ridge, sending volley after volley of rifle fire into the oncoming Rebel ranks. The Federal artillery switched from ball to canister, and shards of steel whistled into the men massed and trudging across the open field. Smoke and dust. Thirst and dying. More screams, more whistling canister and ball. More death.

Armistead ordered his men to increase to double-time, and more gaps opened in the Confederate line. By the hundreds young men—young boys, really—fell dead. Others huddled in fear and cried for deliverance. The Rebel line stalled. Armistead skewered his old black felt hat on the tip of his sword, raised it high into the air, and cried out, "Virginians! With me! With me!"

To the stone wall the Virginians charged, and the Federals fell back. It was the High Water Mark of the Confederacy, some would say. But at that high water mark, a blast of hell-hot air and searing steel doubled Armistead over. He was suddenly tired and had to hold on to a Federal cannon just recently captured by his men. Some were there with him, those same men, only now many lay lifeless.

The High Water Mark of the Confederacy receded, but Armistead was left behind and died. His friend Winfield Scott Hancock was injured and lay nearby. Long after Gettysburg, Lewis Armistead's package reached Almira Hancock; it was Armistead's personal Bible.

As the battered Rebels slowly returned to their lines, some limping, some crawling, some being helped by comrades, while still under Federal fire, George Pickett looked at his men and then at his hand. In it he held the West Point ring Lo Armistead had asked Pickett to give his wife in remembrance of friendships long held.

When the war was over, many resumed their friendships. But for many others it was too late.

For still others, it took a strange twist. Union Gen. William Tecumseh Sherman and Confederate Gen. Joseph E. Johnston were bitter enemies during the war. Johnston finally surrendered to Sherman three weeks after Lee met Grant at Appomattox. Later Johnston and

Sherman became fast friends, and when Sherman died in 1891, Johnston was a pallbearer. It was raining, and Johnston stood hatless throughout the funeral. He contracted pneumonia and died six weeks after the man who had been his worst enemy but became his best friend.

George Wythe Randolph was a Virginia statesman, his name a reminder of the American Revolution, of founding patriots, and of the Declaration of Independence. He was born on March 10, 1818, at Thomas Jefferson's justly famous mountaintop home in Charlottesville; Monticello. He was the youngest of the eleven children born to Jefferson's daughter, Martha, and her husband, Virginia Governor Thomas Mann Randolph. Non-Southerners, non-Virginians in particular, may find it difficult to believe, but the Randolph side of his family was even more distinguished than the Jefferson side. Since the mid-seventeenth century, the Randolphs had been among the most prominent of Virginia families, well situated among the First Families of Virginia, the F.F.V. (which has nothing to do with the cookies by those same initials). They had money, property, prestige, and fame. But for researchers they present a problem. In many cases they not only passed on property and wealth to their heirs, they passed on names as well. As one author puts it, "They were so prolific and the names William, Thomas, and Richard were so often repeated that, in order to distinguish between their branches, one referred to the Randolphs of this or that country estate."[2] George Wythe Randolph came from the Tuckahoe branch, the name taken from his paternal great-great-grandfather's estate at Turkey Island.

That same great-great-great-grandfather, William Randolph of Turkey Island, had been a carpenter in England before sailing to Virginia. Once here he became a friend of the governor and amassed a fortune, making his something of an early American rags-to-riches story. William's uncle never wore rags. He was a favorite of England's Charles I, and he was a poet and protégé of Ben Jonson. The "George Wythe" part of our particular Randolph's name came from Thomas Jefferson's Williamsburg law teacher and friend, signer of the Declaration of Independence, George Wythe.

There is a painting by Jane Petticolas Bradick, now held by the Thomas Jefferson Memorial Foundation in Charlottesville; it's believed the painting was done in 1825, but the date is only approximate. It shows a six- or seven-year-old George on the grounds in front of Monticello, his sisters Ellen (Virginia Jefferson Randolph) and Septimia (Cornelia Jefferson Randolph) watching as young George rolls a metal hoop along, prodding it with a stick. He wears a beaver hat; the girls are arm in arm, wearing frills, and Septimia is carrying a folded parasol. The watercolor was done approximately one year before Jefferson died. The children were unaware of the financial troubles the family was in. George's father brooded so much over his debts and those of his son's father-in-law (we're back to Tom Jefferson now), that he apparently sank into a deep depression, became a recluse, and died in 1828, only two years after Jefferson. By 1830 Monticello had been sold to pay off Jefferson's debts.

George Wythe Randolph and his mother, Jefferson's daughter, went to visit George's elder sister and her husband, Ellen and Joseph Collidge, Jr., in Boston. George stayed, and, for the next four or five years, he studied at Cambridge, Massachusetts, giving his Virginia education something of a Northern twist. Encouraged by his sister's family, when he was just one month beyond his thirteenth birthday, George Wythe Randolph was appointed to the U.S. Naval Academy at Annapolis. He served as a midshipman for six years, much of the time in the navy yard at Portsmouth, Virginia, which got him back down South, to his home state.

In 1837, at the age of nineteen, he took a two-year leave from the navy and moved in with his older brother, Dr. Benjamin Franklin Randolph. He later resigned from the navy and, encouraged by his brother, enrolled in the University of Virginia (conveniently founded by his grandfather, Thomas Jefferson), and took up law.

We have, then, a young man with an excellent if by now financially poor heritage, one who had studied at both Annapolis and the University of Virginia, served aboard the famed USS *Constitution*—"Old Ironsides," and even sailed around the world—a young man with a law degree and a small legal practice at 38 Main Street in Richmond, and one who had organized and led an armed group in battle.

We say "a small legal practice," but among his clients were

Thomas C. Epps (a relative by marriage), George T. Patton (an ancestor of that other George Patton of World War II fame), James M. Taylor (a relative of Zachary Taylor, James Madison, Jeff Davis, and even Robert E. Lee), and Mann Valentine (the "Mann" indicates ties to George's father, Thomas Mann Randolph). The Valentines were among the richest families in Richmond, one of whom would later sculpt the recumbent statue above Robert E. Lee's crypt in Lexington and whose home is now a museum in Richmond. In short, anybody who was anybody went to George Wythe Randolph for legal advice.

There was even talk among his family that George Wythe Randolph someday would take up residence in the White House. What more could a poor but well connected Southern boy want?

In the 1860s, the answer apparently was to lead his state out of the union his family had helped found, had helped establish, and had helped rise to prominence. After South Carolina seceded, after the country that wasn't yet a country captured Fort Sumter, George Wythe Randolph was elected a member of the Virginia Secession Convention. As such, he was sent on a peace mission to confer with President Abraham Lincoln, but it did no good. In the spring of 1861, George Wythe Randolph warned: "We are in the beginning of the greatest war that has ever been waged on this continent." He was right; the years of the Civil War were among the most important ever, not only for this but for any other nation as well.

In 1862 he succeeded Judah Benjamin as Confederate Secretary of War. Questions arose about Randolph's differences with Jefferson Davis over an order allowing Gen. Theophilus Holmes to cross the Mississippi River to aid in the defense of Vicksburg, and he resigned a few months later. Randolph returned to a field command.

He contracted tuberculosis, resigned from the Rebel army, and took his family to France to recover. It didn't work, and he returned to Virginia after the war. In the spring of 1867, Randolph died and was buried near Jefferson in the family plot. The plot still belongs to the family today; among the latest to be buried there, a Jefferson descendant who passed away in 1992.

Not all Civil War participants were this closely connected or got around so much, not even those from the South. George Wythe

Randolph may not be so much an example of the way the Confederacy and particularly Virginia was run, but rather an example of what was wrong. Among its leaders there was a lot of crossbreeding; everybody was related to, indebted to, or married to everybody else. The South was an example of one large extended family using its poorer cousins and field hands to fight a war those cousins and field hands may not have cared about.

The subject of the brotherhood of war continues to be of interest. Long after the war was over, there was a move to return to the South Confederate flags captured during the conflict. Some have been sent back, but there are many states who even now refuse, preferring to retain the spoils of war.

John Howard Jewett, years after the actual contest, if not the controversy, was over, wrote a poem—"Those Rebel Flags":

> Shall we send back the Johnnies their bunting,
>   In token from Blue to the Gray,
> That "Brothers-in-blood" and "Good Hunting"
>   Shall be our new watchword to-day?
> In olden times knights held it knightly
>   To return to brave foemen the sword;
> Will the Stars and Stripes gleam less brightly
>   If the old Rebel flags are restored?
>
> Call it sentiment, call it misguided
>   To fight to the death for "a rag";
> Yet, trailed in the dust, derided,
>   The true soldier still loves his flag!
> Does love die, and must honor perish
>   When colors and causes are lost?
> Lives the Soldier who ceases to cherish
>   The blood-stains and valor they cost?

And Jewett ends:

> Yes, send back the Johnnies their bunting,
>   With greetings from Blue to the Gray;

We are "Brothers-in-blood," and "Good Hunting"
Is America's watchword to-day.

Not all brothers split, one to either side. Often they stayed together. By the time the war was over, five pairs of brothers had received the Union's new Congressional Medal of Honor.

Two brothers from Charlotte fought with the 13th North Carolina—Jack and Jasper Walker. They were together at Gettysburg, where Jasper was wounded on July 1. His leg was amputated and he was sent to a Northern prison.

Meanwhile, his older brother Jack was shot as the South retreated. Jack's leg was also amputated, and he too was sent to a Yankee prison.

They were a familiar pair after the war, the two brothers stumping around town together. On the day Jasper was to be married, he fell and broke his wooden leg. Not to be done in by the accident, he borrowed Jack's artificial leg. It fit, and the wedding went on as planned.

Later, the two brothers often told the story: Jasper was the only man who got married while standing on somebody else's leg.

CHAPTER TWELVE

Clothes Make the Man:
Especially If He's a Soldier

Most of the boys had never worn drawers and some did not know what they were for and some of the old soldiers who are here told them that they were for an extra uniform to be worn on parade and they half believed it.
— Pvt. Theodore Frelinghuysen Upson
100th Indiana

Even today we hear about the *War Between the Blue and the Gray;* several books and a television miniseries used the term. For the most part, the Federal army did stick to the color blue (although there were various shades of blue), but the Confederacy had a hard enough time clothing its men, much less worrying about the color.

Confederates called Union troops "bluebellies," because of the uniforms the Federals generally wore. Union troops sometimes called the Rebels "graybacks," even though the Confederates frequently wore uniforms of other colors—butternut brown, or just about anything they could get ahold of, including blue uniforms taken from dead Yankees.

Things were so bad on the Rebel side, with men wearing bits of this and bits of that, the troops talked not of uniforms but of wearing "multiforms." At Shiloh, members of the 2nd Texas were issued new uniforms made of undyed white wool. They asked, "Do the generals expect us to be killed and want us to wear our burial shrouds?"

Nothing, it seems, was uniform about Civil War uniforms.

The South selected "cadet gray" as its official uniform color, but just because the government said "cadet gray" should be the color certainly didn't mean that's the way it was. Since each regiment frequently seemed to be fighting its own war, why should they all stick to the same color? Especially in the beginning.

At the First Battle of Manassas, one Union artillery unit saw what it thought was a band of friendly Federals heading its way to help out. Wrong. It was a band of decidedly unfriendly Rebels wearing blue uniforms. By the time the Union troops discovered the mistake, they'd been overrun by the blue-clad Confederates.

On the other hand, there was the Battle of Wilson's Creek in Missouri. The Union's 1st Iowa wore gray uniforms, and the Confederacy's 3rd Louisiana wore blue. For the first year or so of the war, you could take your pick of nearly any regiment on either side, and you might find several different units, each wearing different-colored uniforms. Many units, especially Rebel ones, banded together so quickly they fought in civilian clothing.

Troops from out West often wore buckskin. And then there were the Zouaves, both North and South, patterned after French-African troops: red turbans with white bands intertwined with orange tinsel, waist-length blue jackets with gold trim, and loose red trousers. Certainly not the "secret service."

The 79th New York Highlanders was made up of Scottish-Americans, and in the beginning of the war they went to battle wearing kilts. It's unknown what they wore under their kilts. In August of 1861, the army told them they couldn't wear their kilts, so the 79th mutinied. They ended their mutiny when the army aimed an artillery battery at them.

The saying in the modern army is that uniforms come in two sizes, too large and too small. Apparently it was the same in the Civil War. Once issued their usually ill-fitting outfits, the men spent the next several days trading for something that fit better. Often as not, they failed. When you witness a Civil War reenactment these days, or see a nicely produced Civil War film, all of the soldiers wear well-made, well-fitting, usually clean uniforms. The folks whose lives today's reenactors are reliving wouldn't even recognize themselves. The real Billy Yank and Johnny Reb were given pants that were too long or too short, coats with sleeves either hanging beneath the soldier's hands or looking like shortsleeve shirts. "We had quite a time with our uniforms," one Northern recruit remembered. "If they fit, all right; if not, we had to trade around till we could get a fit." He was lucky; he was of average size, and that made it more likely he could find something close to a reasonable fit. "Some of the very tall or short men," he wrote, "were not so fortunate." One of those less fortunate, a man shorter than average, said he "could never find in the quartermaster's department a blouse or a pair of trousers small enough, nor an overcoat cast on my lines." He had to cut off the bottoms of his trousers and roll up his coatsleeves and shirtsleeves.

In March of 1862, young Nelson Stauffer was a volunteer in the 63rd Illinois. He wrote in his diary about being issued a uniform he estimated to be at least twelve sizes too long and nine sizes too big around. Stauffer put on his new uniform in order to cut it down to the right size, but about all he managed to do was to set his comrades to laughing: "I say, soldier, come outen them pants. You don't fool me. I know you're there, for I can see your ears a-worken."

Especially in the beginning of the war, not only was there nothing uniform about uniforms, they were poorly made from shoddy material. Unscrupulous contractors took advantage of the sudden need for government clothing. Shoes made of imitation leather fell apart in the first rainstorm. Shoes always were a problem, and not just those imitation leather ones. Even the leather shoes wore out quickly. It can be argued that the Battles of Antietam and Gettysburg were caused by the South's shoe shortage. Robert E. Lee aimed at Antietam in one year and in another turned his army toward Gettysburg looking for shoes for his almost barefoot army. It's estimated that one third of the Army of Northern Virginia was close to barefoot, their shoes worn so thin.

In the early days of the war there was no such thing as a left or right shoe. Generally, they were just shoes. Everybody, soldiers or civilians, bought or made just plain *shoes*. Sometimes you might switch left and right shoe in order to even out the wear, rather like rotating your car's tires every five thousand miles or so, but for the most part the troops never got around to rotating their shoes. It was through wear and tear that they became left and right. During the war, Northern factories began turning out, not only left and right shoes but offered footwear in a greater variety of sizes.

Southern belles tried their darndest to sew uniforms for their brave boys, but trying doesn't always succeed. Many times the product these young ladies turned out was less than satisfactory.

The Union army also decreed its soldiers should, for some unknown reason, wear leather neckties, cravats the troops called "dog collars" and that they found so uncomfortable they very seldom wore them.

Union Gen. Philip Kearny was a millionaire and had twenty custom-tailored uniforms prepared for him prior to riding into battle. As stated earlier, Stonewall Jackson was one of the worst dressed Confederate officers. Union General Grant was another candidate for the Worst-Dressed Officer award. On any given day he *might* just *might* wear some part of a uniform. Even when Lee surrendered to Grant at Appomattox, Grant was dressed more like some lowly private who'd just slogged his way through the nearest muddy field. General Lee, on the other hand, somehow managed to look fresh. He even had a brand-new uniform he'd carried with him through the war, almost as if he were saving it for some special occasion. The occasion came, and he wore it to a meeting with Grant in Wilmer McLean's parlor at Appomattox.

Hats. Confederate troops wore almost anything they wanted to or found. Union soldiers were issued black felt hats to be worn on dress occasions. One Federal soldier wrote home, "My new hat looks as near like the pictures that you see of the pilgrim fathers landing on Plymouth, tall, stiff, and turned up on one side with a feather on it." He did not, he added, wear it "any more than I am obliged to." Grant usually wore the regulation army "slouch" hat. On the other side of the coin was General Kearny, whose favorite was a gold-braided, French-style kepi. Both Jeb Stuart and George Armstrong Custer wore plumed hats. After Stuart was killed at the Battle of Yellow Tavern, his hat was laid atop his casket as it was carried to Richmond's Hollywood Cemetery; today, it's in the Museum of the Confederacy in Richmond. Stuart was still dressed in his U.S. Army uniform when he took up his Confederate commission, and he even wore it during his first battle as a Rebel, at Falling Waters, Virginia, in July 1861.

Charlie Jennison, head of the Kansas Jayhawkers, was—to be politically correct—height disadvantaged. To make up for his lack of size, he usually wore an enormous fur cap that made him look taller.

As often as possible, when things were quiet, and the two sides were near a river, the rank and file troops called an informal truce, jumped in a nearby river, and washed and cavorted. Major General

Winfield Scott Hancock apparently would have understood that, believing cleanliness was akin to godliness. He always insisted on wearing a clean shirt going into battle. If his shirt became soiled by gunpowder or, Heaven forbid, blood, back he'd go to his tent to change into a fresh one, while the battle raged on around him.

On the subject of cleanliness, troops on both sides were often noted as wearing what appeared to be a strange flowerlike contrivance in their jacket buttonholes. They weren't flowers; they were toothbrushes, and buttonholes just seemed an easy place to carry them.

Fashion, however, can get the best of you. One day down at Roanoke Island, North Carolina, Confederate Capt. Jennings Wise stood wearing a red satin-lined cape. A Yankee marksman saw Wise, saw the cape, and shot and killed the captain.

In the twentieth century, there's a sometimes spirited discussion over whether a man's underwear should be of the boxer or brief variety. Many troops in the nineteenth century would have had no idea what was going on. Or under. They had never worn underwear—or drawers, as they were then called—and when they were issued such items they didn't know what to do with them.

Eventually, they all got used to strange items and strange sizes. A Rhode Island volunteer who stood only four feet eleven inches tall was issued a pair of army drawers that were so long they reached his chin. But things have a way of working out, and he found he didn't have to wear a shirt. He'd have felt right at home with little Charlie Jennison and his big fur cap.

For some Southern troops, having anything at all to wear was the best they could hope for. There's a story that when Robert E. Lee's troops were crossing the Potomac River, headed along the way that eventually took them to Antietam, they took off their uniforms and held them over their heads to keep them from getting wet. They waded across the river wearing only bits and pieces of their worn and dirty underwear.

At the same time, a group of young Maryland ladies were picnicking along the riverbank. They turned their heads in order not to see the shameful condition of the Rebels in their torn and tattered drawers.

Today's modern soldier has winter uniforms, summer uniforms, dress and undress uniforms; uniforms to be worn in the jungle; uniforms to be worn in the desert; even uniforms to be worn in the snow. In the Civil War, Union troops had one kind: hot and woolen. Confederate troops had their own variety: full of holes or nonexistent; cold weather or hot, they wore the same, hoping for a blanket when the weather was wet and snowy.

The Rebels, at least, didn't have one worry their Federal opponents did. They didn't have to worry about whether to wash their new woolen trousers and jackets. This was one time when being issued a too large uniform might work to their advantage. That height-deprived trooper who had to cut down his too large uniform should have waited until after the first rainstorm. Everything shrank.

Since troops both North and South were originally militia units, nearly everything about them varied—their horses' saddles and bridles, their weapons (some carried double-barreled shotguns, some had nothing more than spears), and their backpacks. Troops from Rhode Island carried so much they were known as "pack mules." Underwear, socks, blankets (including one of rubber in case of rain), dress coats, paper and ink, a Bible, pins, needles, threads, tobacco, meat, bread, cheese—you name it. A metal plate, knife, fork, spoon, and cup; a skillet hanging from a hook attached to his belt; and an overcoat tied on top of his knapsack.

At a time when the average soldier was only five feet eight and a half inches and weighed only 143 pounds, the packs Northern soldiers carried often weighed forty to fifty pounds. One Union trooper wrote home, telling his family just what he was forced to carry: "40 rounds ammunition, belt & c . . . 4 lbs; canteen of water, 4 lbs; Haversack of rations, 6 lbs; Musket, 14 lbs; Knapsack at least 20 lbs, besides the clothes we have on our backs." Pack mules, indeed.

One rather wealthy unit from New York City marched off to war carrying haversacks filled with meals cooked by that famous restaurant Delmonico's. Another New York unit, the 10th New York, wasn't quite so lucky. They had so little in the way of uniforms that they formed ranks wearing white shirts and drawers. Except for the first sergeant, of course; he also wore a red sash. Apparently, the

10th's commanding officer didn't like the way his men were dressed and refused to let them march in review. He arrested them and sent them back to camp.

Uniforms didn't fit and they quickly wore out. Frequently there were no replacements. About all the troops on both sides, but especially the South, could do was to take from the dead what clothing their fallen comrades—or enemies—had left behind.

"Submarine Torpedo Boat *H. L. Hunley,* December 6, 1863." In 1995, the *Hunley* was discovered at the bottom of Charleston harbor. It was built for privateering and was not officially part of the Confederate navy. *(Oil on board by Conrad Wise Chapman. Katherine Wetzel photograph, the Museum of the Confederacy, Richmond, Virginia.)*

"Torpedo Boat *David* at Charleston dock, October 5, 1863." This was the first of several "Davids" built by the Confederacy. Inventor Lieutenant William T. Glassells gave them the name David because he hoped to use its slingshot-torpedo to sink Union navy's Goliath, the *New Ironsides. (Oil on board by Conrad Wise Chapman. The Museum of the Confederacy, Richmond, Virginia.)*

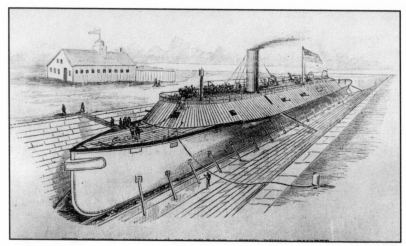

"CSS *Virginia*, ex-USS *Merrimack*." Early 1862, in drydock at the Gosport Navy Yard, now the Norfolk Naval Shipyard at Portsmouth, Virginia. There is no known photograph of the Virginia. *(Artist's sketch. Courtesy of Mrs. A. W. Hasker, Richmond, Virginia. U.S. Naval Historical Center Photograph.)*

Company of 170th New York Volunteers. Card playing was a frequent way of passing time between marching and fighting. Many soldiers considered card playing a sin, and prior to battle they would throw away their cards. If they survived the fight, returning soldiers often picked up their cards and resumed play. *(Mathew Brady photograph. Library of Congress.)*

"Group portrait of Confederate prisoners at Camp Douglas, Chicago."
Camp Douglas was among the largest and worst of the Union prison camps,
housing more that 30,000 Rebels. More than 6,000—20 percent—died of disease, starvation, and exposure to the cold. *(Chicago Historical Society Chicago,
Illinois.)*

Elmira, New York prison. Built along the Chemung River in May 1864 after Gen.
U.S. Grant ordered a halt to an exchange of prisoners with the Confederacy.
More than one-third of the 10,000 Confederate enlisted prisoners held at
Elmira died while in captivity. *(Eleanor S. Brockenbrough Library, The Museum of
the Confederacy, Richmond, Virginia.)*

The Old Capitol Prison, Washington, D.C., was built in 1815 to house Congress after the British burned the original capitol during the War in 1812. In 1861, the Union army turned it into a prison to house such well known prisoners as "Rebel Rose" O'Neal Greenhow and Belle Boyd. *(Library of Congress.)*

Baseball game between teams of Union prisoners at Salisbury, North Carolina, 1863. By the mid-1800s, baseball was well on its way to being an American pastime. In November 1861, an abandoned cotton factory was turned into a Confederate prison at Salisbury. By late 1864 it was overcrowded with 10,000 Federal inmates. Nearly 3,500 died. *(Lithograph of a drawing by Maj. Otto Boetticher who was held at Libby Prison in Richmond. Library of Congress.)*

Confederate torpedoes, shot, and shells in front of the Charleston arsenal, 1865. Civil War "torpedoes" were not self-propelled; marine mines floated on or just beneath the water's surface. Some were set off on contact with a ship, while others were denoted by an electric current from the shore. *(Selmar Rush Seibert photograph, National Archives.)*

"Quaker guns." Rebel troops sometimes mounted logs like cannon to deceive Union forces. Used by the Confederacy at the Battle of Yorktown and here, at Centreville, Virginia, March 1862, near Manassas. *(Photographed by two of Mathew Brady's operators, George N. Bernard and James F. Gibson. National Archives.)*

Entrance to Mahone Mine, Petersburg, Virginia. Union and Confederate troops dug nearly side-by-side tunnels at Petersburg, hoping to break through the other's lines. On July 30, 1864, the Union exploded four tons of black powder in its 511 foot tunnel. The resulting Battle of the Crater saw 3,798 Federal troops killed or wounded and another 1,500 taken prisoner. *(Library Of Congress.)*

State dining room, the White House of the Confederacy, in Richmond, Virginia. The Confederate government leased the home in 1861 for the use of president and Mrs. Jefferson Davis. Davis usually worked at home, preferring to sit on the couch to the right while greeting visitors and discussing battle plans. *(Katherine Wetzel photograph. The Museum of the Confederacy, Richmond, Virginia.)*

"President Lincoln riding through the streets of Richmond, Virginia, April 4, 1865." Lincoln toured Richmond after the city fell, accompanied by only a small armed force. He visited the Confederate White House, sitting in the chair formerly occupied by Jefferson Davis. *(From an original woodcut. Eleanor S. Brockenbrough Library, the Museum of the Confederacy, Richmond, Virginia.)*

President Lincoln and his field commanders at Sharpsburg, Maryland, after the Battle of Antietam. Rarely published print from a broken negative made by Mathew Brady on October 4, 1862. *(Library of Congress.)*

Elizabeth Van Lew. "Miss Lizzie" or "Crazy Bet," as she was sometimes known, was credited with being the Union's most important spy in wartime Richmond. She carried food and messages to Libby Prison inmates and passed on information she smuggled out. *(Cook collection, Valentine Museum Richmond, Virginia.)*

Libby Prison. Shown from the rear, looking over the City Canal in Richmond. Originally built as a warehouse, the Confederacy quickly converted it into a prison after the Seven Days' Battles in June 1862. Libby Prison housed upwards of 50,000 Union soldiers. *(Cook collection, Valentine Museum Richmond, Virginia.)*

Libby Prison, museum. In 1888, a Chicago syndicate purchased the former prison, dismantled it, and shipped the numbered pieces to Chicago where it was rebuilt "brick after brick, just as it stood during the War of the Rebellion." With the reconstructed prison nestled inside a middle ages-style stone building, the museum was located on Wabash Avenue, between 14th and 16th Streets. *(Kaufmann and Fabry photograph, 1892. Chicago Historical Society, Chicago, Illinois.)*

"Libby Prison wood rotting in Indiana." After being used as a museum in Chicago for more than a decade, Libby Prison was dismantled again in 1899. Much of the prison's original timbers were loaded onto railroad cars and sent east to be rebuilt once more as a museum. Fifty-three miles into Indiana the train derailed, and local residents either bought or stole the wood—building this now destroyed Barn. *(Valentine Museum, Richmond, Virginia.)*

Edmund Ruffin was age 67 and a member of South Carolina's Palmetto Guard at Charleston on the morning of April 12, 1861. A fellow Virginian, Congressman Roger Pryor, declined to fire the first shot on Fort Sumter. Ruffin, an ardent secessionist, volunteered; "I was highly gratified by the compliment," he said, "and delighted to perform the service." Gen. Abner Doubleday, who later became associated with baseball, fired the first Union shot. On June 15, 1865, Edmund Ruffin committed suicide. Rather than live again under the United States, the man who fired the first shot at Fort Sumter shot himself in the head. *(Library of Congress.)*

CHAPTER THIRTEEN

Diary of a War Clerk:
John B. Jones

At night. We have a gay illumination. This. . . . is wrong. We had better save the candles.

—John Beauchamp Jones
April 20, 1861[1]

John Beauchamp Jones was born in Baltimore on March 6, 1810, but spent many of his younger years in Kentucky and Missouri, the border country.

Through his marriage to Frances T. Custis, he had Southern "connections," he was related to Robert E. Lee's wife's family. Even George Washington was, as Virginians like to put it, among "John Jones's people." It's doubtful, however, the relationship did John any good, but it certainly did him no harm.

He once served as U.S. Consul in Naples, Italy, but mainly John was a journalist and pulp fiction writer. Before the war he wrote several western novels, including *Wild Western Scenes* and *Freaks of Fortune, or The History of Ned Lorn*. He may be thought of as the Zane Grey or Louis L'Amour of his day. He'd been the editor of the official Whig party newspaper, *The Madisonian,* and editor of the pro-slavery newspaper *The Southern Monitor.* In the spring of 1861, an antislavery mob stormed *The Southern Monitor*'s office, threatening to hang editor Jones.

When America's Civil War broke out, Jones and his family were living in Burlington, New Jersey, across the river from Philadelphia. He believed the North would try to resupply Major Anderson and decided to move South. "I well know," he wrote, "that the first gun fired at Fort Sumter will be our signal for an outbreak of ungovernable fury. . . ." Thinking he'd wind up in a Northern jail, he moved his family south. It was April 8, 1861.

When the South opened fire on Fort Sumter, the Philadelphia *Inquirer* had the following headline: THE BALL HAS BEEN OPENED AT LAST AND THE WAR IS INAUGURATED. John tried to join the dance. Down South, he volunteered for duty with the Confederacy, but he had no military experience and was judged too old for active service. He wrote that "at fifty-one I can hardly follow the pursuit of arms; but I will write and preserve a diary of the revolution." In 1862, at age fifty-two, he volunteered for service in a local artillery battery, where he served for about a month around Richmond.

Jones spent the war as a clerk in the Confederate War Department, first in Montgomery, Alabama, then in Richmond. He was, we might say, an "inside man," working within the Confederate government and as such had knowledge of much that was going on in Richmond and the Confederacy in general.

As we look at such matters 130 years later, he was both a racist and an anti-Semite, a bigot who became a self-imposed refugee. He was also an astute observer.

He began his diary on the day Fort Sumter was fired on, and he continued it throughout the war. Paper of any variety often was difficult to obtain as the war continued, and, while he doesn't specifically mention the problem, it's reasonable to believe Jones, along with printers, newspapers, and other diarists, probably had difficulties finding enough paper. One of Jones's earlier books, *Wild Western Scenes,* was first published in Philadelphia in 1860, and three years later a Georgia publisher wanted to reprint it. He found only enough paper for the first half of the book, and even then the cost was excessive.

He wrote his diary, *A Rebel War Clerk's Diary at the Confederate States' Capital,* with the consent, he said, of President Jefferson Davis. It is both full in its scope and, at the same time, sparse in its language. The first entry into his Diary is dated April 12, 1861.

> *To-day I beheld the first secession flag that has met my vision. It was at Polecat Station, Caroline County, and it was greeted with enthusiasm by all but the two or three Yankees in the train.*

He was moving from Montgomery to Richmond.

Arrived at the Exchange Hotel, Richmond. The news-boys are rushing in all directions with extras announcing the bombardment of Fort Sumter! This is the irrevocable blow! Every reflecting mind here should know that the only alternatives now are successful revolution or abject subjugation. But they do not lack for the want of information of the state of public sentiment in the North.

His final diary entry is dated April 19, 1865, and told of Lincoln's assassination.

In between those two entries are weather reports, crop reports, economic reports, and reports on how the war was faring. In detailed language he told how prices rose and rose again. He rejoiced with the rest of the South at news of that battle fought over the stream called Bull Run. He praised Robert E. Lee and criticized Jefferson Davis. He saw a fervor take over the people of the South. "Never," he wrote, "was there such a patriotic *people* as ours." He told of the arrest of Northern spies and attempts to gun down Confederate deserters.

After the First Battle of Manassas, Jones and the South learned that even a major victory carries a lesson. War means death and injuries. On July 2, wounded began arriving in Richmond from Manassas. Jones noted their coming, saying, "To-day quite a number of our wounded men on crutches, and with arms in splints, made their appearance in the streets, and created a sensation." Cynically and prophetically, he ended that day's entry by adding, "A year hence, and we shall be accustomed to such spectacles."

It *was* less than a year later when Union General McClellan made his "On to Richmond!" move. Confederate troops dug in around the capital city and called Robert E. Lee the "King of Spades."

"We are now so strong," Jones wrote in his diary, "that no one fears the result when the great battle takes place." That "great battle" wasn't a single event, it was a whole week's worth, the Seven Days' Battles. The Union was pushed back, Richmond was put under siege, and Robert E. Lee was in full command of Confederate troops in Virginia.

What genius! what audacity in Lee! He has absolutely taken the greater portion of his army to the north side of the Chickahominy, leaving McClellan's center and left wing on the south side, with apparently easy access to the city. This is (to the invaders) impenetra-

ble strategy. The enemy believes Lee's main forces are here, and will never think of advancing. We have so completely closed the avenues of intelligence that the enemy has not been able to get the slightest intimation of our strength of the dispositions of our forces.[2]

Jones was even more ecstatic over the new Confederate commander in a later diary entry.

The President publishes a dispatch from Lee, announcing a victory! The enemy has been driven from all his entrenchments, losing many batteries.

Yesterday the President's life was saved by Lee. Every day he rides out near the battle-field, in citizen's dress, marking the fluctuations of the conflict, but assuming no direction of affairs in the field. . . . [O]nce, when the enemy were about to point one of their favorite batteries in the direction of a certain farm-house occupied by the President, Lee sent a courier in haste to inform him of it. No sooner had the President escaped than a storm of shot and hail riddled the house.

The Confederate secretary of war had nothing to do with the Rebel victories, Jones believed: "He is, truly, but a mere clerk." Jones thought it was all due to Lee. That same day Jones saw "thousands of bluejackets—Yankee prisoners" paraded through Richmond.

General Reynolds, who surrendered with his brigade, was thus accosted by one of our functionaries, who knew him before the war began:

"General, this is in accordance with McClellan's prediction: you are in Richmond."

"Yes, sir," responded the general, in bitterness; "and d—n me, it is not precisely in the manner I anticipated."

Four or five thousand prisoners have arrived.[3]

As a diarist, Jones recorded the good and the bad of life in Richmond under siege. He wrote of the war news as reported by the Richmond newspapers; and he told how those same newspapers often carried no news of the fighting, perhaps because they didn't want to frighten the already horrified Richmond citizens, perhaps to keep the North from learning more about what was happening.

Reading Jones's diary you learn just how bad, certainly how expensive, life in Civil War Richmond was. On May 23, 1862, he wrote:

Oh, the extortioners! Meats of all kinds are selling at 50 cts. per *pound; butter, 75 cts.; coffee, $1.50; tea, $10; boots, $30 per pair; shoes, $18; ladies' shoes, $15; shirts, $6 each. Houses that rented for $500 last year, are $1000 now. Boarding, from $30 to $40 per month.*

At the same time, Jones's salary was twelve hundred per year. Everybody was hurting. On New Year's Day 1861, the Richmond *Daily Dispatch* sold for one cent per copy and lump coal went for six dollars per load. By November of 1864, newspapers sold for twenty cents and coal was ninety dollars per ton. Flour, when it could be had, went for upward of eight hundred dollars per barrel.

When there was no flour, the women of Richmond rioted—the "Bread Riot" of April 2, 1863—and Jones told about the affair. "A few hundred women and boys," Jones wrote, "met as by concert" and demanded food. He told of meeting "a young woman, seemingly emaciated, but yet with a smile" who said the crowd was "going to find something to eat." John Jones personally opposed the riot and later testified in court against some of its participants. Yet in telling about the day's events, "I could not for the life of me refrain from expressing the hope that they might be successful." He even pointed the rioters in the "right direction to find plenty in the hands of the extortioners."

Life was tough for Jones's family as well. Once he wrote of how one of his daughters gave up her own small ration of meat to feed her cat. The cat died anyway.

Clerk Jones became farmer Jones, planting vegetables in his backyard. Despite his garden, John lost twenty pounds during the first two years of the war, adding in his diary, "The shadow of the gaunt form of famine is upon us, and my wife and children are emaciated."

A city long noted for its hospitality, Richmond under siege discovered a new way to entertain: starvation parties. Society "would assemble at a fashionable residence that before the war had been the abode of wealth," wrote another diarist, Edward Alfriend. There would be music and dancing, "but not a morsel of food or a drop of drink was seen."

They also devised "banting," a system not unlike potluck suppers of another day. Richmond society continued to dine in some semblance of style, only each guest provided a dish or a drink. "I'll give you a nice coffee," another diarist wrote, asking, "Will you give me something sweet?"

With clothing in short supply, Jones bought two undershirts from a Rebel soldier marching through Richmond. They had bloody bullet holes in them, and John's wife Frances had a hard time getting the stain out. Still, John Jones was happy to get them.

As the war wore on, as prices rose higher, Jones began selling off his possessions in order to survive. He once commented, "We have hardly enough money to live until the next pay-day."

He and his family watched as the dead and wounded were brought to Richmond. He counted Union soldiers as they were marched to confinement at the dozen or so prisons in the Confederate capital city. He saw, and didn't like, black troops recruited in March of 1865. And in April of that year, Jones looked on as the Confederate army set fire to warehouses and almost destroyed the city in doing so.

The night of April 2, he wrote: "All is yet quiet. No explosion, no conflagration, no riots, etc. How long will this continue? When will the enemy come?"

He stood watching as thousands took everything they could and fled the city. He and his family didn't evacuate Richmond. "I remain here," he wrote, "broken in health and bankrupt in fortune, awaiting my fate, whatever it may be. I can do no more. If I could, I would."

The next day, he saw Federal soldiers posted at the Capital Square, posing for pictures in front of the Confederate capitol building. Robert E. Lee's arthritic wife, Mary, had refused to leave the abandoned city. "I saw a Federal guard promenading in front of [Mrs. Lee's] door," Jones wrote on April 4, "his breakfast being sent to him from within."

Jones doesn't mention attending the event, but the day after Abraham Lincoln walked through the defeated city his diary contains two short paragraphs.

> *The cheers that greeted President Lincoln were mostly from the negroes and Federals comprising the great mass of humanity. The white citizens felt annoyed that the city should be held mostly by negro troops. If this measure were not unavoidable, it was impolitic if conciliation be the purpose.*

Mr. Lincoln, after driving to the mansion lately occupied by Mr. Davis, Confederate States President, where he rested, returned, I believe to the fleet at Rocketts (Landing).[4]

It was just twelve hours after Jefferson Davis and the Confederate government abandoned Richmond. Lincoln and his son Tad came ashore at Rocketts landing and, accompanied by only a small armed guard, walked most of the way to the Rebel White House. He was cheered by hundreds of newly free blacks. Former slaves surrounded the small party and knelt before Lincoln, calling him "Messiah." It embarrassed the president and he told them to stand. "You must kneel to God only," he said.

"Thank God I have lived to see this," Lincoln said. "It seems to me," he added, "that I have been dreaming a horrid dream for four years, and now the nightmare is gone." He walked toward the Confederate White House, only recently abandoned by Jefferson and Varina Davis. Inside, Lincoln looked around and climbed to Davis's second floor office. He couldn't resist it; the President of the United States sat in the chair formerly occupied by the President of the Confederate States.

Lincoln looked around at the small office, then jumped up and said, "Let's go! Let's look at the house." He and Tad ate lunch and then went sightseeing around the city, riding in an open carriage. They stopped briefly at the former Confederate capitol and at Libby Prison. Everywhere he went blacks cheered Lincoln and whites turned their backs or remained indoors.

The same day President Lincoln walked the streets of Richmond, John B. Jones wrote, "I feel that this diary is near its end." On April 10, 1865, Jones added:

My diary is surely drawing to a close, and I feel as one about to take leave of some old familiar associate. A habit is to be discontinued—and that is no trifling thing to one of my age. But I may find sufficient employment in revising, correcting, etc. what I have written. I never supposed it would end in this way.

Then, the words he did not want to write:

It is true! Yesterday Gen. Lee surrendered the "Army of Northern Virginia." His son, Custis Lee, and other generals, had surrendered a few days previously. . . .

All is lost! No head can be made by any other general or army—
if indeed any other army remains. If Mr. Davis had been present, he
never would have consented to it; and I doubt if he will ever forgive
Gen. Lee.

Jones learned of the assassination of Abraham Lincoln on the six-teenth, first believing "it might be an April hoax." It was not, of course, and on the nineteenth he ended his four-year-long diary: "Yesterday windy, to-day bright and calm." Lincoln had been shot by John Wilkes Booth, "an actor."

"I suppose," Jones recorded, Booth's "purpose is to live in history as the slayer of a tyrant; thinking to make [himself] the leading character in a tragedy, and have his performance acted by others on the stage."

The last words in his diary: "It was a dastardly deed—surely the act of a madman."

CHAPTER FOURTEEN

Sex and the Single Soldier: Married Ones, Too

We have a good spring of water and the health of our Regt. is good except some disease that I feel a delicacy in spelling them out to you as you are a female person but however I reckon you can't blush at little things these times. It is the POCKS and CLAP. The cases of this complaint is numerous, especially among the officers....

—J. M. Jordan, C.S.A.
February 8, 1864, Letter to his wife

America's Civil War came in the middle of the Victorian Age, so the picture we have is of prim and proper soldiers sitting around a campfire between battles, wiping tears from their eyes as they dream of home. Well, they weren't all so prim and proper. The average Civil War soldier was twenty-five years old; many were younger. Still, that's pretty old when you consider the draft age of World War II onward— pretty old when you think how very young the pilots who flew mission after mission over Germany were, the men the British claimed were, "Overpaid, oversexed, and over here." Pretty old when you think about *their* children, who slogged through the mud of Vietnam, and when you consider the number or Asian-American children left behind when the United States pulled its troops out.

Civil War soldiers were old enough to know better, certainly old enough to know about sex and to practice it. In fact, they practiced it so often, you could say they finally got it right, or we wouldn't be here. They practiced it so often it was like voting in Chicago: early and often.

J. Kimball Barnes was a Northern soldier stationed in Beaufort, South Carolina. On Christmas day, 1862, he wrote home to his friend George Starbird, saying his primary objection to the war was that he missed having sex with white women. In his words, there was "nothing but these damn negro wenches" in Beaufort. Plainly and probably honestly, he told his friend, "I can't get it hard to go to them."

Soldiers' letters home frequently were candid about such issues as sex; however, nineteenth-century relatives and modern descendants often censored descriptions of ladies of delight. These letters sometimes have whole sections marked out and deleted. The army obviously didn't censor J. Kimball's letters. It's all right there; his letters preserved in the Schoff Collection in the University of Michigan's Clements Library.

By early March, he'd apparently overcome his objection and indulged, frequently taking his business to black prostitutes. By then there were white hookers around, but J. Kimball and many others often preferred blacks because, as he wrote his friend Starbird, many of the white prostitutes in Beaufort carried venereal diseases.

Troops North and South took full advantage of prostitutes, just as prostitutes took full advantage of the troops. Soldiers called it "going down the line," and the line wound from North to South, Billy Yank to Johnny Reb. Richmond held one of the largest prostitute populations in either North or South. These ladies of the evening (daylight, for that matter) often were known as "Cyprians," and Rebel troops on leave in the Confederate capital spent many an hour with them. One such group of Cyprians operated a house across from the Young Men's Christian Association (YMCA) Hospital. The hospital superintendent complained to authorities that he was having trouble keeping the recuperating soldiers from running, walking, or hobbling across the streets. The sight of young women parading half-dressed in front of open windows often was too much for the troops, no matter how ill or wounded they might be. Patients sneaked out to visit these Cyprians so often, the hospital superintendent seriously worried about their health.

Other Richmond Cyprians operated in boardinghouses or former office buildings; they leaned from windows and stood in doorways, often as not their clothing in partial if not almost total disarray, making provocative gestures. One group of prostitutes openly solicited on the Confederate Capitol grounds.

In Washington, D.C., they were also called "Cyprians"—and "fallen angels," and "daughters of Eve," and "gay young chicks." As time went on, their numbers grew and prospered. By 1862, according to the Washington provost marshal, the city had 450 bawdy houses. Almost daily they poured into the capital. Almost as if they were soldiers themselves. Hundreds of these "gay young chicks" were recruited in Philadelphia, Chicago, St. Louis, and every farm in between. By 1863, the Washington *Star* estimated there were at least seventy-five hundred prostitutes in town, not including the perhaps more refined and certainly better-kept mistresses of more affluent soldiers, politicians, and hangers-on.

Francis B. Wilkie was a war correspondent in town to report on preparations to bring the South to its knees. Meanwhile, Washington was being brought to its knees. Wilkie claimed the Union capital probably "was the most pestiferous hole since the days of Sodom and Gomorrah." "The majority of women on the streets," he added, "were openly disreputable." Wilkie believed that, "every possible form of human vice and crime, dregs of scourings and scum had flowed into the capitol (sic) and made of it a national catch-basin of indescribable foulness."

Eli Veasie was a Union soldier from Massachusetts. On April 20, 1863, he wrote his friend Jeremiah Norris about a recent visit to Washington, saying, "I had a gay old time I tell you. . . . Lager Beer and a horse and Buggy [and] in the evening Horizontal Refreshments or in Plainer words Riding a Dutch gal—had a good time generally I tell you."

In 1941, just as another war was getting under way for the United States, Margaret Leech wrote her Pulitzer Prize-winning history, *Reveille in Washington*. In it, she says, "Entire blocks on the south side of Pennsylvania Avenue were devoted to the business [of pleasure]." There were, she wrote, brothels known as "the Ironclad," "Fort Sumter," and "Madam Russell's Bake Oven." A Mrs. Hay ran "the Haystack," and a Mrs. Wolf operated "the Wolf's Den."

One such house of pleasure was family owned and operated. Figuratively speaking, they did their level best to contribute to the cause. At first the business included father, mother, and three daughters—Kate, Anna, and Matilda. The father *enlisted* in the army, but his daughters *solicited*, keeping up the family's good (or bad) name in the field of pleasure.

All of this was in a small area within sight of the White House, an area sometimes known as "Marble Alley." City officials hoped to sanitize most of the town by winking at bars and bawdy houses in Marble Alley.

Union Gen. Joe Hooker may have contributed his name to the action. Margaret Leech claims another section of town was known as "Hooker's Division." From that, some say, came the name "hooker" for those engaged in the trade. Another version of the name comes from the practice ladies of the evening had of walking up to a soldier and hooking onto his arm.

As for the Light ladies (you remember Kate, Anna, and Matilda?), when the war briefly moved to Gettysburg, Pennsylvania, so did they. While the battle raged on for three days, for three days and nights the girls did what they had been doing back in Washington—until a fight broke out, which turned into a free-for-all, which led to the arrest of Kate, Anna, and Matilda, which led to their being ushered out of town, which led to their return to Washington, which led to their joining forces with an organ grinder and a monkey. The organ grinder cranked out his mechanical music; the monkey took up the collection; Kate, Anna, and Matilda danced. They danced so hard their clothes fell off; happened every time. Police finally arrested them, took them all, including the monkey, before a magistrate. A slap on their girlish wrists, and they (sans simian) were back in business.

The Light ladies weren't the only ones who plied their trade by following the troops. Sisters Mary and Mollie (or Molly) Bell were either patriotic ladies dressed as men and fighting with Jubal Early under the names of "Tom Parker" and "Bob Martin," or they were "common camp followers." They spent two years fighting (or something) in the Shenandoah Valley until a Rebel captain accused the two of "aiding in the demoralizing of General Early's veterans." Mary and Molly were taken to Richmond's Castle Thunder Prison, where they spent the next three weeks. Finally, they were sent back to their home in the southwestern part of the state. Still wearing men's uniforms.

Both the Union's George Custer and the Confederacy's Jeb Stuart were known to frequent prostitutes. Custer had Annie Jones, who followed the Union army into Virginia and followed Custer into his tent. Actually, she followed several other officers as well, but Custer was her favorite. So much so that, if you believe Annie's after-war account of it, Gen. Judson Kilpatrick became jealous. She said Kilpatrick believed Annie spent so much time with Custer, Kilpatrick was left to sweat it out alone. Kilpatrick complained to Gen. George Meade, charging Annie Jones with being a spy for the Confederacy.

An individual identified only as a "Southern Lady" wrote Rebel President Davis about Jeb Stuart.

> *If General Stuart is allowed to remain our commanding general of cavalry we are lost people. I have been eye witness to the maneuvering of General Stuart since he has been in Culpeper (Virginia). . . . Gen. S. loves the admiration of his class of lady friends too much to be a commanding general.*

Stuart's aide, however, came to the boss's defense. Captain William Blackford wrote, "Though he dearly loved to kiss a pretty girl, and the pretty girls loved to kiss him, he was as pure as they . . ." In a presidential memo, Jeff Davis offered a solution: "[C]leanse your attentions to the ladies or make them more general."

Down in Savannah, Georgia, a member of the 1st Michigan Engineers was shocked at the situation in that sleepy Southern town. James Greenalch wrote home to his wife, "I am satisfied from what I have seen that some of the women . . . have been convinced that the Yankees have horns but not horns on the top of the head." Greenalch claimed to have been innocent. "I would expect," he wrote, that "if I had ben (sic) guilty of what I have seen [I would have] some plague or sin come upon me for it."

According to Union artilleryman J. L. Bassett, Baltimore, "is known . . . as a sporting place, and fast women are all the go these days." Bassett spent several days there before continuing on to Washington. As for the embattled nation's capital, it was, he said, "a hard place full of Officers, Soldiers, and fast Women; we went into some hard places, but came out all right."

Prostitution was such a big problem in Nashville, the military brass finally got fed up with these "daughters of Eve." They loaded some of them onto a boat and shipped them north. Not, we might add, to the delight of cities along the way, Louisville and Cincinnati.

Authorities in those cities raised a ruckus and shipped the girls back to Nashville, all at government expense. It amounted to an unpaid vacation for the otherwise hardworking working girls.

Nashville frequently tried to rid itself of prostitutes by shipping them out of town. Apparently they never succeeded. One such attempt is a good example. City fathers sent a couple of girls North and almost as soon as they got there they headed back South. Historian Bell Irvin Wiley says they were "as bold in their sightseeing as they were loose in their morals." Following the Battle of Nashville, the pair hopped into a carriage and rode out to the scene of the fighting, where they fell into the hands of a troop of Rebel cavalrymen. The Confederates thought they were spies, not hookers, and sent them under guard to a hotel in Franklin. When the Union took Franklin, the Federals also took the two young ladies. To quote Wiley again, "Yankee horsemen mounted the whores on a mule and brought them safely back to Nashville."

Finally, Nashville officials gave up trying to ship the prostitutes out. Instead, they tried to control the situation by setting aside a district for their use, even building a hospital where the Cyprians could seek a cure for their various occupational diseases.

If Nashville was bad, Memphis seemed worse. Or better. "Memphis," a local newspaper complained, "is the great rendezvous for prostitutes and 'pimps.'" The city, it said, "can boast of being one of the first places of female prostitution on the continent. Virtue is scarcely known within the limits of the city."

Nashville, Memphis, and Washington, D.C., weren't the only cities that tried setting up legal red-light districts, a term, incidentally, that may have come when railroaders hung their red lanterns outside bawdy houses to let other trainmen know where they were in times of an emergency. New York tried it, with the police department endorsing the idea. They all got the bright idea to round up all the bawdy houses, all the hookers, prostitutes, and ladies of the evening, and they relocated all the lower class taverns to one place. They would, you might say, keep all of the city's bad eggs in one basket.

St. Louis's city fathers favored such a plan, but St. Louis city mothers did not. With the encouragement of local church officials they intervened, and the idea never was put into effect.

Both New Orleans and Norfolk used the plan at one time or other. New Orleans tried it in the nineteenth century, and Norfolk tried it in the twentieth.

New Orleans's red-light district was known as Storyville, named after Alderman Sidney Story. Storyville existed from 1897 to 1917, when it was broken up at the request of the U.S. Navy. Where Storyville once existed, with Basin Street as one boundary, a federal housing program known as the Iberville Project sits now. Storyville was virtually the birthplace of jazz. Most of the large houses of ill repute had pianists to help customers wile away the time waiting for their favorite ladies. Some even had small bands. Several early jazz tunes, even some later rhythm and blues songs, grew out of the prostitutes' use of drugs and their realization that, in many cases, their only escape was death. "The House of the Rising Sun" is just one such song that comes to mind.

Norfolk, Virginia's enclave of sin, wasn't quite so famous, unless you were a sailor or lived nearby. Just before World War II broke out, Norfolk set aside the waterfront area known as East Main Street. For a generation it was notorious for bars, burlesque, and bawdy houses. Now it's banks, baseball, and bankruptcies; home to several financial institutions; a park for the city's minor league baseball team; and the location of many once-famous but now broke retail giants.

J. Kimball Barnes, whom you'll remember from his letters from Beaufort, South Carolina, apparently was correct in his assessment of prostitutes and venereal disease. Beginning in 1870, the Surgeon General's office issued six volumes entitled the *Medical and Surgical History of the War of the Rebellion*. In them, the surgeon general claimed that from May 1, 1861, to June 30, 1866, there were 197,036 cases of venereal disease, resulting in 168 deaths. It was estimated that in the twelve months beginning with the firing on Fort Sumter, one out of every twelve Union soldiers suffered from venereal disease. For the entire run of the war, it was eighty-two cases for every thousand men. And remember, this was just in the Union; there are no such records for Confederate troops, but you can bet your stash of Confederate money, boys, that they were just as sexually active, just as subject to disease as their Northern brothers, and the ladies of Southern evenings were just as agreeable as their Northern counterparts. If there was any difference, it was only that Northern troops were better paid, and so more likely to be able to afford the pleasures of the flesh.

What a later generation would call "protection" were called "French envelopes" by Civil War soldiers—condoms, generally made of lambskin. They were no better than twentieth century lambskin condoms and despite, in some cases, being warranted against leaking, they did. "Before You Sow Your Wild Oats, Learn the Truth About the Crop," one product advised. Not too many "sowers" took the advice.

Ah, yes. Those prudish Victorians of America's Civil War.

CHAPTER FIFTEEN

Liberty Lost:
Prison Camps

My heart aches for the poor wretches, Yankees though they are, and I am afraid God will suffer some terrible retribution to fall upon us for letting such things happen. If the Yankees ever come to southwest Georgia and to Anderson(ville) and see the graves there, God have mercy on the land!

—Eliza Frances Andrews
January 22, 1865, private diary

Their names may be forgotten, but what happened to those held prisoner during America's Civil War must be remembered. On both sides of the war, men and women were locked away in dark prisons or held in outdoor camps under blistering sun and freezing snow. They were fed too little and lived and died under primitive conditions. Their "crimes" were getting caught while fighting for their countries.

Together, the two sides had more than 150 prisoner of war camps. Some originally were old forts, some buildings or warehouses. In some cases, the prisons themselves provided tents; in others, inmates had to make do as best they could. But whatever they were, prisons and prison camps were more lethal than the war itself. More than two and a half times as many troops were imprisoned than had fought at the Battle of Gettysburg. And more than ten times the number died in Civil War prisons than in the fight around that one small Pennsylvania town.

Shortly after General Sherman captured Atlanta, a group of Union soldiers gathered around a campfire, congratulating themselves on taking one of the most sought-after cities in the Confederacy. Out of the night a band of men, no more than skeletons, wandered into the firelight. The Union troops were horrified. Here, covered with sores, barely clothed in rags, here with hip and knee bones visible beneath stretched skin, were men the likes of which had not been seen before in America. Here, standing before them, were survivors of Camp Sumter, the prison known as Andersonville. Here were prisoners whose likes would not be seen again until the Allies threw open the gates to Hitler's death camps after World War II.

Union troops had heard rumors of Andersonville Prison, but those reports only hinted at conditions. After winning the Battle of Chattanooga, some Federal troops wanted to push on and free those held at Andersonville, but the Union command felt Atlanta must first be captured. After Atlanta was taken care of, then the prisoners at Andersonville could be freed. Conditions couldn't really be as bad as they'd been rumored to be, could they?

It's hard to compare rumor with reality, but from February 1864 to April 17, 1865, forty-one thousand Union soldiers shuffled into the stockades of Andersonville. At one point, they died there at the rate of one hundred per day. And for three months, after Andersonville first opened, the prisoners didn't even have tools for burying their dead. All told, more than thirteen thousand Union prisoners died at Andersonville.

It was small, covering just twenty-six acres, and the available water—ironically enough, from a branch of a creek called Sweetwater—wasn't nearly enough for the thousands held in the camp. The prisoners drank from the creek, washed in the creek, and their privies drained into the same creek; it was more sewer than Sweetwater.

Often, the prisoners' only shelter came from tree branches, bits of wood planks, a few tent parts, and whatever shreds of blankets the soldiers had with them when captured. They blistered in the summer and froze in the winter. Food was mainly cornmeal made with the cobs ground up in it. A "deadline" just fifteen feet from the stockade was just what the name implied; anyone crossing that deadline would be shot. Dead.

Inside was a band of between 150 and 500 Union prisoners known as the "Raiders." Sometimes they traded information to the Rebels for food and better treatment. Other times they robbed, beat, killed, and controlled their fellow inmates.

Their chief was William "Willie" Collins, nicknamed "Mosby" after the Rebel horseman. He stood just under six feet tall and was one of the largest of the thugs in camp. He claimed to have been born in England. He enlisted almost as soon as the war began but grew bored sitting around Washington and went AWOL—Absent Without Leave, as we'd say today. He returned to his unit and was injured at the Battle of Second Manassas, in late July 1862. The Confederates captured Willie but paroled him. His military career was replete with tales of going AWOL, of malingering, of running off and avoiding duty. He was wounded a second time, this time in a fight with his own men, after which he surrendered to a nearby Rebel unit. They sent him to Andersonville, and he became the leader of the Raider element.

Finally tired of Willie and the Raiders, Confederate guards and a group of Union prisoners known as "Regulators" fought the Raiders into submission. A court comprised of other prisoners tried and convicted many of the Raiders. They executed six of them, including Willie Collins.[1]

Actually, they had to hang Willie twice. The first time, the rope was so old it broke, and angry Regulators had to do the job again. The second time it worked, with one onlooker calling out, "Dead, dead, dead."

Twenty-six thousand prisoners looked on that day as Willie and the five Raiders spun at the ends of their ropes. One inmate who still had his watch said it took twenty-seven minutes for the last of them to die. Even those who hated the Raiders most would not forget the hangings, and for days several prisoners wrote about the event in diaries they kept.

As in other Civil War prison camps, inmates at Andersonville tried several times to escape. In early 1864, the Confederates discovered a tunnel prisoners had dug. Some inmates believed a fellow prisoner, Thomas Herburt, had informed on them. Herburt was a one-legged Canadian immigrant whose incessant ramblings about the battle earned him the nickname "Chickamauga." They called him "Poll Parrot" for his large nose and "Pretty Polly" because he was anything but handsome.

Frequently, Herburt tried to talk with the Rebel guards. On one day in May his fellow inmates believed he'd talked about their tunnel, so the prisoners went after him, threatening to kill him. Pretty Polly climbed to the top of the prison gate and yelled for camp commandant Capt. Henry Wirz to save him.

Wirz arrived, riding an old white mare and wearing two pistols. One of the pistols had a broken spring and the other was never loaded. Still, Captain Wirz spoke with authority when he aimed a revolver at Herburt, demanding to be told what the prisoner wanted.

The other inmates were out to get him, Herburt claimed. Wirz apparently wasn't impressed and told him to get back behind the deadline or he'd be shot. The commandant turned to a guard, told him to shoot if the inmate refused to leave, then he rode off on his white horse. Thomas "Chickamauga" Herburt may have thought Wirz was bluffing; the guard didn't. Herburt sat down, saying he'd rather be killed outside the deadline by his enemies than inside by his friends.

The guard was a green recruit, but not so green he couldn't miss a sitting target. He shot Herburt in the head. It was the end of the day before the camp surgeon saw the prisoner. By then it was too late, and in the early hours of the next morning Pretty Polly Herbui . died.

Captain Henry Wirz was the commander of the inner stockade at Andersonville, the only Confederate official executed for war crimes by the Federal government after the war. Later he was exonerated, which certainly didn't help him, since it happened posthumously. Wirz was hanged November 10, 1865, in the yard at the Old Capitol Prison in Washington. He was interred in the Washington arsenal yard near the graves of those hanged earlier for the assassination of Abraham Lincoln. Four years later he was reinterred in Mount Olivet Catholic Cemetery in Washington. Wirz had been a lifelong atheist, but just before he was executed, he was attended by a Catholic priest; he affirmed his belief in God.

For years, his tomb was marked simply WIRZ. Later someone, believed to be an anonymous sympathizer from South Carolina, added another stone that reads, CAPTAIN, C.S.A. MARTYR.

By April 6, 1865, only fifteen prisoners were left in Andersonville. The rest had been shipped out, 3,425 going to Albany, Georgia. One trainload of emaciated inmates paused at the Smithfield, Georgia, depot while a group of young girls were having a picnic nearby. Starved as they where, the men still whistled and shouted to the girls. At first the girls turned away, but then they saw the looks in the men's eyes. They saw them, and they gave the men the food they'd prepared for their own lunch—not much, but all they had—sandwiches, fried chicken, and iced tea.

On May 4, the last two prisoners died at Andersonville, and the Confederacy closed the prison gates for good.

Not much is left of Andersonville today, only one brick wall and remnants of railroad tracks that carried prisoners to where many would spend their final days on earth. Stakes mark the location of the stockade and the deadline.

And there are graves at Andersonville, thirteen thousand small white markers. At first, not even the small markers were in place.

Paroled Confederate calvary Col. Joel Griffin was given a job at the cemetery. It was in foul shape. Some graves were so shallow, animals rooted among exposed bodies. Griffin enlisted some local blacks, newly freed slaves, to help clean up the mess. Local whites objected to former slaves being hired.

In July of 1865, nurse Clara Barton went to Andersonville, where she met Griffin. He showed her around the cemetery, a vast area outside the prison stockade, and she was stunned. Rough-cut markers with crude numbers were the only identification. Mass graves had as many as 100 to 150 bodies to a trench. The number of dead staggered Clara Barton.

Former prisoner Dorence Atwater had kept a record of those who died at Andersonville. Atwater, Griffin, and Clara Barton worked to identify them. Thanks to their efforts, all but 460 of the dead were identified. Their graves now are marked simply: UNKNOWN U.S. SOLDIER.

After the war, Clara Barton became, as some called her, a "professional angel." She was the first president of the American Red Cross, and more than thirty years after America's Civil War, Clara Barton rushed to the scene of the May 31, 1889, Johnstown, Pennsylvania, flood.

Following days of hard rain, an aging dam holding back a lake privately owned by a resort gave way. Andrew Carnegie was one of the lake and resort's owners, as were many others of Pittsburgh's monied elite; apparently, they didn't use their money to repair the lake's dam.

Water rushed into Johnstown and killed twenty-two hundred people. At age sixty-seven, Clara Barton led the Red Cross team into the ravaged city, remaining in Johnstown for five months to aid the survivors. Ten years later, at the age of seventy-seven, she was back on the battlefield, serving in hospitals in Cuba during the Spanish-American War. In 1912, at the age of ninety, she lay dying. Perhaps her mind drifted back to the war years of 1861–1865, years during which she tried desperately to overcome societal restrictions against women going onto battlefields. Her last words were, "Let me go, let me go!"[2]

Lieutenant David Van Buskirk of the 27th Indiana, the Monroe County Grenadiers, may have been the most unusual prisoner of war detained by either side. It was an age when the average soldier stood only five feet eight and a half inches. Ulysses S. Grant was just over five-seven; he wouldn't have been allowed to join the 27th Indiana, much less command the unit. No one shorter than five-ten was allowed in the Grenadiers, and in all, the unit counted more than a hundred six-foot-plus soldiers. Still, David Van Buskirk literally was head and shoulders above his own crowd, at six feet ten and a half. His uniform had to be handmade.

Rebel troops captured Van Buskirk near Winchester, Virginia, and held him at Richmond's Libby Prison. President Jefferson Davis wasn't short, about six feet two inches, and when he heard about Van Buskirk, he just had to meet this giant of a man. Davis reportedly looked up at the captive and said simply, "My God!" Calming down somewhat, Davis said, "I'd shake your hand, son, but I'm afraid you'd break mine."

"I'm as gentle as a lamb, Mr. President," Van Buskirk answered, laughing at the "little" Confederate leader.

Davis wanted to know if the lieutenant had any brothers as big as he was. "One, sir, but we ain't so big compared to our sisters," Van Buskirk said, grinning. "Back home in Indiana, I have six sisters," he boasted, and "when they told me good-bye, as I was standing with my company, they all walked up, leaned down, and kissed me on the top of my head."

While Van Buskirk was held prisoner at Libby, his guards put him on display. Every night they'd take him into town and charge the public to see the man called "The Biggest Yankee in the World." The lieutenant didn't mind too much. Other prisoners starved, but Van Buskirk took his cut of the gate in food—all he could eat, and he could eat a lot. In the four months Lt. David Van Buskirk was held prisoner at Libby, he gained twenty-five pounds.

The "Yankee Giant" was exchanged in September 1862, returned to military service, and was promoted to captain. After the war he returned home to Gosport, Indiana, where he was elected county treasurer; he married, and had two children—there's no word on the size of his offspring. But circus mogul P. T. Barnum tried to get David Van Buskirk to join his freak show. David said no; he'd had enough of being on display as he ate his way through a hungry Richmond.

More than fifty thousand Union officers were held in Libby Prison, three buildings joined together, each about 110 by 44 feet, four stories high. They were built as warehouses by tobacco merchant John Enders, but he died before they were finished, and Northern-born Luther Libby rented them and put up a sign saying L. LIBBY & SON, SHIP CHANDLERS. When the war started, orders to vacate the buildings came so fast, he didn't have time to remove his name; so it became known as Libby Prison. That was just after the First Battle of Manassas. From then until April 3, 1865, when Federal troops marched in to Richmond, Libby served as the South's largest prison.

In July of 1863, Order No. 163 directed that two Federal captains held at Libby were to be executed in retaliation for the deaths of two Confederate officers. Two months earlier, Confederate Captains William F. Corbin and T. G. McGraw had been captured in Kentucky, charged as spies by Gen. Ambrose Burnside, convicted by a military court-martial, then executed by the North. Now, by lots, Union inmates at Libby Prison chose Capt. Henry Washington Sawyer of the 1st New Jersey Cavalry and Capt. John M. Flinn of the 51st Indiana Infantry.

Sawyer asked Richmond provost marshall Gen. John Winder for permission to write his wife. Winder agreed, but warned Sawyer the completed letter would be read before he sent it on. Quickly, Captain Sawyer began writing. When he was finished, he stood and read the letter out loud.

My Dear Wife—I am under the necessity of informing you that my prospect looks dark.

This morning, all the captains now prisoners at the Libby military prison drew lots for two to be executed. It fell to my lot.

The Provost-General J. H. Winder assured me [he] will permit yourself and my dear children to visit me before I am executed. . . . My situation is hard to be borne, and I cannot think of dying without seeing you and the children. . . . If I must die, a sacrifice to my country, with God's will I must submit; only let me see you once more, and I will die becoming a man and an officer. . . .

Farewell, my dear wife, farewell my children,
farewell, mother. . . .[3]

A reporter for the Richmond *Dispatch* had attended the drawing of lots. In telling of the event, he claimed that Sawyer "begged those standing by to excuse him, and turning aside, burst into tears."[4] Captain Flinn, the reporter added, "said he had no letter to write home, and only wanted a priest."

Federal spies in Richmond quickly sent word to Washington. The Union responded that if Captains Sawyer and Flinn were killed, the North would execute two Confederate prisoners, Capt. Robert Tyler of the 8th Virginia Infantry and Gen. William Henry Fitzhugh "Rooney" Lee, Robert E. Lee's second son.

Rooney Lee had been wounded in the leg at the Battle of Brandy Station, the largest cavalry battle ever fought on the American continent. He was recuperating at a friend's home known as Hickory Hill. On June 26, 1863, Union troops raided the home, capturing young Lee. They held him at Fort Monroe until March 1864, when he was paroled.

In the end, none of the four—Sawyer, Flinn, Lee, or Tyler—was executed.

Richmond's Libby Prison housed only officers. Other prisons in Richmond, including one on Belle Isle in the middle of the James River, were used for enlisted men. G. E. Sabre, of the 2nd Rhode Island Cavalry, described Belle Isle in his diary.

The prison camp was situated on the extreme lower end of the island. . . . The ground was low, wet and flat. . . . The area occupied by the

*prisoners was not over the size of an ordinary regimental camp—
say four acres. Around the whole was an embankment about three
feet in height, somewhat resembling in appearance a hasty field de-
fence. . . . Here was the fatal "dead-line," outside of which, encir-
cling the whole camp, were a chain of sentinels, ready to carry out
their instructions to kill at every opportunity. . . . Still further from
this were the guard and officers' quarters, cook house, hospital and
graveyard. A ridge of low hills surrounded and overlooked the camp.
Here were posted, at different points, four pieces of artillery, charged
with shell and canister, and pointed to rake all parts of the camp.*[5]

One day the Belle Isle camp commander's dog got too close to the
starving prisoners; two prisoners coaxed him to come closer. It was
the last time the dog's owner saw the animal. Similar incidents—kidnapping dogs and turning them into stew—occurred so frequently,
it wasn't long before there wasn't a dog left on Belle Isle. The men
had found a way to supplement their meager diet. The prisoners
were so successful at luring dogs into their pots that the Richmond
Enquirer warned its readers to keep their pets at home. If the animals
wandered too close to the Yankee prisoners, the newspaper claimed,
they would be "instantly devoured by the ravens of the North."

John Ransom of the 9th Michigan Cavalry, who would also be held
prisoner at Andersonville, wrote a diary including the time he was
held at Belle Isle. His January 8, 1863, entry reads:

*All taken outside today to be squadded over—an all day job and
nothing to eat. The men being in hundreds and some dying off every day, leave vacancies in the squads of as many as die out of them,
and in order to keep them filled up have to be squadded out every
few days, thereby saving rations. Richmond papers are much
alarmed for fear of a break among the prisoners.*

If squads fell below the usual number, they were reorganized,
"squadded over." If ten men died out of an inmate population of one
hundred, instead of ten men in ten squads, the remaining ninety
would be squadded over into ten men in nine squads. Since rations
would be handed out on a per-squad basis, this would mean the
ninety men individually would receive no more rations than before
the other ten died. With food short, the weather at times harsh, as
many as thirty Union prisoners a day died on Belle Isle.

Today, the site of Belle Isle Prison lies under the Robert E. Lee Bridge over the James River. It's part of the City of Richmond's river parks system. There's not much left of the prison site, only a berm or two thrown up to mark the outlines of the prison. In the summer, visitors cross a pedestrian bridge, picnic lunch in hand. Once on Belle Isle, they dine on sandwiches and beer where hundreds of prisoners died of hunger and want.

Libby Prison was torn down in the late nineteenth century. Only a marker bolted to a flood wall remains where the prison once stood at Twentieth and Cary Streets. The building's beams and bricks, planks and rafters, were taken to Chicago where they were reassembled in conjunction with the Columbian Exposition, the "Libby Prison Museum." After a decade of only mediocre success, the museum was demolished. Bits of Libby were given to the Chicago Historical Society. Other parts were loaded onto a train, to be sent on a world-wide tour, but the train crashed east of Chicago and planks and rafters were sold (or stolen, the story isn't clear) to a nearby farmer. They became part of a barn and stood in an Indiana cornfield until the 1960s. During the Civil War centennial, visitors tramped through the barn and around the owner's house and crops until he got tired of the crowds, had the barn torn down, and sold the planks and rafters. A marker was erected, but someone stole it.

The final owner of the remnants of Libby Prison intended to use them to build a restaurant, the "Libby Prison Steak House," complete with a Rebel Room and a Yankee Room. The idea never took hold, and today, all that's left of Libby sits in a steel barn in Southern Indiana, rotting away. Strangely, it's not too far from Gosport, Indiana, the home of David Van Buskirk, the Union officer who reigned for a while as the "Biggest Yankee" at Libby.

Elmira, New York, was in the middle of a state grown prosperous by the Civil War. Yet, in this booming economy, Confederate prisoners housed there died at an alarming rate: 24 percent of the Confederates held there died. That's a conservative figure; some sources put Elmira's mortality rate as high as 32.5 percent, almost one-third. In three months, with 8,347 prisoners in the camp, 2,011 had to be admitted to the camp hospital. More than 775 of those died; more than one-third of the prisoners admitted to the hospital. The camp surgeon notified the U.S. War Department that "at this rate, the entire command [of prisoners] will be admitted to the hospital in less than a year and 36 percent will die."

The camp, he reported, stank to the high heavens, that a river flowing through the ground had, much like that at Andersonville, formed a gummy pond "green with putrescence, filling the air with its messengers of disease and death." Despite the prosperity of the surrounding countryside, the surgeon was unable to get straw for bedding. That forced a good many of his hospital's patients to lie on the bare floor and die there. A Texas soldier put it simply: "If there was ever a hell on earth, Elmira prison was that hell."

Local Elmira residents apparently welcomed the prison. To many, having the Confederates in the neighborhood was something of a thrill. While thousands died inside the stockade, an entrepreneur of somewhat doubtful ethics built an observation platform on a public road outside the prison grounds. For ten cents each, he allowed curious civilians to peak at the Rebels living and dying on the other side of freedom.

One of the nation's greatest writers and entertainers, Samuel L. Clemens, is buried in Elmira, New York, not far from the site of the former prison. He'd been a journeyman printer and Mississippi riverboat pilot. When America's Civil War began, Clemens joined a pro-Confederacy unit in his native Missouri but quickly realized army life wasn't for him. He quit, changed his name to Mark Twain, and took to writing. In later years, he published Ulysses S. Grant's autobiography.

While the Union prison at Elmira lacked adequate medical facilities, Federal officials didn't even bother with a hospital at the Rock Island, Illinois, prison, and eighteen hundred Confederate prisoners suffered and died there in a smallpox epidemic.

Orders went out in mid-1863 to build a prison on Rock Island, situated in the middle of the Mississippi River. Captain Charles A. Reynolds of the quartermaster department built eighty-four prisoners' barracks, each one hundred feet long, twenty-two feet wide, and twelve feet high. They all faced eastward—that is, toward Illinois and away from Iowa. Each of the barracks had twelve windows, two doors, and two roof ventilators. And each building had its own kitchen located eighteen feet to the west of the barracks and separated by a wall from the sleeping quarters.

Each barracks building had sixty double bunks, meant, the builders claimed, for one hundred twenty prisoners. Six rows of buildings, fourteen barracks to a row, the buildings were thirty feet apart.

Around them all ran a stockade thirteen hundred feet long, nine hundred feet wide, and twelve feet high. Sentries patrolled a boardwalk outside the fence, four feet from the stockade top; every hundred feet there was a sentry box.

In December 1863, 5,592 prisoners were shifted to Rock Island, some after a fire destroyed several barracks at Chicago's Camp Douglas Prison. The rest had been taken by Grant at Lookout Mountain and Missionary Ridge, the battles of Chattanooga and Chickamauga.

The prisoners were cold, wet, and despondent; quickly the temperature dropped from the freezing mark to zero, then to 32 *below* zero. Southern troops always lacked adequate uniforms; nothing prepared them for subzero weather.

Then the smallpox epidemic hit, and the prison surgeon general finally declared some of the barracks to be a hospital and filled them with sick inmates. It was too late. By the end of December, 94 prisoners were dead of smallpox. The next month, another 231 died. By February, the death toll was 346.

The weather and pox also affected the guards; 171 Union soldiers guarding the Rebels died of disease and exposure suffered while on duty at Rock Island.

Not in sheer numbers, but in percentages Rock Island, Illinois, was the worst Union prison. Of 2,484 prisoners held there, 1,922 died—77.4 percent. A Union doctor said of Rock Island Prison: There is "a striking want of some means for the preservation of human life which medical and sanitary science has indicated as proper."

As in every other prison, North and South, prisoners at Rock Island made elaborate escape plans. One problem, of course, was the Mississippi River. If the prisoners managed to dig a tunnel without being discovered, they had to crawl through it without being found. If they succeeded in getting past the guards, they were faced with swimming the Big Muddy, about four hundred feet wide at that point. Needless to say, escaping from Rock Island Prison wasn't easy. Only forty-one prisoners managed to escape the island and elude the guards.

When President Lincoln issued an Amnesty Proclamation, nearly eighteen hundred Confederate prisoners at Rock Island took the oath of allegiance. They would join the Union army if they were not assigned to fight in the South. Instead, they were to be sent to garrisons out West, which would free those Federal troops on duty in, say, Utah, to be sent East to do battle with the Confederacy.

When orders were delayed, Rebels still loyal to the Confederacy began re-recruiting those who had defected from the Southern cause. About thirteen hundred of the Rebels-turned-Union returned to the Southern side.

When word reached the North about the treatment Federal prisoners received at Andersonville, some Northern prison officials began to retaliate. Rations were reduced and the quality of food got worse. Treatment of those caught trying to escape ranged from riding a rail, to hanging by the thumbs, to death.

Rock Island Prison was closed down in July of 1865, and in August the buildings were turned over to the U.S. Ordnance Department, which used the barracks to store weapons captured from the Confederate army. The last of the original buildings was torn down in 1909 after serving as an officers' barracks. The land formerly used for a Civil War prison now is part of the Rock Island Arsenal—the commanding general's mansion, a golf course, machine shops, and officers quarters—and cemeteries, one for the North and one for the South. Long, straight rows of white headstones. Headstones and bitter memories of the Andersonville of the North.

At Fort Delaware on Pea Patch Island the ground was so soggy that buildings holding Confederate prisoners were often in danger of toppling over. More than twenty-four hundred Rebel prisoners died at Fort Delaware, many due to typhoid fever. Much of the prison remains today, and across the river in New Jersey, the U.S. government has erected a monument to those who died at Fort Delaware.

* * *

Abraham Lincoln said that Chicago, more than any other city in the North, was responsible for America's Civil War. Chicago was given the sobriquet "Windy City" because of its blustering officials, not for any excessively high winds, and during America's Civil War they lived up to the nickname.

"After Boston," the president said, Chicago "has been the chief instrument in bringing this war on the country." Editor Joseph Medill of the Chicago *Tribune* had asked Lincoln to lower Chicago's draft quota. In a letter to Medill, the president said, "The Northwest has opposed the South as New England has opposed the South. It is you who are largely responsible for making the blood flood as it has. You called for war until we had it. You called for emancipation and I have given it to you. Now you come here begging to be let off from the call for men which I have made to carry out the war you have demanded."[6]

In September 1861, Camp Douglas was built about four miles southeast of downtown Chicago. The area has long since been incorporated into Chicago. The site of Camp Douglas now is the site of the Robert Taylor Homes project, the Illinois Institute of Technology, and Comiskey Park, home of the Chicago White Sox. The Stephen Douglas monument isn't far away. The stockade fronted Cottage Grove, then ran west four blocks to what is now Martin Luther King Drive. East 31st Street (then called Ridgley Place) was the northern boundary, with East 33rd Place (formerly College Place) on the south.

Intended to house Union army recruits, the camp was named for U.S. Sen. Stephen A. Douglas, who had lost to Abraham Lincoln in the election of 1860 and who owned much of the property in the area. The camp's smallpox hospital was located at the site of the original homestead at Camp Douglas. Originally, Henry Graves owned the land, and the area was known as "Cottage Grove" because of the Graves family cottage and other cottages nearby. One boundary of Camp Douglas was the road (now street), still known as Cottage Grove—better, we suppose, than "Graves Street," though it's ironic that the site of the Graves homestead became a graveyard.

Even while it served Union recruits, Camp Douglas was a place of death. In December 1861, several cases of measles were reported among the 4,222 Federal troops. By January 18, 1862, at least 42 had died of the disease. By no means would their deaths be the last at Camp Douglas.

The first major influx of prisoners came after U. S. Grant's victory at Fort Donelson, the victory that saw him demand "no terms except unconditional and immediate surrender," a demand that gave him the nickname "Unconditional Surrender" Grant. More than thirteen thousand Rebels surrendered at Fort Donelson; seven thousand of them were sent to Camp Douglas.

When the Confederate officers arrived under terms of the Fort Donelson surrender, many still wore their swords and carried their pistols. Chivalry was not yet dead, and the code of chivalry allowed "officers and gentlemen" to carry their weapons into captivity. Needless to say, this and other parts of "the code" were soon dropped.

By the time the war ended, Camp Douglas had housed more than thirty thousand Confederate prisoners. In excess of six thousand died of malnutrition and the elements. It took several years and three burials for their bodies to come to rest. First they were buried at the prison. Next they were exhumed and taken to an area called Lincoln Park, along Lake Michigan.

Lincoln Park is near what is known as Chicago's Gold Coast, high-rent, high-rise, a prime area for the twenty-something generation to play and work off excess energy. An area where the Camp Douglas prisoners once were buried is now part of a softball field. It was admitted at the time that the individuals who exhumed the bodies from Lincoln Park in the nineteenth century may have left some bones behind. One of these days, following a hard spring rain, those bones may turn up when some twentieth-century hotshot hits a hard grounder down toward first base.

Undoubtedly it will cause quite a stir, with reports of mass murder being carried by the local media. A few years back, when a grader digging at the site of a shopping center uncovered several bodies, the Chicago media ran with the story for days: Mass Murder; Multiple Killings, Death and Destruction, Bodies, Bodies, Bodies. The media never noticed the bones carried remnants of clothing from another era. Finally, someone recalled that a nearby hospital had been used for many fatally injured in the great Chicago fire. It was at the hospital that many of those injured died; they were buried in the hospital graveyard. Only then did the media settle down and stop running stories of some crazed killer on the loose.

Back to Camp Douglas. The bodies of the camp's Confederate prisoners were exhumed for a second time and taken to Chicago's Oak Woods Cemetery, where they rest along with former city mayors and state governors. Other prisoners are buried in what is now a parking lot of an African-American–owned funeral home. Until his recent death in 1996, the owner flew a Confederate flag over their graves, despite frequent protests from his neighbors. Funeral home owner Ernest A. Griffin was a founder of the Confederate Prisoner of War Society and the Stephen A. Douglas Association and was the grandson of a black private in the Civil War who enlisted at Camp Douglas. His grandfather, Pvt. Charles H. Griffin, fought with the 29th Regiment, U.S. Colored Troops, Company B.

As for the Confederate prisoners who lay beneath his parking lot, Ernest Griffin said he honored those who died, not their cause nor the flag he flew over their graves.

The bodies of more than two hundred Union soldiers are buried about ten miles to the north, in Rosehill Cemetery. They came from the Battles of Fort Donelson, Shiloh, and Vicksburg. A monument to the Chicago Board of Trade Battery proclaims: MILES TRAVELED BY TRAIN, 1,231. MARCHED, 5,266. When the Confederate bodies were first exhumed in 1867, there was talk of burying them next to the Union graves, but families of the Union troops buried at Rosehill objected.

By 1903, Oak Woods Cemetery had almost disappeared in a swamp. It took a Federal grant to save it. Ill feelings are hard to heal. In 1992 there was a proposal to give the Confederate monument at Oak Woods landmark status; local residents objected.

The numbers are appalling. Of 214,000 Confederate soldiers held by the Union, 26,000 died, a full 12 percent. Of 194,000 Union troops captured by the South, 30,000 died, more than 15 percent. In many prisons the percentages were much higher. In the hills of Salisbury, North Carolina, one-third of the prisoners held captive there died; at least 24 percent succumbed at Elmira, New York; more than 77 percent on Rock Island. They died of malnutrition, of disease, of untended wounds.

They were held prisoner not because they were thieves or murderers, but merely because they were on the wrong side of a war that neither North nor South could afford, imprisoned by systems that could not or would not care for them.

CHAPTER SIXTEEN

Liberty Found:
Prison Escapes

We paid the guard $7.50 to "look the other way" while we went over the fence. We made it on foot back to Middle Tennessee, which we reached about the 1st of July. My regiment still being in prison, I enlisted in Company G, Ninth Tennessee Cavalry.
—Pvt. J. T. Branch
Co. G, 9th Tennessee Cavalry

American history and folklore are rich in horror stories of Civil War prisons. Numerous diaries survive, attesting to the inhumanity. Yet many of those same diaries also attest to the superhuman efforts some prisoners made to escape.

In January of 1864, inmates at Richmond's Libby Prison began a tunnel to freedom. It wasn't their first tunnel, but it was certainly the most successful.

The first attempt ran into solid rock and was abandoned. The next idea was to cut into the sewer running under the street between the prison and a nearby canal, but water began leaking into the tunnel.

Finally, a plan worked: They cut through the kitchen fireplace, slid down the chimney into the cellar under the hospital, and dug a 53-foot-long tunnel under the guarded street. They would lower each other through the fireplace, then crawl to freedom, ending in the safety of a shed outside the prison walls.

They had a few smuggled-in pocketknives for digging, a large chisel, and a wooden split-box (a spittoon). One man would dig out the dirt, fill the container, and pass it back to an assistant who would haul the earth and gravel out, concealing it in straw and rubbish in the cellar.

For seventeen days they dug, led by Col. Thomas E. Rose of the 77th Pennsylvania Volunteers and Maj. A. G. Hamilton of the 12th Kentucky. Come Tuesday, February 9, they went for it. One of the original planners of the escape, Col. Frederick Bartleston of the 100th Illinois Volunteer Infantry, wanted to go but couldn't; simply put, he was too big to fit down the chimney.

Only about 25 prisoners were in on the secret, but at the last minute, many more joined in, 109 in all. One by one they began slipping down the chimney and through the tunnel. But they'd made a mistake; the tunnel was too short. Instead of coming up inside the shed where they could not be seen, the tunnel ended in the middle of the street. The prisoners popped up into the night, and Rebel guards watched, too surprised to stop the escapees.

Once outside, Colonel Rose went for help. He hid in the home of Richmond's leading Union spy, Elizabeth Van Lew. When he thought it was safe, he left "Crazy Bet" and headed down the Virginia peninsula, hoping to reach the Union-held Fort Monroe. He didn't make it. When he was within a mile or so of the Federal lines near Williamsburg, he was captured and returned to Libby.

In all, 48 of the 109 who crawled out of Libby were recaptured. Two others drowned, but 61 made it safely back to Union lines. And Colonel Bartleston, who helped plan the escape but was too big to slip down the chimney? He was exchanged for a Confederate officer and released. On June 27, 1864, however, he was killed at the Battle of Kennesaw Mountain in Georgia.

In June of 1863, the Civil War was raging into its third year. On the Mississippi River, Gen. Ulysses S. Grant was making a final drive on Vicksburg.

General Joseph "Fighting Joe" Hooker got his nickname by accident, not by vicious combat or even barroom brawls. During the 1862 Peninsula Campaign in Virginia, an Associated Press report listed: Fighting-Joe Hooker—that is, to say Joe Hooker was fighting that day, not that Hooker was an especially tough fighter. In any event, a Northern newspaper editor picked it up, dropped the hyphen, and the general thereafter was called "Fighting Joe." Such is the road to fame.

There was another "Fighting Joe" in the war, and he was on the other side, Confederate Gen. Joseph "Fighting Joe" Wheeler. Apparently Wheeler earned his nickname because of his "dogged aggressiveness."

General Robert E. Lee beat Fighting Joe Hooker at Chancellorsville and headed north. He would take the war out of Virginia, into Union territory, and look for shoes along the way. At least, Lee's men hoped they'd find shoes, since many were barefoot. The Army of Northern Virginia didn't know it, but it was heading for Gettysburg.

A year before the big prison break at Libby, a smaller escape began about one hundred miles away, at the foot of Colley Avenue in Norfolk. Forty-seven Confederate officers were held onboard the *Maple Leaf,* a Union side-wheel steamer docked on the Elizabeth River at Fort Norfolk. The fort had been used often since the Federals captured Norfolk in May of 1862, a convenient place to jail Southern prisoners before they were exchanged for their Northern counterparts. Conditions there were as bad as any other Civil War prison: too many prisoners, too little food and water.

Just before the *Maple Leaf* steamed off on the morning of June 9, 1863, forty-five more prisoners were loaded onboard, most of them invalids from North Carolina units and Braxton Bragg's Army of Tennessee. The *Maple Leaf* normally was used as a "truce ship," ferrying Confederate prisoners to a point where they'd be exchanged. Not this time, though; they were to be taken to Fort Delaware, one of the North's worst prisons.

By the time the *Maple Leaf* sailed, there were ninety-seven prisoners onboard, all, according to a later newspaper report, well educated and well dressed. Not many guards were posted, just under thirty, none of them especially well trained or experienced at handling prisoners of war. While they were in port, the guards had kept a vigilant watch over the prisoners, but as soon as the *Maple Leaf* left the dock, the situation changed. The guards grew negligent, trusting to the water and the prisoners' own apparent submission to their fate.

They weren't submitting; they were scheming.

Just before five that afternoon, with the *Maple Leaf* just six miles north of Cape Henry Lighthouse at the southern rim of Chesapeake

Bay, the prisoners struck up conversations with their guards. Some of the prisoners were even dining with the ship's officers. One prisoner, Capt. Eugene Homes of Louisiana's Crescent Regiment, was in the pilothouse. Suddenly he reached over and tapped the ship's bell three times. Prisoners all over the ship seized their guards' weapons and, with the Rebel Yell ringing in their ears, the Yankees gave up.

Reversing engines, the former prisoners aimed the ship south. They wanted to turn the vessel over to the Confederate navy, but there wasn't enough coal to make the trip. So they headed for a point about fifteen miles south of Cape Henry, near the Virginia–North Carolina line, where they prepared to abandon ship. At least twenty-seven of the Rebel prisoners were too sick or wounded to escape; several others had taken an oath to cooperate with their Union captors and wanted to stay onboard the *Maple Leaf*. Finally, seventy-one Confederates rowed ashore in small boats, armed with rifles, sabers, and handguns from the ship's armory.

While the escapees marched toward the Outer Banks of North Carolina, the Federal officers retook control of their ship and headed for Fort Monroe to inform Union authorities.

The nearest Confederate lines were a sixty-mile hike away from the escapees. Between them lay five small but difficult rivers, all heavily guarded by Federal troops. So they had to try their luck in Virginia's Great Dismal Swamp, four thousand square miles of trackless marshes, high grass, bogs, poisonous snakes, bears, and assorted other wild animals. Not to mention Union troops sometimes so close, the escaped Rebels could hear them talking. But they made their way through, taking help wherever locals offered it. Three times they managed to hop onboard trains.

And on June 26 they trudged into Richmond, "dirty, fagged out, used up, but as happy a set of 'rebs' as ever wore the gray," one of the escapees later wrote.

At first, the escape from the *Maple Leaf* was taken as a good sign in the Confederate capital, a good omen. But not for long. Within a week, news reached Richmond of two major defeats: Grant had taken Vicksburg, and, even more devastating, Lee had lost at Gettysburg.

* * *

Prisoners were crowded into inadequate housing, both North and South. Prisoners both North and South were given insufficient food and clothing. Prisoners died at an alarming rate. Despite living conditions horrible beyond belief, despite deprivation and loss of personal freedom, the human spirit of those captured and held prisoner worked, and worked hard, at survival.

Prisoners weren't always mistreated. Sometimes they were allowed reading material, although one Andersonville prisoner complained that the only book he found to read was *Gray's Anatomy*. Usually they were allowed to receive mail and could write one-page letters home, even though both incoming and outgoing correspondence were heavily censored. At the Federal prison on Johnson's Island, near Sandusky, Ohio, they were allowed exercise and recreation, including, as one former inmate noted, "Nearly [every] evening [prisoners] are engaged in a game they call 'base ball.'" He admitted he didn't understand the game, "but those who play it get very much excited over it."

In some cases prisoners were allowed to set loose their more creative natures. At Point Lookout, Maryland, for instance, one inventive inmate built a steam engine. The engine, however, was stationary and didn't go anywhere.

Unlike some of the prisoners, who did.

CHAPTER SEVENTEEN

Deserters:
I Shirked. I Skedaddled.

Our men are deserting quite freely. It looks very blue to them, and the fact that Sherman marched from Atlanta to Savannah without seeing an armed Confederate soldier is well calculated to make them despondent.
—Confederate Capt. Charles Minor Blackford
August 10, 1864[1]

Around the turn of the century, a worldwide movement began quickly and almost as quickly ended: anarchism, that theory whose followers scorn organized government. One reason anarchy never got anywhere was that the only thing the participants agreed on was they didn't want to get together to agree or even disagree on anything. It reminds you of comedian Groucho Marx: "I don't care to belong to any club that will accept me as a member."

The Confederacy was made up of "sovereign states," usually unable even during the pressure of war to give up their principles of decentralization and states' rights. State governors might proclaim loyalty to the Confederacy, but they were often slow in obeying the government's orders, orders such as the 1862 draft law.

The Confederacy was so democratic, it might be argued, that its troops felt they had the right to ignore any order they didn't like. They disobeyed orders in the field; in camp, they resented the better conditions under which the officers lived, and they deserted.

Especially in the beginning of the war, volunteer Southern troops felt they had the right to go home anytime they wanted. At one point, General Lee said, "Our ranks are very much diminished—I fear from a third to one-half of our original numbers." If Rebel troops wanted to leave, they simply gave up and went home. Confederate Capt.

Charles Minor Blackford understood. "It is hard," he said, "to maintain one's patriotism on ashcake and water."

In April 1864, the Richmond *Dispatch*, obviously recognizing the problem, carried this item:

> *Harboring a Deserter—A novel mode of [locating] deserters from arrest was disclosed before Commissioner A. H. Sands a day or two since. There being some suspicion that a man named J. H. A. Bowlar, a deserter from the Confederate service, was about the premises of Mrs. Louise Lankford . . . a guard was dispatched to search her house. In one of the rooms was a bed on which were two females who claimed to be very sick; but having instituted a fruitless search about every other part of the house, and there being some doubts in their minds as to the truth of the statement made by the professed invalids, the officers of the law insisted upon examining the bed upon which they lay, when Bowlar was found [hiding between] the two women.*

Bowlar, obviously, had located an unusual and perhaps congenial way of hiding from the law. Perhaps too congenial. "The discovery," according to the newspaper account, "was a lucky one for Bowlar, for when rescued from his hiding place he was in a very exhausted state, and had he remained there much longer in all probability would have suffocated."

Bowlar was arrested, tried by court-martial, and drummed out of the service. His moment of perhaps "very exhausted" freedom didn't last long, however. He was drafted again "for another branch of the service."[2]

The desertion situation only got worse. Less than a year after Bowlar was found, literally, hiding between the sheets, Richmond newspapers carried "General Lee's Last Appeal," invoking "all good citizens, wherever it is in their power, to place before deserters and absentees from the army the last appeal that General Lee will ever make to them, to return to their duty and resume their place under the flag."[3] Referring to Lee, the article declared, "No man has a kinder and more benevolent heart; no official, civil or military, has a more honest and profound sympathy with the private soldier." The general "feels their suffering as his own; and they [the deserters] are aware of the fact." Robert E. Lee needed their help and would pardon any deserter who returned to duty.

Not many did. Later, the Confederate government itself offered a pardon to all deserters who would return to duty. It was "General Order No. 3," and was more than a carrot-and-stick approach; it carried a threat—return or "suffer the consequences."[5]

Frequently, in Richmond, Southern troops who deserted and were captured were "lodged in the Castle . . . upon the charge of desertion." It was either Castle Thunder or Castle Lightning; both prisons were used to handle deserters and others of doubtful loyalty.

General Order No. 3 recorded a long list of soldiers being held, and the list grew longer. In the closing days of the war, prisons meant for Yankees were used for Rebels, those who preferred to desert rather than chance death as the cause lost all hope.

Over the length of the war, 13 percent of the Confederate army deserted. It wasn't quite so bad for Northern troops; only 9 percent took off. Of four hundred thousand troops listed on the Confederate rolls at one point, more than half were absent, although many could have been ill.[4] General Beauregard called desertion an "epidemic." In one month, 8 percent of Lee's Army of Northern Virginia went, as we'd put it "over the hill." On the road to Appomattox, General Lee commented that his army seemed to melt away into the countryside.

Sometimes the folks at home helped out, sending troops boxes of clothing to be worn when the soldier deserted. At the first opportunity, the soldier would change out of his uniform into civilian clothing, and just walk out of camp, hoping not to be noticed, and if he was noticed, not to be recognized. Just as frequently, the deserter—who wanted nothing more than to go home to his family—would be caught, sent before a court-martial, sentenced to death, and shot. Sometimes within a matter of hours.

There was a virtual epidemic of desertion among Union troops after their May 25, 1862, rout by Rebels at Winchester, Virginia. General Nathanial P. Banks, ten-term member of Congress and former governor of Massachusetts, was head of the Department of the Shenandoah. Banks saw his troops, including an otherwise unidentified Wisconsin soldier, running off. Banks cried, "Stop, men. Don't you love your country?" To which the soldier replied, "Yes, by God, and I'm trying to get back to it just as fast as I can!"[5]

On the Union side, eighty thousand deserters were caught and re-turned at gunpoint to the ranks; twenty-one thousand Confederates were sent back into service in the same manner. There's no record of how many Rebel troops were executed for desertion, but at least 147 Yankee deserters were captured and sent before firing squads.

It even happened in the middle of the streets of Richmond. Confederate war department clerk John Jones, writing in his diary, commented on "the spectacle of men deserting our regiments." And it wasn't just late in the war. In 1862, Jones told of letters the war department received from privates in North Carolina regiments demanding they be transferred "or else they would serve no more."

The next year Jones wrote about a man running down Franklin Street in Richmond, apparently a deserter wearing civilian clothing. A uniformed soldier, Jones recorded, "took deliberate aim with his rifle" and fired. But the rifle misfired, and both Jones and the deserter stood transfixed as the soldier fired again. Again the rifle misfired. The shooting had drawn a crowd of curious onlookers. Later, Jones added, "Desertion is the order of the day, on both sides. Would that the men would take matters in their own hands, and end the war. . . . Let every man in both armies desert and go home."

During the war, refugees and deserters from both armies were a constant problem in Richmond. How were they to be fed, since most were without funds? Where were they to be housed? How were they to be controlled when they became hostile, as they sometimes did? Many of the problems were handled by individuals, private charities, and the Richmond city government. The Richmond YMCA, for example, frequently appealed on behalf of the soldiers' families taking refuge in the city, and the appeal was answered time and time again. However, by early July 1864, the supplies gathered by the agency and the remaining funds were so meager that the YMCA felt it could "accomplish but little" in the way of helping the poor. The situation was so desperate that the city council considered taking action against the refugees.

> *All persons who are not liable to military duty, and all others whose presence is not, by their being employed in some useful and legitimate occupation, required in the city [are ordered] to leave it and*

remain away until a change in the state of affairs renders it desir-
able for them to return.

The resolution was withdrawn only when it was decided it would do more harm (alerting the enemy to just how desperate the situation was) than good (ridding the city of its unwanted human surplus). But the idea would be brought up again later in the war.

They were young, middle-aged, and old. They were farmers and me-chanics, lawyers, and even ministers of the gospel. They answered their government's call, whether the call came from Washington or Richmond. Some at first were enthusiastic, then their enthusiasm wore thin; others ran at the first sound of battle. Some didn't wait that long. Many signed up for ninety days or less, and when their tour of duty was over, they went home.

William Wagner was a young volunteer from North Carolina. In early 1861, he wrote home: "Dear wife if we do get in a fite all we can do is to trust God above us and try an fite thrue the best way we can but I hope to God we may be sucsesful whar Ever we go."

CHAPTER EIGHTEEN

The Gentler Sex:
Women Who Spied, Women Who Fought

Sewing and knitting for "our boys" all the time. It seems as if a few energetic women could carry on the war better than the men do it so far.

—Louisa May Alcott
October 1861, private diary

Ancient Greek and Roman bards often told stories of brave men going off to battle while their women remained in the background, caregivers and keepers of the home front. Those same storytellers also sang and wrote of heroines who fought valiantly and defied Rome and Caesar to defend England, women who led lesser souls—both men and women—in battle to protect the lives they held dear. They fought in Ireland and India, in England and France; and they fought in America, standing side by side with men, facing equal danger at every turn. In America's Civil War many women did just that. Not content by any means with keeping the home fires burning, Civil War women set out to set the world itself on fire.

Thomas Jordan was Phil Sherman's West Point roommate. When war broke out, he was on the staff of Gen. Winfield Scott. He was a Southerner at heart, but, instead of immediately leaving Washington after the fall of Fort Sumter, he stuck around, studying Scott's plans for the coming war. He set up a network of spies, about fifty individuals, amateur and professional—those in it for fun, those in it because of their beliefs, those in it for money. When Jordan left Washington for Richmond, he put in charge of the spy network a widow named Rose O'Neal Greenhow. In the Northern capital they called her "Wild Rose." One hundred miles south, in Richmond, she was known as "Rebel Rose."

Rose O'Neal Greenhow's late husband, Robert, was a U.S. State Department official. Rose herself was long a leader in Washington society. When Robert died in 1854, Rose was thirty-six, not old by today's standards, but the nineteenth century was different; she was well past her prime. In the mid-1800s young ladies often married while still in their teens. Thirty-six-year-old women today barely feel their biological clock ticking.

Still, Rose was considered by some "irresistible." In her parlor on 16th Street, in Washington, she received the likes of President James Buchanan (he was the nation's first bachelor president), Senator William Seward of New York (who later became Secretary of State), and—it's believed—even Secretary of War Edwin Stanton (before he became secretary). Certainly, Senator Henry Wilson of Massachusetts, chairman of the Senate Military Affairs Committee, visited Rose; he wanted to marry her, or at least that's what Rose said in her autobiography, *My Imprisonment,* published in 1863, and military reports indicate Wilson was a frequent visitor to Rose.

Rose claimed she obtained military maps and secrets from Wilson, passing the information on to the Confederacy. Letters to Rose Greenhow from an obvious admirer are signed "Yours ever. H." As in *H* for Henry Wilson. Rose claimed Wilson gave her information regarding Federal troops under Gen. Irvin McDowell. She claimed to have a map used by the senate to mark the location of Union army troops around Washington. The map, she said, also had a dotted red line, marking the Federal army's planned march south.

Wilson denied ever giving Rose Greenhow any information, and handwriting experts say the letters signed *H* were not written by Henry Wilson, even though they were on official U.S. Senate stationery, bearing the letterhead of the 36th Congress. Years later, Grant's secretary, Hamilton Fish, reported hearing a conversation in which Wilson admitted having a relationship with Rose Greenhow. The conversation, however, was with Thomas Jordan, the same Thomas Jordan who had been an aide to General Scott. The same Thomas Jordan who had set up the Rebel spy network for Rose Greenhow.

Early in July 1861, Rose sent Confederate General Beauregard a message: General Irvin McDowell had been ordered to march on Richmond and would leave Washington on the sixteenth. Five days later, Beauregard's Rebels met McDowell's Federals at Bull Run. The Battle of Manassas turned into a triumph for the Confederacy and the Great Skedaddle for the Union.

Beauregard later commented, "Having Madame Greenhow in Washington City was like having a personal representative on the Union army's command staff. I could not have had better information."

General George McClellan agreed. "This woman," he said, "is a dangerous and skillful spy. She invariably knew my plans better than Lincoln did." He added that the Rebels had their hands on "detailed orders before some of our own commanders received them."

Still, Wilson denied giving Rose Greenhow any information, and apparently most people believed him. He went on to become vice president under Ulysses S. Grant.

Wilson had been a cobbler, started up a shoe factory, then turned to politics as a Whig. He joined a movement whose very name squelches confidence, the Know-Nothings. The Know-Nothing Party was anti-Catholic and anti-immigrant. Originally, it began as two secret societies, which restricted membership to native-born Protestants, the Order of United Americans and the Order of the Star-Spangled Banner. It went national after papal nuncio Monsignor Gaetano Bedini came to the United States to adjudicate a Protestant-Catholic property dispute. Members of the joint order were pledged to vote for no one except native-born Protestants. The name *Know-Nothings* came when outsiders asked about the orders. They were told to answer "I know nothing."

In mid-1862 the Union caught Rose Greenhow in the act and jailed her in the Old Capitol Prison, but that didn't stop her. She knitted presents for her friends on the outside and hid coded messages in the knitting; knit one, purl two, the Yankees are coming, the Yankees are coming. While still in jail, she even sent a carrier pigeon with a personal message to Confederate President Davis. And she continued to direct her network of spies.

For a while, Rose Greenhow had the youngest of her four children staying with her in prison, eight-year-old "Little Rose," as she was known. But Little Rose was taken ill, or at least her mother's guards thought so, and mother and child were released from prison and expelled from the city.

She went to Richmond, where she met with Jefferson Davis, who apparently sent her to Europe to raise funds for the Confederacy. She took Little Rose with her and placed her daughter in a convent school in Paris. Rose O'Neal Greenhow claimed she was entertained by crowned heads all over Europe.

On September 1, 1864, she tried to slip back into America on-board the blockade runner *Condor*. They were headed for the port of Wilmington, North Carolina, when the *Condor*'s crew sighted the Union ship *Niphon*. Trying to avoid the *Niphon,* the *Condor* ran aground, crashing into the remains of another Confederate block-ade runner the Union had sunk months earlier.

Rose remembered her days in the Old Capital Prison and wanted no more of them. Besides, she still had work to do for the Confed-eracy. She and two other Rebel spies took to a small boat, but wave after wave slammed the boat against the *Condor*. Suddenly Rose was washed overboard, pulled down by bags of English gold coin she had been given to aid the Southern cause. She carried them tied to her waist to keep from losing them.

The next day her body washed ashore; and the gold that caused her to drown was stolen; her body was unceremoniously dumped back into the waves. One day more and, for the second time, the body of Rose O'Neal Greenhow washed ashore. This time she was recog-nized and given final rites at a Catholic church in Wilmington. She's buried there now.

Years later, "Little Rose" Greenhow married and became an ac-tress. She returned to America and settled in California.

Pauline Cushman, on the other hand, spied for the Union. An ac-tress before the war, she pretended to be fervently "secesh." She wasn't, and passed on information to General Rosecrans—the goings and comings of Southern troops in Kentucky and Tennessee. She was caught, and General Hood sentenced her to hang. She escaped the noose, however, when Union troops—using information Pauline had provided—rushed in and saved the day.

Belle Boyd probably was the most notorious Southern spy, and she was proud of it. She was, if you will, a celebrated spy, which is cer-tainly any oxymoron. Her career began when she was seventeen. She killed a Federal soldier who tried to remove a Confederate flag she flew over her home in Martinsburg. She flirted, cajoled, and wangled information from Union troops, then passed messages on to Stonewall Jackson. Once, she even eavesdropped on a Federal council of war held in the army's Front Royal, Virginia, headquarters. At least twice she was jailed—like Rose Greenhow, in the Old Capitol Prison—and twice paroled.

Belle Boyd collected "trophies," brass buttons she had been given or had taken from Union officers she seduced into providing her with information. All of this "without being beautiful," a New York *Tribune* correspondent wrote, adding, "she is very attractive. Is quite tall, has a superb figure, and intellectual face, and [dresses] with much taste." Looking at her picture, it's easy to agree; she had an angular face (maybe that's what was meant by "intellectual"), a long nose, and buck teeth.

But she knew how to flirt and she did it well and often. Some Northern newspapers, however, claimed she took it a step farther, calling her "an accomplished prostitute."

Once, while riding with two Confederate officers not far from Union lines, Belle's horse bolted. The two uniformed Rebels knew they'd be shot by Federal pickets if they tried to help her. Belle, however, made it safely to Union lines, where a Union soldier stopped her horse. He and a companion even offered to escort Belle Boyd back to Confederate lines, and off they went, Belle Boyd and two unsuspecting Union soldiers as escorts. One of the Federals started complaining about "cowardly rebels." When they reached Confederate lines, she announced, "Here are two prisoners that I have brought you." And here, she said to the Yankees, "are two of the 'cowardly rebels.'" The Confederates were so embarrassed by it all they set the two unsuspecting Yankees free.

Early in 1862, she was in Front Royal, Virginia, but wanted to go home to Martinsburg. She applied for and was given a pass by the Union army commanding troops at Front Royal. Belle boarded a train, but before it even left the station, a Federal officer marched in and said he had a warrant for her arrest. Off the Martinsburg train, and onto one headed for Baltimore, Belle Boyd was under arrest. She spent the entire trip waving a Confederate flag out the window.

In Baltimore, she was jailed. More or less. The army didn't have any idea what to do with her, so they put her in a hotel. A week later she was put back on the train for Martinsburg but kept under surveillance. When she asked for a pass to go through the lines to Richmond, the Union army's provost martial in Martinsburg was happy to get rid of her. On the train for Richmond, she talked with a New York *Tribune* reporter, the same one who said she had an "intellectual face."

> [S]he pleads guilty to nearly all the charges made against her, as far as they refer to conveying information to the enemy, carrying letters and parcels from rebels within our lines to those without, and performing acts of heroic daring worthy of the days of the Revolution.

She informed on the Union for Gen. Richard Taylor, for Stonewall Jackson, for anyone who would listen to her. And apparently what she wrote in her autobiography, *Belle Boyd in Camp and Prison,* was true. How important the information was that she passed on is questionable, but there's no doubt she did pretty much what she claimed to do.

Once, when she was captured and jailed in Washington, prison superintendent William Wood asked if there was anything he could do to make her "stay" more comfortable. She asked for a rocking chair and wood for the fireplace. It was the middle of summer, but she said the fire would make her more comfortable. She got both chair and fire. She even got a husband, or at least a boyfriend, another Confederate prisoner named McVay whom she agreed to marry. They threw notes into each other's cells.

Belle Boyd never was brought to trial. Instead, she was paroled to Richmond. Apparently, she had spent too much time in jail singing songs of the South, and her keepers wanted to get rid of her.

Either on a mission for the Confederacy or a mission she made up for herself, Belle Boyd left on a trip to Europe. She didn't get very far. The blockade runner she was on was captured by the Union navy off Wilmington, and Belle was paroled to the South. Her engagement to Lieutenant McVay didn't stop her from flirting with a Union sailor while onboard the Federal vessel. The sailor, Samuel Hardinge (or Harding or Hardings), helped her win her freedom. Belle had not stayed in the South, as ordered by her parole; she had run to Canada, then to England. In August 1864, Belle and Hardinge were married in England, where he'd been discharged from the U.S. Navy. A short while later, Hardinge returned to America. He died in New York, never to see Belle again.

Not much is known about Hardinge. Was his discharge from the navy voluntary or forced? When he died, it was in a New York prison, but it's not known why he was there.

That left Belle, still in England, broke, and with an infant daughter. So she wrote her autobiography, but it didn't bring in anywhere near as much money as she had hoped. In 1866 she turned to the stage, first in Manchester, England, then in America. She toured in a play called *The Honeymoon*, appearing in New York, Ohio, and Texas. She married twice more, first to an English military man. It was an unhappy marriage, but happy or not, they moved to Stockton, California. She was pregnant with her second child when, as she later wrote, "My health was failing. . . . Just previous to the birth of my little son my mind gave way and my child was born in the asylum for the insane. . . . My boy was buried there."

Belle recovered and later gave birth to two other daughters, but she and her husband never reconciled completely. In 1884 she divorced him and, six weeks later, married again. Husband number three was Nat High, an actor seventeen years younger than Belle. Nat High gave her the incentive to resume her stage career. This time it was a one-woman show in which she lectured and told of her life as a spy: *The Cleopatra of the Secession*. But America's Civil War had been over for more than two decades, and there wasn't much interest in her. Belle Boyd died of a heart attack in Wisconsin. It was Monday, June 11, 1900; she was fifty-six, ten years older than Rose O'Neal Greenhow was when she had died.

Was she a Cleopatra or just a spy? Was she a flirt or a prostitute?

Her hometown was no longer in Virginia; the western counties had "seceded" from Virginia in 1863 to form West-by-God-Virginia. Her hometown no longer wanted Belle, so she's buried in Evansville, Wisconsin, a small town in the tourist area known as "the Dells." Four members of the Grand Army of the Republic—ex-Union soldiers—lowered her into her grave. Southern through and through, Belle

Boyd was laid to rest in Northern soil. Finally, in 1919, a Confederate veteran donated a tombstone for the celebrated spy. It reads:

BELLE BOYD
CONFEDERATE SPY
BORN IN VIRGINIA, DIED IN WISCONSIN
ERECTED BY A COMRADE

Allan Pinkerton, who headed a Chicago private detective agency and
who went on to help form the beginnings of the U.S. Secret Service,
had a special way of determining if a woman had the ability to be a
spy. He used phrenology, the "science" of reading the bumps on an
individual's head.

There is, however, no information on whether he checked the
bumps on the head of one Elizabeth Van Lew of Richmond. Miss
Lizzie, as she was sometimes known, was a small, birdlike, undoubtedly eccentric woman who lived near Libby Prison. Her father, John
Van Lew, was a prominent Richmond merchant when he died in
1843. He'd been well known among Richmond society, entertaining
such personages as Chief Justice John Marshall.

Edgar Allan Poe is said to have read his poem "The Raven" during a party at the Van Lew Mansion. Not far from Libby Prison, the
Van Lew home was demolished in 1911.

Elizabeth Van Lew was born in the South but educated in the
North, and upon her father's death immediately freed their slaves,
including Mary Elizabeth Van Lew (slaves generally were given the
name of their owners). Miss Lizzie sent Mary Elizabeth to Philadelphia to be educated and later brought her back to Richmond. In a
service held in Richmond's St. John's Church, the former slave married Wilson Bowzer on April 16, 1861, four days after the firing on
Fort Sumter. The St. John's congregation was white, but Elizabeth
Van Lew had enough political pull, you might say, to have several of
her slaves and former slaves married in the church. Almost as soon
as he married Mary Elizabeth, Wilson Bowzer left town, heading for
Philadelphia. After the war, Mary Elizabeth and her father, Nelson,
joined Wilson in Pennsylvania.

Elizabeth Van Lew openly proclaimed her allegiance to the Union,
sort of obfuscation of her spying by open admission of her loyalties;

she became known as "Crazy Bet." She and her mother sneaked messages in and out of Libby, sometimes using false-bottom plates,
sometimes in a pinprick code on pages of books.

Elizabeth's mother, Eliza, died in 1875, and the loss took a lot out
of Crazy Bet. With the help of her niece, Elizabeth Louisa Klapp, Miss
Lizzie continued to hound both the state and city governments. In
many ways she was way ahead of her time. For example, she questioned why women property owners had to pay taxes but weren't allowed to vote.

To the outside world, Mary Elizabeth Bowzer still appeared to be
a slave and Miss Lizzie "rented" her to, of all places, the Confederate White House. Die-hard slaveholders apparently believed slaves either were too dumb or too dedicated even to think of such things as
spying on their beloved white masters. Such slaveholders generally
didn't bother keeping ideas or events to themselves, certainly not
written material. After all, most blacks couldn't read or write. Mary
Elizabeth Bowzer could read, and she picked up a lot of information
about the Confederacy while working inside Jefferson Davis's own
home. She slipped information out of the Confederate White House
and over to Miss Lizzie, who slipped them to the Union army. During this period, the Davis's house caught fire; it's believed Mary Elizabeth was responsible.

When it came time for Jefferson and Varina Davis to evacuate Richmond, they discovered someone, very likely Mary Elizabeth Bowzer,
had stolen the Confederate First Lady's horse and saddle, hoping to
keep Mrs. Davis a prisoner in the town when the Yankees took over.
A descendant, McEva Bowzer, says Mary Elizabeth wrote a diary about
her times as a spy. The book, however, is now lost and only rumors
and memories are left.[1]

The years of working undercover for the Union cost Elizabeth Van
Lew her fortune, and soon she was destitute. She tried to sell her
Richmond mansion, but there were no takers; the people of Richmond held a grudge against her. It was only due to funds given her
by Union Gen. George Sharpe, along with help from families of Federal soldiers she aided, that she survived. Her neighbors shunned
her, but after Ulysses S. Grant was elected president, he made Elizabeth Van Lew Richmond's postmistress. The Federal government

paid Crazy Bet fifteen thousand dollars for services she and her mother performed while aiding the Union during the war.

She died in 1900 at the age of eighty-eight, but there were few mourners. For years, her grave lay unmarked in Richmond's Shockoe Hill Cemetery. It wasn't until residents of Boston took up a collection that a headstone was placed over the Union's chief source of information in Richmond during the Civil War. The plaque reads:

She risked everything that is dear to man—friends, fortune, comfort, health, life itself, all for one absorbing desire of her heart—that slavery might be abolished and the Union preserved.

Sara Emma Edmonds was both spy and soldier. Born in Canada, she ran away from home to avoid marrying a man she didn't like. Wearing men's clothing, she became Franklin Thompson, and when the war came to America, "Frank" enlisted. During McClellan's Virginia Peninsula Campaign, Emma, or Frank, began spying; she shaved her head, tinted her skin black, wore a wig, and pretended to be a runaway *male* slave. She learned about the Rebel defenses, was even given a gun and put on picket duty. She slipped back to the Federal side, taking all the information *she* had gained while pretending to be a *he* back to the Union troops.

Later, Sara (whom everyone still thought of as Frank) dressed as a *woman* in order to spy, taking on the identity of an Irish baker named Bridget and crossing through the Confederate lines. Wandering about in a rainstorm, she discovered an injured Rebel officer and sat up all night with him; he asked her, should he not live, to give his pocketwatch to a Confederate friend and tell him where the officer was. The next day the man was dead, and true to her word, Sara or Bridget took his watch to the Confederate commander in the area, then led a burial party back to the dead Rebel. While the Rebels set about moving the dead soldier, Sara slipped away, went back across the lines, and turned over information about Confederate defenses; however, she did not mention the burial party gone to retrieve that dead Rebel officer. So well and so often did Sara Emma Edmonds change her identity, it wasn't until twenty-five years later that it was known for certain that Franklin Thompson was really a woman.

* * *

It didn't take nearly that long to learn about Lt. Harry T. Buford. Buford fought in the First Battle of Manassas, a young, independent officer, attached to no specific unit. But Lieutenant Buford really was a woman, Cuban-born, New Orleans–reared Loreta Janeta Valazquez. She later told her own story, one that had doubters then and has a whole new set of disbelievers today. She claimed she wore a fake beard to cover her smooth chin; a wire frame beneath her uniform made her appear more masculine. She paid for her own supplies and equipment and carried with her a black servant named Bob. Apparently, Bob was unaware that his master was really a mistress in disguise. At Manassas, Valazquez claimed, masquerading as Buford allowed her to act as a courier for Confederate Gen. Bernard Bee, he who gave Thomas J. Jackson the nickname "Stonewall" that same day.

Still acting as Lieutenant Buford, Valazquez borrowed women's clothing from a slave and turned spy, which put her in Sara Edmonds's class, a woman pretending to be a man pretending to be a woman. According to Valazquez, she made her way to Washington and mingled with society, where she met Abraham Lincoln and had no trouble moving around town. In fact, she later reported, it was disconcertingly easy to pry information from Union officers.

She preferred fighting to spying and returned to the guise of Lieutenant Buford; she and Bob went to Tennessee but avoided capture in the Union victory at Fort Donelson. She also claimed to have fought at the Battle of Shiloh with the 11th Louisiana where, while helping to bury the dead, her right arm was wounded by shrapnel. When a doctor examined her, "I perceived by the puzzled expression that passed over his face," she wrote, that "he was beginning to suspect something." Still, he said nothing, but patched her up and sent her on her way.

She headed for Richmond, where "some lynx-eyed detective was not long in noting certain feminine ways I had." Her true sex discovered, Loreta was thrown into Richmond's Castle Thunder Prison. The prison superintendent's wife befriended Valazquez, and, thanks to Provost Marshal General John Winder of Richmond, she again got her wish to serve the South. At least she said so in her memoirs. She claimed Winder made her a spy, sending her off dressed again as Lieutenant Buford with dispatches. The "dispatches," however, were only blank sheets of paper and a letter that explained Winder was testing her loyalty. Lieutenant Buford proved her value and returned to Richmond, not to fight, as she had hoped, but to spy—still as a man.

Others fought and others spied. Jennie Hodgers dressed and served under the name of Albert J. J. Cashier, keeping her secret for sixty years.

Keith Blaylock didn't want to fight, but when the Confederacy drafted him, he went along, as did his wife, Malinda, who enlisted as "Sam" Blaylock. After Keith rubbed poison ivy over his body, the doctors released him, saying he wasn't fit for duty. "Sam" then went to the unit commander, admitted being Malinda, and went home to North Carolina with Keith.

Mary Walker didn't spy, and she didn't fight. Rather, she saved lives. She was the first woman doctor in the U.S. Army. After the war, she was given the U.S. Congressional Medal of Honor. But in 1919, when Congress decided too many Medals of Honor had been awarded, they revoked Mary's. She refused to give it up and was buried with it in her hand. In 1977, not only was her medal reinstated, but the U.S. Post Office issued a stamp honoring Dr. Mary Walker.

The actions of these women were not "above and beyond the call of duty," at least not to them. To Belle Boyd and Elizabeth Van Lew, to Mary Walker, Rose Greenhow, Pauline Cushman, Loreta Janeta Valazquez, and many others, fighting and spying for their beliefs was the only thing they *could* do. To them, fighting battles and carrying information across enemy lines offered proof enough of their right to believe as they chose and to act as they believed right.

CHAPTER NINETEEN

To Err Is Common:
Bungling Through War

I am too much out of temper to write about the defeat, or I would give you an account of mismanagement and stupidity that would make you grieve for the course intrusted to such heads.

—Gen. Theophilus Hunter Holmes, C.S.A.
October 18, 1862

Eighteen-sixty-four was about as bloody as any other year in history. The new Union commander in the east, Ulysses S. Grant, lost 41 percent of his original strength, fifty thousand troops in all. Robert E. Lee lost fewer men, a total of thirty-two thousand, but since he had fewer to start with, the 46 percent of the Army of Northern Virginia lost in May could never be replaced.

First there was the Battle of the Wilderness, the brush thick and the firing even thicker. Rifle and cannon sparks set trees and leaves on fire. You really couldn't call the Battle of the Wilderness a battle between armies, not as such. It was just each man fighting by himself in individual, often hand-to-hand, combat. Two days later the two sides came together again at Spotsylvania and then once more at the North Anna River.

On May 11, 1864, at Yellow Tavern, not far from Richmond, Confederate cavalry chief Jeb Stuart was killed. He had graduated thirteenth in his West Point class of forty-six in 1854. While a student at the Point, he picked up the nickname "Beaut" or "Beauty," a satirical reversal of how many thought him to be, for he was decidedly not handsome—a large, prominent nose and wide nostrils, a florid face and broad forehead.

James Ewell Brown "Jeb" Stuart was fireplug stubby, about five feet nine inches tall, massive, and nearly square. He was vain and wore a thick, curled mustache; a long, heavy beard covered a weak, child-like chin. By the Peninsula Campaign, he'd taken to wearing a plume in his hat in honor of his professed ancestry, the Royal Stuart line to the Scottish throne. Stuart added a gold-trimmed sash and a flowing cape. Splendidly dressed and sitting atop a horse, no one re-membered he was fireplug short. He seemed handsome and mag-nificent and dashing; he was what every other Southerner believed every Rebel looked and acted like. He agreed and, to add to his self-portrait, insisted he be accompanied everywhere by a banjo-playing corporal named Sam Sweeney (once, as a prewar blackface minstrel, Sweeney even played for Britain's Queen Victoria), a servant named "Mullato Bob" playing the bones, and a group of singers, dancers, and fiddlers.

One night when some of his troops were missing, laughing it up in a Richmond theatre, Stuart rode his horse inside, rounded up his boys, and set them back to work. Now he was gone, his black-plumed hat resting on his flag-draped casket as he was carried to Rich-mond's Hollywood Cemetery.

He was as brave as he was vain, as courageous as he was flamboy-ant. In other words, he made the almost perfect cavalry leader.

In the Battle of Cold Harbor on June 3, more than seven thousand troops died in the first seven minutes. Ulysses S. Grant said Cold Har-bor was the only battle he regretted.

And then came July 30.

For a while things had settled down around Richmond, but not so in the lines around Petersburg. Or, rather, *under* the lines. The Union army was digging a tunnel under Confederate lines. It would turn out to be a fiasco, albeit a deadly and exciting one.

Coal miners made up much of the 48th Pennsylvania. Peacetime mining engineer turned soldier Col. Henry Pleasants heard some of his men grousing that "we could blow that damn fort out of existence if we could run a mine shaft under it." So, Pleasants took the idea to heart and put his regiment to work doing just that. They would tun-nel under the Rebel redoubt only 150 yards away, set explosives, and when the blast went off, storm the Southern forces.

General George Meade didn't think much of the idea, but didn't stop Pleasants. The Pennsylvania miners planned to dig a shaft 511 feet long under the Rebel lines with several separate tunnels going off in different directions. They'd rig a ventilation shaft to create a draft, thereby carrying fresh air into the tunnel. When everything was ready, they'd load the tunnel with four tons of gunpowder.

By mid-July, Southern miners had done a piece of work themselves. Rebel troops knew what was going on, or at least had a pretty good idea what it was. What they didn't know was when it would happen. Confederate troops set to work digging, tunneling, probing for the Union project. They knew it was around somewhere. They heard Yankee picks and shovels but couldn't break through to the enemy's side.

In the meantime, they began their own tunnel. They called it "Mahone's Mine" and hoped it would take them under the Union's Fort Sedgewick. Sometimes Union and Rebel tunnels were only feet apart.

The North scheduled its big event for dawn on Saturday, July 30. Just before the fuse was lit, however, General Meade ordered a change in the order of battle; Maj. Gen. Ambrose Burnside was to send in his white divisions first, apparently because Meade lacked confidence in his inexperienced black troops. General Grant agreed to the change. He later claimed Meade believed if the tunnel project went wrong, "it would then be said, and very properly, that we were shoving these people (the black troops) ahead to get killed because we did not care anything about them." That couldn't be said if the Union put white troops in front.

The change in plans demoralized troops of both races. It didn't help that Meade named as leader of the assault thirty-two-year-old Gen. James Hewitt Ledlie, who wouldn't go near the place on the day it was scheduled to be exploded. He was snugly tucked away in a bombproof shelter four hundred yards behind the lines. To make it even easier on himself, he borrowed a bottle of rum from the brigade surgeon and proceeded to get drunk. His may have been the best idea of all.

Dawn, that July Saturday, literally came up like thunder. The gunpowder blew a hole 170 feet long, 60 feet wide, and 30 feet deep. It created the *Crater*. More than 275 Confederates were buried instantly, an entire Rebel regiment and artillery battalion. And just as quickly, Confederate forces around the *Crater* ran off.

Instead of charging around the blasted-out hole, Union forces ran into the *Crater*. Ran in and stopped. It was like nothing they had ever seen. They looked around in amazement. Two more Yankee divisions followed them into the *Crater*. They, too, stopped and looked around, equally amazed. It didn't help matters that, in planning the affair, no one thought to include ladders with the onrushing troops. Once they got in, they had to climb out, hand over dirt daub, all the time ducking Confederate gunfire, holding on to their rifles, fighting back, and generally being scared as hell.

While the amazed Federals stopped to look around, the confused Rebels stopped running and headed back for the edge of the *Crater*. They began shooting the Federals like fish in a barrel. The black soldiers Burnside had wanted to use but whom Meade pulled out to avoid political repercussions finally had to be sent in to save the Union troops who had been floundering around.

In the end, the *Crater* remained a no-man's land. In the end, also, fifteen hundred Confederates were lost, at least thirty-five hundred Federals were killed or wounded, fifteen hundred Union troops were taken prisoner, and twenty U.S. flags were captured by the South.

Grant called it a "stupendous failure, the saddest affair I have ever witnessed in the war."

The Petersburg *Dispatch* called the attempt to undermine Confederate defenses "Grant's imitation earthquake," and said it was no "great shakes after all." The Richmond *Whig* said about all the explosion did was terrify "all the babies and frightened a few of the old ladies of Petersburg." Things on the front, the *Whig* said, "go on again as usual."·

The Battle of the *Crater* also marked a change in attitude among Southern troops, at least partially because black troops had been used against them. Phoebe Yates Pember, the matron of Chimborazo Hospital in Richmond, wrote that until the *Crater*, the Confederate soldiers she treated had not been bitter toward their Northern counterparts. They accepted the fighting, she believed, and she quoted her patients as simply saying, "They fit us, we fit them."

But the white Rebels felt the North's use of black troops was a "mean trick," and that changed the way her hospitalized charges looked. "Eyes gleamed," she wrote, "and teeth clenched as they showed me the locks of their muskets, to which the blood and hair still clung, when, after firing, without waiting to reload, they had clenched the barrels and fought hand to hand."

The South's biggest blunder came less than a year later, on April 2, 1865, a Sunday. Confederate diarist John Beauchamp Jones wrote that "a soft haze rested over the city. No sound disturbed the stillness of the Sabbath morn."

Confederate President Jefferson Davis was in St. Paul's Episcopal Church, listening as the Rev. Charles Minnegerode intoned, in his thick, thundering German accent, "The Lord is in His Holy temple. Let all the earth keep silence before Him." Minnegerode paused as the church sexton passed a telegram to Davis.

The Union had broken through Robert E. Lee's ranks. Richmond was lost.

At once, Davis stood up and left the church; he walked down Ninth Street to his office at the war department. A witness said an "ominous fear fell upon all hearts," and then other church-goers were summoned to leave. Finally, Reverend Minnegerode himself was called to the vestry room. The city was to be evacuated, he was told. When the priest returned to the chancel, he found the congregation had beaten him to the door; they were on their way out. He tried stopping them but had little success. Some returned to take communion, but Reverend Minnegerode could no more stop his congregation from leaving St. Paul's than General Lee could stop the Union forces from pushing through his lines.

By midday, Richmond's banks were open, their customers retrieving all of their valuables but leaving behind the now worthless Confederate money and bonds. Chimborazo Hospital Matron Phoebe Yates Pember watched "from the hill on which my hospital was built." Later, she wrote,

I walked through my wards and found them comparatively empty. Every man who could crawl had tried to escape a Northern prison. Beds in which Paralyzed, rheumatic, and helpless patients had laid

for months were empty. The miracles of the New Testament had been re-enacted. The lame, the halt, and the blind had been cured.

Those who were compelled to remain were almost wild at being left in what would be the enemy's lines the next day; for in many instances they had been exchanged prisoners only a short time before. I gave all the comfort I could, and with some difficulty their supper also, for my detailed nurses had gone with General Lee's army, and my black cooks had deserted.[1]

What happened to other patients, especially those caught in the middle of the fire, isn't certain.

The day Richmond fell it housed more than 200,000 people, well above the prewar 39,910 counted in the 1860 census. They all seemed to be trying to leave at once. Refugees and deserters vied for use of city streets already clogged with military movement.

Then came the South's biggest blunder. They destroyed their own capital city. It wasn't Union forces that burned Richmond; it was the Confederacy itself.

When the Confederate government abandoned Richmond, it wanted nothing left behind that the Yankees could use. Despite locals' pleas, Rebel troops under Gen. Richard S. Ewell set fire to tobacco warehouses. In a postwar report to Robert E. Lee, Ewell denied the charge. He claimed it was rioters, not his troops, who nearly destroyed Richmond. The evidence, however, is against him.

Phoebe Pember saw "warehouses and tobacco manufactories fired, communicating the flames to the adjacent houses and shops, and soon Main Street was ablaze."[2] Ten thousand hogshead of tobacco were on fire.

A strong wind sprang up and burning fragments of tobacco blew toward the city's business district. Confederate warships anchored in the James were torched and bombed, including the still unfinished CSS *Virginia II* and several other ironclads. To the north, the army's arsenal also exploded. Shells flew high into the smoke-filled air; red-hot metal rained down and started more fires.

Stragglers and scavengers roamed the city, robbing and sacking stores and homes. They carried with them their spoils from pillaged store to plundered home—paintings, chairs, household goods. An elderly woman rolled a horsehair-covered sofa along the street on its castors. Down Broad Street the looters went, to Central Station, but the last train had left them behind.

The last remnants of Confederate Gen. Joseph B. Kershaw's brigade was guarding the lines east of Richmond but left and went clattering through the city, heading south to join Lee on the road to Appomattox. They fought through streaming crowds trying to leave the burning city and finally reached Mayo's Bridge. The rear guard galloped over the bridge, and Gen. Martin W. Gary shouted, "All over, good-bye; blow her to hell." Tar-filled barrels had been placed under the bridge, and following General Gary's orders Col. Clement Sulivane signaled his men. Engineers put those tar-filled barrels to the torch; flames reached for the already rose-pink skies, and fire from the two railroad bridges burned high into the night.

The night sky that had been a warm pink, turned red hot.

Sparks flew, flames racked the ten-story-high Gallegro Flour Mill, and still the fire spread from Seventh to Fifteenth Street, Main to the James. "The old war-scarred city seemed to prefer annihilation to conquest," one retreating Rebel said.

Ships of the Confederate navy, including the *Patrick Henry*, used as a naval academy, were destroyed when sparks ignited gunpowder. As was the yet unfinished CSS *Virginia II* at Rocketts Landing.

Almost as soon as Confederate forces left the city, the people began tearing Richmond apart. Refugees and deserters, spies and criminals, gamblers and speculators—all who had only recently strayed into the city—roamed the abandoned city's streets. The guards at the state penitentiary ran off, and the prisoners broke loose to steal what they could and destroy what they couldn't take with them. It seemed the whole city was running around confused, not knowing whether to evacuate, to put up a defense, to give up, to plunder, to burn, or to hide. They did some of each.

Crowds gathered outside government warehouses, raiding stores of food and whiskey, the latter poured into the streets, with women and children dipping rags to drink, others kneeling to lap at the flowing liquor.

All that is left today of the *Crater* in Petersburg is a series of rolling mounds, all covered with grass now. Peaceful. All that the big explosion did was to kill more men, North and South; the lines of trenches remained the same. The blunder lay in an ill-placed, poorly planned, poorly executed scheme.

Between seven hundred and eight hundred buildings were destroyed by Confederate troops in fires they set as they left the Confederate capital: banks, hotels, government offices, private homes. Everywhere, there was desolation. Burning Richmond was worse than a blunder, it was a crime. Richmond need not have been destroyed. The North didn't want to level the city, and burning warehouses full of tobacco harmed Southerners more than it did the Federal army.

But then, as Robert Burns wrote: "Oh, would some power the giftie give us/ to see ourselves as others see us! It would from many a blunder free us."

CHAPTER TWENTY

Battlefield Medicine:
Malpractice Makes Imperfect

Poor George was a good boy and an excellent soldier. He told the boys when shot he was sorry to lose his leg but was grateful his life was spared. And told the Surgeon after the Second amputation he knew he was bound to die and if his leg had been properly taken off at the first he would have lived.

—Pvt. Harry Lewis
July 20, 1862[1]

The timing of the Civil War was all off. There is never a *good* time for a war, but America's Civil War came along at a time when the art of killing far outstripped the art of healing.

Of the approximately 3,000,000 soldiers and sailors who fought in the war, more than 600,000 died, about 360,000 for the North and another 258,000 for the South. Of that total, less than one-third, about 200,000, were either killed outright or died of wounds in battle. The other two-thirds died of disease. It was infection that took their lives, not bullets or cannonballs. Usually, it was due to the physicians' almost total lack of knowledge about infection.

It was not unusual to see a surgeon go from one patient to another without even so much as wiping his hands, not to mention washing and sterilizing himself and/or his instruments. Surgeons of the day praised what they called "laudable pus," saying it was a good sign. They even bragged about how fast they could amputate a man's arm or leg. Speed was important when they lacked morphine or chloroform—or chose not to use them.

The Union's medical inspector general believed "the smart [pain] of the knife [was] a powerful stimulant." Many surgeons agreed and fell back on Samuel Gross's *Manual of Military Surgery* as a how-to text.

In it, Gross said that anesthesia should be used only in extremely serious cases, not especially for amputation. "It is astounding," Gross wrote, "what little suffering the patient generally experiences . . . even from a severe wound or operation." Surgeons felt that using anesthesia led to complications. Union army surgeon Frank Hamilton had his own idea. He claimed anesthesia caused gangrene.

Fortunately, not everyone agreed. Confederate surgeon Edward Warren said, "The discovery of the anaesthetic effects of chloroform is the great surgical achievement of the age." He and some other surgeons welcomed the booty from one of Stonewall Jackson's Shenandoah Valley raids: fifteen thousand cases of chloroform.

The South frequently had little chloroform or any other medicine, especially during the beginning of the war; all pharmaceutical companies were located in the North. Confederate physicians (notice, at no time do I use the word *healers*) relied on herbs, plants, and what we now refer to as home remedies. Which may have been to the patients' benefit, considering what some Union physicians and surgeons used.

Civil War physicians also believed in the medicinal use of arsenic and strychnine. They even used something called calomel to stop diarrhea. Arsenic and strychnine we now know are poisons. As is calomel, which is mercury. Union Surgeon General Dr. William A. Hammond tried to prevent the use of calomel and was forced out of the army by physicians who believed in the drug's alleged curative powers.

Hammond also got into trouble over irregularities in the army's liquor contracts. He was taken before a court-martial and dismissed from service in 1864. Fifteen years later his case was reviewed; he was restored to the rank of brigadier general and put on the retired list. After the war he practiced in New York and studied diseases of the nervous system.

As in every war, Civil War soldiers often criticized their medical corps. For instance, a Rebel soldier from Alabama wrote home, saying "I believe the Doctors kill more than they cour (sic)," adding "doctors haint Got half Sence." On August 9, 1862, Pvt. J. W. Love of North Carolina was stationed outside Petersburg when he wrote home:

T. G. Freman is Ded and they is Several mor that is Dangerous with
the feever. they have been 11 Died with the fever in Co A since we left
kinston [North Carolina] and 2 died that was wounded so you now
See that these Big Battles is not as Bad as the fever.

Another Confederate said that in every regiment, "there were not less than a dozen doctors from whom our men had as much to fear as from their Northern enemies." It was bad enough, troops believed, to be killed on the battlefield. They liked even less the probability that if wounded, the physicians' and surgeons' "cure" would kill more than it healed. During a two-month period in 1862, surgeons in Richmond performed 580 amputations; 245 of them ended in death. It is said that more arms and legs were amputated during the Civil War than in any other war in American history.

Captain Alfred Bell of the 39th North Carolina Regiment blamed Abraham Lincoln for the illnesses afflicting his men. The Union president, Bell believed, "ought to burn in a hell ten thousand times hotter than fier (sic)." In a letter to his wife, Bell claimed that six out of every seven men in his regiment were ill.

His men weren't the only ones. E. J. Ellis was a Rebel officer from Louisiana. From his camp near Tupelo, Mississippi, he wrote his brother Stephan, "Look at our company—21 have died of disease, 18 have become so unhealthy as to be discharged, and only four have been killed in battle."

North and South, alcohol was the most commonly used drug, not as an antiseptic, since doctors knew nothing of sepsis, but as whiskey. It was often given to wounded soldiers taken to field stations after a battle. The idea was to prevent shock. It wasn't exactly successful, but it was a very popular remedy among the troops.

There were, of course, other remedies. In 1861, a committee of New York City hospital physicians prepared a *Manual of Directions* for use in Union army hospitals. It offered *Drinks for the sick* (toast water, apple tea, rice water, and plain lemonade), proposed *Articles of diet for the sick* (egg brandy, milk punch, sago posset, and oatmeal gruel), and suggested *External applications* (water and vapor baths, poultices). There was even something known as "evaporating lotions."

Cold water, spirit and water, equal parts; a solution of muriate of
ammonia, a dram to the pint; a solution of sugar of lead and opium,

*a half dram of each to the pint of hot water, are frequently ordered
as lotions. They are to be applied by means of a single layer of muslin
or linen, which is to be kept constantly moist with the lotion.*

The manual suggested using blisters, leeches, and enemas, the last
said to be "injections . . . intended to be either purgative, sedative,
or nutritious." It prescribed opium with no hesitation but suggested,
in the making of wine whey (goat's milk and wine), that in this "and
all other articles containing alcoholic stimulants, specific directions
should be obtained from the medical attendant, as to the proportion of wine or spirits to be used. . . ."

The many illnesses didn't just happen. One of the problems was
the caliber of men recruited. As the war began, the Confederacy took
just about anyone who had two feet. It wasn't until the fall of 1862
that Rebel authorities began giving physical exams prior to enlistment. When they finally began examining volunteers, the examination didn't do much as far as weeding out the sick. The army believed
anyone who could stand up to active work as a civilian could stand
up to life in the military. It didn't matter if the volunteer were partially deaf, didn't have all ten fingers, and might have only one eye.
Obviously the doctors didn't enforce the regulation calling for physical examination; otherwise, how could women join the army and not
have their secrets exposed?

Frank Richardson wrote his mother in early October of 1862.

*[The new recruits] are like little children, never away from home be-
fore, can't take care of themselves, and need someone to force them
to wash themselves and put on clean clothing, when they start out
to march and load themselves with more baggage than two men
should carry. These are the men which for the most part compose our
sick and fill up our hospitals.*

Unlike their Northern opponents, Southern recruits generally were
from rural areas and had not been immunized to childhood diseases.
Like a child going into kindergarten, when they joined up, they carried with them some diseases they faced at home. In return, they took
from others diseases they weren't used to.

An inadequate diet didn't help matters either. Rebel troops very
seldom saw fresh vegetables or fruit. When they were able to find,
say, an apple or other fruit, they ate it even if it was not ripe. Their

rations likely were only half cooked, since they were overly anxious, we suppose, to eat what little they had.

Americans today tend to assume their drinking water is safe. During the Civil War they didn't even think about it. To find water, the troops dug shallow holes, which often as not were too close to their garbage dumps.

Just as their water holes were near refuse piles, so, too, were their tents likely to be too near their latrines (they called them "sinks"). Richard Waldrop was a private from Virginia when he wrote: "Dec. 3, 1863 . . . On rulling (sic) up my bed this morning I found I had been lying in—I won't say what—something though that didn't smell like milk and peaches."

When they remained in camp for any length of time, such as at Petersburg or Vicksburg, Rebel soldiers littered for all they were worth, tossing bones, apple peelings, and rinds, along with other scraps of food, into their trenches. There was no policing of their camp, in the modern military sense. An official count of the dead and dying at the South's camp near Corinth, Mississippi, showed that more Rebels died from diseases than were killed in the nearby Battle of Shiloh—and Shiloh, remember, was one of the deadliest battles of all time.

As the capital of the Confederacy, with most of the eastern military action occurring in Virginia, Richmond virtually became one large hospital, one vast complex with patients coming in and the dead going out. An estimated 60 percent of all Rebel wounded were treated in Richmond during the war. Most of them more than once. Confederate surgeon Joseph Jones estimated that every Rebel soldier was sick or wounded an average of six times during the war.

Neither side believed the war would last long. Both North and South confidently forecast victory. It was a confidence that, on the Union's side, suffered greatly in July of 1861 at the First Battle of Manassas. Northerners began to have doubts; Southerners had their beliefs reinforced. People on both sides began looking differently at the war; this thing would last longer and cost more in lives and money, than either Washington or Richmond believed.

More than one-fourth of Confederate forces at Manassas were from Virginia, and when the dead and dying began arriving in Richmond, the seriousness of it all began to take form and substance. War is not for the faint of heart.

They came by train, the first time railroads were used to evacuate large numbers of wounded soldiers. They came in growing numbers. There were so many dead, arriving so quickly in the summer heat, Richmond residents complained about the odor around the railroad depot. Grave diggers couldn't keep up with their work and left the casualties of war stacked up where they'd been unloaded from the trains. Grave diggers were pushed so hard, a Confederate surgeon later wrote, they buried the dead in mass graves, often graves so shallow that a summer shower would leave the bodies exposed. Richmond's joyous sounds of summer turned into a long funeral dirge as the slain were carried off to Hollywood and Oakwood cemeteries.

The wounded were everywhere. Warehouses, homes, and churches quickly became makeshift hospitals; no one was prepared for the thousands upon thousands who would be wounded in the months and years to come. The Confederacy built thirty-two general hospitals in Richmond during the war, and at least thirty homes and businesses were used to house the ill and wounded. Conditions in these "hospitals" were horrifying.

One of the largest of Richmond's hospitals was Winder, on the western edge of town. Ninety-eight pine buildings were constructed; it held up to forty-three hundred patients at a time. One hospital, Grant or Wayside Hospital, even advertized for patients, placing ads in Richmond newspapers:

> Sick and disabled soldiers on furlough or honorably discharged with the service, who are temporarily detained in Richmond, Va., will be comfortably provided with food, quarters and attention at the Wayside Hospital, corner of Franklin and 19th.

A twenty-eight-year-old spinster, as such "elderly" young ladies were known at the time, Sally Tompkins wanted to help the wounded. Ten days after the First Battle of Manassas, she opened at her own expense a private hospital in the downtown home of Judge John Robertson. Officially, it was known as Robertson Hospital. Unofficially, it was called "Aunt Sally's." It had a capacity of only twenty-one, but she treated those twenty-one so well that, in 1863 when the Confederate government decided to close all private hospitals and transfer the patients to the larger military facilities, Aunt Sally was allowed to continue. Allowed to continue? She was encouraged—by Jefferson Davis himself, who gave Sally Tompkins a military commission with the rank and pay of an army captain. She returned the pay but kept the rank. By the time the Union army rode into Richmond in April of 1865 and she closed her hospital's doors, Sally Tompkins had treated a total of 1,333 sick and wounded men. Only 73 died while in her care.

Chimborazo General Hospital's 150 buildings overlooked downtown Richmond. Named after a mountain in South America, Chimborazo was, at the time, the largest hospital in the world. It had its own herd of cows for milk (200 at one time), its own bakery (10,000 loaves of bread per day), its own icehouses (five of them), and even its own canal boat to ferry in the wounded—and to ferry out the dead. Chimborazo was divided into five divisions and had the capacity to care for 3,000 soldiers at one time. Over the course of the war, Chimborazo treated more than 77,800 soldiers. The next largest medical facility was the Union's Lincoln Hospital in Washington; it treated only 46,000 patients.

Chimborazo's success was due to two people, surgeon-in-chief Dr. James B. McCaw and hospital chief matron Phoebe Yates Pember. Together, they utilized sunlight and fresh air, herbal remedies and old wives' tales, to heal the wounded and stop the suffering. They did a pretty damn good job of it, too. Not only did Chimborazo have a relatively low mortality rate, the lowest of all government-run hospitals until World War II, but at the end of the war it was operating at a profit.

Except for minor illnesses or wounds, the normal hospital stay in the Civil War was six weeks. For more serious cases, including diarrhea (known as "the Virginia quick-step"), a soldier could be hospitalized for up to a year. Today's "case management" hospitals would scream bloody murder at such long stays.

Hospital food, naturally, was derided. Both Johnny Reb and Billy

Yank told of having chicken soup, or "shadow soup," as it was called, and one provided a recipe.

A chicken was provided and hung up in the sun where its shadow would strike into the kettle. A quantity of water was put into the kettle and the shadow boiled therein. Salt, pepper, and other spice were added to make it palatable, and it was served out.

Another wounded soldier complained that the food served in the hospital was so bad, "we had to 'shoo' and knock for some time before we could tell what was on our plates other than flies."

Many hospitals were nothing more than homes for contagion, with regular outbreaks of mumps, measles, pneumonia, smallpox, and other equally deadly diseases. That same Alabama soldier who said he believed doctors killed more than they cured? Well, he wrote his wife in 1862, saying "I never want to go to a horse pital again men are dying there constant."

He was right. Then, as now, sometimes a hospital is no place for the sick.

When the war began, there were only 115 doctors in the Union army's medical corps. That included one surgeon general, 30 surgeons, and 84 assistant surgeons. After Fort Sumter, 27 of these left the North and headed for the South and the Confederate forces. By the end of the Civil War, more than 13,000 doctors had served in the federal army. Thirty-two surgeons died in battle; 83 others were wounded (ten of these died later), and 281 died from various diseases. More than 3,500 physicians and surgeons served the Confederacy, including Dr. Hunter Holmes McGuire, who was Stonewall Jackson's chief surgeon. It was McGuire who, after Jackson was injured at Chancellorsville, amputated the general's left arm; Jackson, however, developed pneumonia and died two days later. After the war, Dr. McGuire resumed his private practice and went on to become the 45th president of the AMA, the American Medical Association.

For the first time, women served in the U.S. Army medical corps. It was only twelve years before the war, in 1849, that a woman graduated from an American medical school: Elizabeth Blackwell. She and her sister Emily, who was also a doctor, organized the New York Infirmary for Women and Children. When the Civil War broke out, Elizabeth Blackwell organized women's relief activities, activities that became the U.S. Sanitary Commission. It was inspired by Britain's Sanitary Commission in the Crimean War eight years earlier.

It was in the Crimean War that Florence Nightingale served as one of the world's first female nurses. Nightingale took her brigade of women nurses to the British army depot at Scutari, Turkey; she swept into the mess she found at Barrack Hospital and brought order and discipline and cleanliness. She was possibly one of the first women to be named "Florence." Until she came along Florence generally was a man's name. Apparently Ms. Nightingale's father hoped for a boy. When his soon-to-be-famous daughter arrived, he was disappointed at the baby being a girl, so he gave the infant a masculine name. She became so famous, others began calling their daughters Florence, and the practice stuck.

The U.S. Sanitary Commission was formed to do for the soldiers what the soldiers' own government could not or would not do, primarily drag the hygienic standards of army camps screaming into the nineteenth century. They set up a home in Washington for discharged soldiers, cared for the wounded, and sent various supplies to the troops in the field.

Perhaps the most famous woman doctor in the Civil War never was recognized by the U.S. Army as a doctor. Mary Edwards Walker of New York graduated from Syracuse University Medical School in 1855. The army wouldn't take her as a doctor, so for three years she served as an army nurse. In 1864 she became the first woman assistant surgeon in the U.S. Army.

Dr. Walker was also very active in the fight for women's rights, adopting the costume made famous by suffragette Amelia Bloomer. Later, Dr. Walker said to heck with it, gave up the bloomers, and wore male clothing for the rest of her life.

Another woman doctor, Esther Hill Hawks, tried to serve in the army—her husband was also an army surgeon—but the army said no. So did Dorothea Dix, the head of the army's corps of nurses.

Nurse Dix, who later became famous as a reformer of insane asylums, was the first Superintendent of Army Nurses. Dix wanted only middle-aged, "plain" women as nurses. She thought Dr. Hawks was too young and too pretty, so she said no.

Dr. Hawks spent most of the war as a schoolteacher for young black students. Finally, she was allowed to tend to wounded troops of the 54th Massachusetts, made of "men of color."

Among the most famous of Civil War nurses was Clara Barton, and she never tried to join Dorothea Dix's fledgling army nursing corps. Dix, after all, wanted only "plain-looking" women who would not distract the wounded from the job of getting well, and Clara was not "plain-looking." She also was independent, an ambitious loner who wanted to get things done by herself, traits that would have alienated her from Dix.

Let others, the "gentle, the quiet, and the plain," work in Dorothea Dix's nursing corps. Clara Barton preferred to wade hip-deep in the muck and mire of war. While Dix might make speeches about the "horde of eager women" flocking to help her, Barton kept quiet. When approached to speak out for herself and her work, Barton wrote:

> *I make gruel, not speeches.*
>
> *My business is stanching blood and feeding fainting men; my post the open field between the bullet and the hospital.[2]*

Speaking of bullets, Barton was a dead shot with a revolver. She was physically strong, at home with a hammer and saw, and could drive a wagon team. Her father once said Clara was "more boy than girl."[3] She went on to form the American Red Cross. In one of her few written remarks, Clara Barton declared:

> *If I were to speak of war, it would not be to show you the glories of conquering armies but the mischief and misery they strew in their tracks; and how, while they march on with tread of iron and plumes proudly tossing in the breeze, some one must follow closely in their steps, crouching to the earth, toiling in the rain and darkness, shelterless like themselves, with no thought of pride or glory, fame or praise, or reward; hearts breaking with pity, faces bathed in tears and hands in blood. This is the side which history never shows.[4]*

During a visit to General Hospital Number Ten for Colored troops (yes, as in everything else, "Colored troops" had separate hospitals), Barton met Susie King Taylor, a fourteen-year-old, slender girl who had been born a slave on a plantation near Savannah. It was illegal, but her master's daughter had taught her to read and write. She married a soldier in the 1st South Carolina Regiment, the first regiment of black troops formed. When the 1st South Carolina went off to war, she went off with it as a laundress.

Taylor taught many of the members of her husband's unit to read and write, and they taught her how to fire a rifle, and how to take one apart and put it back together. When the troops were wounded or taken sick, she learned how to nurse them.

Clara Barton met Susie King Taylor, and Taylor wrote in her journal that Barton was "very cordial" toward her. Together they moved from bed to bed in the hospital, with Barton touching the wounded soldiers' cheeks and soothing them with what was described as "her soft musical voice."

Susie King Taylor wasn't actually trained as a nurse. As far as can be determined, the honor of being the first black woman to be *trained* as a nurse goes to Mary Eliza Mahoney, and that wasn't until fourteen years after the Civil War was over, in 1879, that she graduated from the New England Hospital for Women and Children.

The National Archives in Washington holds journals of nurses who worked during America's Civil War. Journals about black nurses are separate from those of white nurses.

For a short time, Louisa May Alcott served as a nurse in Georgetown before going on to write the novel *Little Women.* Alcott, as did many others—male and female, soldier and nurse—kept a journal. In October 1861, she wrote "I've often longed to see a war, and now I have my wish. I long to be a man; but as I can't fight, I will content myself with working for those who can." In late 1862, things looked, or smelled, different; she frequently wrote home to her family, letters later published in her book, *Hospital Sketches.*

> *The first thing I met was a regiment of the vilest odors that ever assaulted the human nose, and took it by storm. . . . I must bear it. I did, armed with lavender water, with which I so besprinkled myself and premises, that . . . I was soon known among my patients as "the nurse with the bottle."*

Alcott's supervisor from December 1862 to January 1863 was Hannah Ropes, who was a New England–born reformer and abolitionist. She'd even taken part in the "Bloody Kansas" brawls where both sides killed nearly anyone who even appeared to disagree with them. Hannah Ropes had, as they say, friends in high places, including Senator Henry Wilson.[5] When Wilson was injured in early 1862, Hannah Ropes helped nurse him.

She worked at Union Hospital in Georgetown, then just outside Washington, D.C. After the fierce fighting at Antietam, she wrote her mother.

> *The house (hospital) has been full of sufferings of such a complicated nature as you can hardly conceive. We have been up from six in the morning till one at night, and then laid down ready to jump at a moment's warning. . . .*

She attended services at a nearby church on Sunday.

> *It was an impressive sight. The church was full of beds, the chaplain stood near the entrance between the beds, and a few singers sat on stools behind him. The nurses were fanning the sickest patients; and near one bed sat the mother of the sick man. I think they all felt the better for the services. I only wore my cap and stood among the patients. Outside, the rumble of army wagons made almost indistinct the words of the speaker. The doctor told me yesterday that I must spend four hours outdoors. Today, upon the strength of such a charge, Miss Stevenson (a fellow nurse) and I got into the horse cars and rode into Washington, up to the Capitol, winding round to the Depot. . . . I don't know how long we shall be able to hold out; we shall stay till longer stay would make us only a care to others. Our house is one of constant death now. Every day some one drops off the corruption of a torn and wounded body. It is more from the worn condition of the soldier before the wound, and the torture of exposure on the field, added to the forced removal in heavy wagons to the hospitals, than to the dangerous nature of the wounds.[6]*

Hannah Ropes died January 20, 1863, a victim of typhoid pneumonia.

Frequently, nurses North and South blamed surgeons for poor hospital conditions. Kate Cumming was born in Edinburgh, Scotland, in 1835 but moved to Alabama as a young girl. She served as a nurse in the Confederacy, and she kept a diary in which she wrote of her distrust of surgeons. "The amount of good done," she claimed, "is not near what it might be if things were better managed."

Cumming added that "Someone is to blame for this state of affairs. Many say that it is the fault of Dr. Foard, the medical director." She was used to treating the sick. Treating the wounded was something else again. "Seeing an enemy wounded and helpless," Cumming wrote, "is a different thing from seeing him in health and power. The first time I saw one in this condition, every feeling of enmity vanished at once." Things didn't get better. Eleven days later she wrote:

> A stream of blood ran from the table into a tub in which was the arm. It had been taken off at the socket, and the hand, which but a short time before grasped the musket and battled for the right, was hanging over the edge of the tub, a lifeless thing. I often wish I could become as callous as many seem to be, for there is no end to these horrors.[7]

Kate Cumming's comments about physicians ring just as true today. In the twentieth century, nurses and doctors still blame each other when things go wrong. It may be this competition that keeps both groups going strong.

Earlier we mentioned Hannah Ropes's complaint of the wounded's "forced removal in heavy wagons to the hospital." If a soldier was wounded, but didn't die in battle, he had a good chance of dying later, often on the way to a hospital.

In the 1980s, a group of Chicago aldermen wanted to buy advanced life-support ambulances, the kind with the latest telemetry equipment, the latest of everything that could go toward saving lives. The vehicles themselves would have been more utilitarian than luxurious in ride and style. Mayor Richard J. Daley spoke out against the plan. He said, if you were on your way to a hospital, perhaps to die, you'd rather go in something like one of the old, soft-riding Cadillacs. As usual, Mayor Daley got his wish; the council turned down the plan to buy modern ambulances. And a few months later, he got to ride in one of the old non–high-tech ambulances. He died in his doctor's office and was taken to a hospital in one of the old-style vehicles he had praised.

Richard J. Daley's son, Richard M., now holds the office, and when Richard M.'s wife, Maggie, was injured in a 1996 household accident, her bodyguard didn't bother with any form of ambulance when he transported her to the hospital. They rode in a limousine.

* * *

Wounded Civil War soldiers would have welcomed any ambulance other than what was available, because what was available was pretty bad. First, however, the wounded had to get to where the ambulances were kept, back at the field hospital. If they couldn't walk, they had to depend on friends to help out or to wait for a team of stretcher-bearers. Lots of luck.

Stretcher-bearers were among the worst troops in the army. Each regiment was to provide twenty-five to thirty men as stretcher-bearers. Now, who are you going to assign? Your best soldiers? Your top marksmen? Usually, those assigned to Civil War ambulance duty were the loafers, bums, and scoundrels. Musicians sometimes also were pressed into service when not off tooting some martial tune.

You've finally made your way to the field hospital a mile or so back from the battle. A doctor checks you over and decides you need to go to a regimental hospital farther away from the fighting. Call in an ambulance. Take your pick, either a two-wheel or four-wheel horse-drawn wagon.

They didn't even have that choice at the Battle of Manassas. Like many of the troops they were meant to aid, Union ambulance drivers got scared, turned around, and drove back to Washington as fast as possible. Many of the Union troops at Manassas left their weapons in the field. Ambulance drivers were worse; they left the wounded behind.

Neither the two-wheeled nor the four-wheeled variety had springs, but the smaller variety was worse. It bounced, swayed, and tossed the wounded men from side to side and up and down. Union soldiers called it the "avalanche," because they were so unstable, the wounded men tended to slide out of them. The larger, four-wheel ambulances weren't much better. Anywhere from half a dozen to ten men were squeezed in, driven over rough-and-tumble roads (if there *were* any roads nearby), and transported back to where, if they were still alive, they faced the surgeon's saw.

Nurse Hannah Ropes was right. Getting to the hospital was not, as a later ad would say, half the fun.

A Michigan soldier summed up the situation, even as he tried to make fun of the seriousness of it all.

> *I hope you will pardon me for not wrighting before but a hole through*
> *my leg caused by a minney [ball] has caused me some inconvenience*
> *as it has kept be from doing enny verry big running around. the ball*
> *went in a little above my knee and came out just under my a-s so it*
> *made a pretty big hole.*[8]

Both sides also used ships to transport the wounded. In five months,
the U.S. Hospital Steamer *Charles McDougall* transported 12,299 sick
and wounded soldiers.

But, as usual, whether they were transported by two-wheeled or
three-wheel wagon, by railroad, or by ship, the end result was the
same: too many deaths. The following is a description of a Union
field hospital written by Dr. J. R. Weist of Ohio. It is vivid. It is startling.
It is very strong stuff.

> *There are a few tents and improvised tables. . . . Wounded men are*
> *lying everywhere. What a horrible sight they present! Here the bones*
> *of a leg or an arm have been shattered like glass by a minnie ball.*
> *Here a great hole has been torn into an abdomen by a grape shot.*
> *Nearby see that blood and froth covering the chest of one choking with*
> *blood from a wound of the lungs. By his side lies this beardless boy*
> *with his right leg remaining attached to his body only by a few shreds*
> *of blackened flesh. This one's lower jaw has been carried entirely*
> *away; fragments of shell have done this cruel work. Over yonder lies*
> *an old man, oblivious to all his surroundings, his grizzly hair mat-*
> *ted with brain and blood slowly oozing from a great gaping wound*
> *in the head. Here is a bayonet wound; there a slash from a saber.*
> *Here is one bruised and mangled until the semblance of humanity*
> *is lost. . . .*
>
> *The faces of some are black with powder; others are blanched with*
> *thirst, and many suffer horrible pain; yet there are few groans or com-*
> *plaints.*[9]

A soldier's chance was one in 65 of dying in battle, one in 10 of being wounded, one in 13 of dying of disease. In any case, it wasn't
good. Bullets broke bones, wounds became infected, surgeons
transferred germs from one patient to himself to another patient,
and then often prescribed medication that killed as often as it
cured.

When one unit was being formed in the midwest, a would-be en-listee objected to the motto on the regimental flag: "Victory or Death."

"How shall it be changed?" an officer asked him.

The recruit answered: "Make it victory or pretty damned badly wounded, and I'm your huckleberry."

CHAPTER TWENTY-ONE

Villains and Scoundrels:
In All Shades of Blue and Gray

Mr. Butler gets letters almost daily, that he will be poisoned or assassinated, and that leagues are formed, sworn to accomplish it.
—Sarah H. Butler, wife of Gen. Benjamin F. Butler, U.S.A.
May 15, 1862

Jefferson Davis, the first and only president of the Confederacy, almost was the sixteenth president of the United States. Going into the Democrats' 1860 convention, Davis was a United States senator from Mississippi and a frontrunner for the presidential nomination.

After eloping with his boss's daughter, Sarah Knox Taylor, in 1835, Jefferson Davis resigned his commission in the army. He became a Mississippi planter. A decade later, in 1845, he turned to politics, winning a seat in the U.S. House of Representatives, but he resigned to rejoin the army during the Mexican War. He went back into politics after the war, first as a U.S. senator, then as secretary of war under President Franklin Pierce. It was while he was secretary that he introduced the breech-loading rifle to the army, a weapon that, when it came down to the Union against the Confederacy, would be a major factor. But he also introduced camels to the army, believing that since they worked well in the deserts of Egypt, they'd do just fine in the deserts of the American Southwest. They didn't. Among other reasons for the camels' failure, the hard-riding U.S. cavalry troops apparently didn't like the idea of riding a camel sidesaddle in the approved Arabian style; even when equipped with more-or-less regulation saddles, the camels didn't work out. A few of their descendants are still around now, and once a year residents of Arizona hold camel races.

Leaving President Pierce's cabinet, Davis returned to the senate. He was there in 1860 when fellow politicians began talking about him as a presidential candidate. In the Democratic presidential convention that year—held in, of all places, Charleston, South Carolina, at a time when secession talk in the South was turning from whispers to screams—the name of Jefferson Davis came up frequently in debate for a presidential nominee. For fifty-seven unsuccessful ballots the Democrats tried to find a consensus candidate. And each of the fifty-seven times, the man leading the cries for Jefferson Davis was a delegate from Massachusetts, Benjamin Franklin Butler.

The Democrats split three ways and the party couldn't come up with a candidate, and so they left Charleston to try again later. But Davis always remembered the man who tried so hard to get him nominated for U.S. president. Three years later, Jefferson Davis—president not of the United States but of the Confederacy—ordered Benjamin Butler hanged on the spot if he was ever caught.

Abraham Lincoln was elected president in 1860, and almost from the beginning he had several reasons—all bad—to remember Butler.

Shortly after the South fired on Fort Sumter, Massachusetts Governor John Albion Andrew, a Republican, named Democrat Benjamin Butler a brigadier general in the state militia. Not much later, when President Lincoln called for the states to send troops to put down the rebellion, Massachusetts sent Butler to Washington.

Butler became one of Abe Lincoln's first politically appointed generals. It was one of a handful Lincoln made early in the war, hoping to soothe the ruffled feelings of the opposition party. In Butler's case, it may have been one of the worst appointments Lincoln made. Benjamin Franklin Butler, it could be said, was the most incompetent of all the incompetents Lincoln appointed. His was a military career whose chief distinction seemed to be raising cain and causing trouble—before, during, and after the war.

Butler took command of the District of Annapolis, Maryland. Early in 1861, he occupied Baltimore. It was a time when Maryland was wavering between Union and Confederacy, a time when, in a completely unconstitutional move, Abraham Lincoln locked up the Maryland legislature to prevent it from voting to secede.

Even after losing Fort Sumter in South Carolina, the Union still held Fort Monroe in Virginia, and Benjamin Butler was assigned there. When Virginia slaves by the dozens crossed the battle lines looking for freedom, their owners demanded they be returned under provisions of the Fugitive Slave Act. General Butler refused, and in a completely unauthorized move, said since Virginia had seceded from the Union, she had no right to demand anything under Federal law. The runaway slaves were, Butler declared in a letter to the secretary of war, "contraband of war." From then on, runaway slaves in particular and blacks in general often were referred to as "Contrabands."

A year later, Butler took command of Union forces occupying New Orleans. The residents there didn't really resist the Union forces, mainly because they didn't want ships under admiral-to-be David Farragut bombarding the city many called the most beautiful in America. Butler, however, wasn't at all popular.

He issued an order saying no demonstration would be tolerated supporting the Confederacy or any activity in "disrespect to the Stars and Stripes." A local gambler, William Mumford, took that as a challenge. He chopped down the staff carrying the Union army's newly raised Union flag, betting the new Federal commander would do nothing about it. Mumford lost. Butler had Mumford arrested, found him guilty of treason, and promptly hanged the man. It was the first time anyone had been found guilty of treason against the United States since the War of 1812.

Not even John Brown fell into that category. His offense was treason against the Commonwealth of Virginia, not the United States.

Not long after the Mumford incident, a New Orleans lady, perhaps deliberately trying to provoke the Federals, began wearing a dress made from a Confederate flag. And, bravely if foolishly, she marched up and down the streets of New Orleans's French Quarter. Butler sent a squad of soldiers to arrest her, then sentenced her to deportation to Ship Island off Biloxi, Mississippi, in what is now the Gulf Island National Seashore. He held her there in exile for two years.

New Orleans, especially the Vieux Carré—the city's old downtown—has many beautiful old homes with iron-filigreed balconies overhanging city streets and sidewalks. Some of the local ladies took to dumping water off the balconies, using Union troops walking beneath them as targets. The ladies quite often and quite literally showered abuse on the Federal soldiers. Even David Farragut wasn't immune; one woman dumped the contents of her chamber pot onto the future admiral's head.

On May 15, General Butler issued an order that ladies who insulted Northern troops "shall be regarded and held liable to be treated as a woman of the town plying her avocation." Now, implying that a Southern lady was "a woman of the town," a woman of ill repute, was too much. Residents took to calling him "Beast" Butler. News of what became known as Butler's "Woman Order" reached Richmond, and, Southern gentleman that he was, Confederate President Davis acted immediately. He branded Benjamin Butler a felon and an outlaw, not subject to the laws of civilized nations. If Gen. Benjamin Franklin Butler was captured, the order continued, he was to be hanged on the spot.

Pottery makers in the South made clear their opinion of Butler. They painted his picture on the bottom of chamber pots.

About the same time of the New Orleans incident, "Beast" Butler took on another nickname: "Spoons." Allegedly, he amassed a small fortune by absconding with Southern silverware without the nicety of reimbursing the owners. Lincoln heard about the "spoons" charges and recalled Butler to Washington.

Political general he was, Butler gained another post, serving under Grant in the trenches outside Richmond. Butler tried to straighten the James River below the city, hoping to make it easier for Union ships to get to the Confederate capital. He ordered his troops, primarily black soldiers, to dig what came to be known as the Dutch Gap Canal. They removed more than 66,000 cubic yards of earth and set about blasting away at trees and rocks along the way. It didn't work, and the James continued to flow peacefully on its way to the Atlantic.

Benjamin Butler was unimpressive, to say the least—balding, overweight, and cross-eyed. One Union officer called him "the most shockingly disreputable general I have ever clapped my eyes upon." Butler apparently felt the same way about his superior, General Grant, saying Grant "no more comprehends his duty or his power than does a mongrel dog."

By virtue of his early political promotion, Butler was the senior-most officer Grant had in the East. So, even though he disliked the man, Grant sent Butler to capture Fort Fisher, which as guarding the port of Wilmington, North Carolina. "Beast" Butler's idea was to load an old ship with 215 tons of gunpowder and send it against the fort. About all it did was make a lot of noise. The New York *Herald* called it "a ridiculous fizzle." That did it; Grant relieved Butler of command. "Beast" Butler's, "Spoons" Butler's military career was over.

After the war, Butler was elected to Congress. The man who tried fifty-seven times to force the Democrats to take Jefferson Davis on as a presidential candidate changed parties. A year after the war ended, Butler was elected to Congress as a Republican. Except for one term, he remained in Congress until 1879, and took a leading role in the impeachment of President Andrew Johnson. Butler left Congress and, after several failed efforts, was elected governor of Mas-sachusetts. In 1884 he ran for president. Thankfully, he lost. Nine years later, Benjamin Butler died. To the North, he'd been an in-competent general and a sleazy if successful politician. To the ᵕouth, he'd been a scoundrel through and through.

Nathan Bedford Forrest was also a scoundrel, but at least he was a soldier of outstanding abilities. He was illiterate, with only about six months' formal education; his letters read as if written by someone to whom English was a second language. Forrest was older than many others when he first joined up—one month shy of his forti-eth birthday—and considerably richer. He was a wealthy, self-made businessman who grew cotton and livestock, and held real estate and slaves.

Union Pvt. William J. Mays wrote about an incident he claimed to witness. "There were two Negro women and three little children," according to Mays, "standing within twenty-five steps of me, when a rebel stepped up to them and said, 'Yes, damn you. You thought you were free, did you?' and he shot them all." The Rebel allegedly was Nathan Bedford Forrest. Private Mays said that four of the five Ne-groes Forrest attacked fell to the ground. One child remained stand-ing. In Mays' words, Forrest then "knocked it in the head with the breech of his gun."

When Bedford Forrest, as he usually was called, was only fifteen years old he was described as "six feet two, lithe and powerful of build, with steady eyes, altogether, a man of striking and commanding presence." His biographers say Bedford Forrest struggled with his emotions throughout his life; a violent, passionate man, he emphasized discipline and order.

When his native Tennessee voted to join the Confederacy, Forrest couldn't wait to volunteer. He enlisted as a private in the Tennessee Mounted Rifles along with his youngest brother, Jeffrey, and his fifteen-year-old son, William. No one, least of all Tennessee Governor Isham Harris, who knew Bedford Forrest, expected Private Forrest to remain long at that rank.

Harris authorized Forrest to raise his own cavalry regiment. Bedford Forrest did just that, paying for the regiment's equipment out of his own pocket. The governor then commissioned Forrest lieutenant colonel, and the new officer went to work confiscating enemy arms and equipment and even kidnapping a couple of Union sympathizers. Apparently, he hoped to hold the two men hostage and exchange them for two pro-Southern men Federal troops had caught.

In February of 1862, Lt. Col. Bedford Forrest commanded the cavalry unit attached to Fort Donelson, on the Cumberland River. Two of the South's most incompetent generals were in charge of Donelson, Generals John B. Floyd and Gideon J. Pillow. The newly appointed Union commander in the area, Ulysses S. Grant, surrounded Fort Donelson. With the help of a naval flotilla, it looked as if the Federals were about to win. With Grant away on the morning of the fourteenth, the Confederate troops broke. It was a success and it seemed the Rebels, about fourteen thousand of them, were on their way to freedom. But Generals Pillow and Floyd began arguing and for some reason, no one knows why, decided to return to the fort. By this time, Grant was back in charge, and it became obvious the Union would take the fort, and consequently many Southern lives, if the Rebels fought on.

Floyd and Pillow didn't want to surrender, so they handed over command to the third-ranking officer, Simon Bolivar Buckner. Floyd and Pillow escaped across the shallow river to safety.

Bedford Forrest also didn't want to be caught, so, instead of giving up, with the permission of General Buckner he took his own command and several hundred volunteers from other units and waded across an ice-covered river.

Forrest was one of the South's top cavalry officers, yet for someone who spent so much time in the saddle, he had a hard time riding. Friends say Bedford Forrest had frequent bouts with boils on his buttocks. They occurred so frequently and were so severe that often it was all he could do to mount a horse. The man who earned the nickname "Wizard of the Saddle" frequently had trouble sitting in one.

Maybe it was the boils that caused his bad temper. He had frequent arguments with fellow officers and particularly disliked Gen. Braxton Bragg. After the Battle of Chickamauga, when Forrest thought Bragg should have kept the Yankees on the run, Forrest approached his commanding officer. Forrest was only four years younger than Bragg, but Bragg, who was far better educated than his cavalry officer and far more experienced, looked at least fifteen years older. The tides of war had washed nooks and crannies into Bragg's heavily bearded face.

Not only had Bragg not followed up on his Chickamauga victory to Forrest's satisfaction, he had made several changes in his cavalry corps, changes that Forrest did not welcome. Bedford Forrest took a ten-day leave to cool off, but it didn't help. When he returned, he was still in a towering rage. Welcoming him back, Bragg extended his hand in greeting, but Forrest wouldn't touch it. Looking his superior officer in the eye, Forrest told him:

> *I have stood your meanness as long as I intend to. You have played the part of a scoundrel, and are a coward. If you were any part of a man, I would slap your jowls and force you to resent it. You may as well not issue any more orders to me, for I will not obey them. And I say to you that if you ever again try to interfere with me or cross my path, it will be at the peril of your life.*

With that, Nathan Bedford Forrest stalked off, took his cavalry to Texas, and never fought under Bragg again. Bragg chose to overlook the matter. It wasn't because he was a coward, but he knew if he pushed the issue, Jefferson Davis would have to court-martial Forrest, and Bragg thought the younger man was too important to the cause of the South.

One of the most shameful instances of the Civil War occurred on April 12, 1864, and Nathan Bedford Forrest was right in the middle of it. He was a major general by then, the only man on either side to rise from private to general. He sent 1,500 men to, as it was put, "attend to" Fort Pillow in Tennessee. More than 260 black and 295 white troops were stationed there. The Rebels attacked at dawn, driving through the pickets and surrounding the fort. Forrest arrived about mid-morning to take personal command of the attack.

Once he had his men in place, Forrest sent a surrender ultimatum to Maj. William Bradford, the fort's commanding officer. Bradford asked for an hour to decide, but Forrest say he'd give him only twenty minutes. Finally, Bradford sent back word: "I will not surrender."

With that, the Confederates swarmed into the fort. With their almost three-to-one advantage, they had little difficulty, and when it was all over, Federal losses included 231 killed and 100 seriously wounded. Another 200 or so were taken prisoner, about one-third of them black. Among the Union troops lost was Major Bradford, reportedly captured then subsequently shot "while attempting to escape."

Achilles V. Clark was a sergeant with the 20th Tennessee when he took part in the attack on Fort Pillow.

> *The poor deluded negroes would run up to our men fall upon their knees and with uplifted hands scream for mercy but they were ordered to their feet and then shot down. The white men fared but little better. I with several others tried to stop the butchery and at one time had partially succeeded but General Forrest ordered them shot down like dogs, and the carnage continued.*[1]

Six days after the attack, the Richmond *Sentinel* ran the following account as taken from the Mobile, Alabama, *Advertiser and Register:*

THE CAPTURE OF FORT PILLOW

> *Forrest attacked. . .with Chalmers' division yesterday. The garrison consisted of three hundred white and four hundred negro troops. The fort refusing to surrender was carried by storm. Forrest led Ball's brigade and Chalmers led McCulloch's. They both entered the fort*

simultaneously and an indiscriminate slaughter followed. One
hundred prisoners were taken, the balance of the garrison were slain.
The fort ran with blood. Many jumped into the river and were
drowned or shot in the water. Over one hundred thousand dollars
worth of stores were taken. Six guns were captured. The Confederate
loss was seventy-one. Lt. Col. Reid, of the 6th Mississippi was mor-
tally wounded.[2]

Other Southern accounts claimed the high loss among black troops occurred when the Union forces were fighting their way back to the river's edge, hoping to get away. Northern accounts, however, said the Federal troops surrendered as soon as the fort was overrun but were shot down in cold blood by the Rebels. The Confederates, the North claimed, shouted "No quarter! No quarter! Kill the damned niggers. Shoot them down!" A member of the Union garrison later recalled the incident.

[A]s soon as the rebels got to the top of the river bank, there com-
menced the most horrible slaughter that could possibly be conceived.
Our boys saw they were overpowered, threw down their arms and held
up, some their handkerchiefs and some their hands in token of sur-
render. . . . [N]o sooner were they seen than they were shot down, and
if one shot failed to kill them, the bayonet or revolver did not.

Some reports said the black soldiers were killed, massacred if you will, after the garrison had surrendered, that some blacks were buried alive, that tents housing Federal wounded were burned.

Almost immediately the Federal government ordered an inquest into what came to be called the Fort Pillow Massacre. Bedford Forrest denied it all.

The controversy continued after the war, when, as a civilian in 1871, Forrest appeared before a joint congressional committee. He testified for several hours, all the while maneuvering, dodging, and evading questions. He answered with phrases such as, "I presume," or "I heard," or "I do not remember." Later, he supposedly told a friend, "I have been lying like a gentleman."

The congressional committee was doing more than investigating the Fort Pillow Massacre. It had been called to look into atrocities committed by the newly formed Ku Klux Klan.

Nathan Bedford Forrest, the man who had been called the "Wizard of the Saddle," was the first Grand Wizard of the Ku Klux Klan. In his biography of Forrest, Brian Steel Wills questions whether Forrest was, as many others claim, the Klan's Grand Wizard.[3] If he truly was the Grand Wizard, it would be ironic, since during the war cavalry General Forrest was known as "the Wizard of the Saddle." Wills says Forrest "denied even being a member of the organization, much less commander of it." Wills quotes Forrest as saying he tried to stop the Klan, "disband it and prevent it." Forrest's biographer quotes the general as claiming "I did suppress it." All of which sounds much like former Nazi SS officers who, during war crimes trials, admitted to being in the SS but claimed they'd been forced to join and then as members did everything possible to prevent the atrocities they were charged with.

Union Gen. Benjamin Butler denied being a beast, denied ever stealing anybody's silverware. His political constituents in Massachusetts apparently believed him, sent him back to the U.S. Congress after the war, and even elected him governor.

Nathan Bedford Forrest never admitted he did anything wrong. He is quoted as saying, "War means fighting, and fighting means killing." Some, however, would argue there's a big difference between killing and slaughtering, a difference never learned by the Wizard of the Saddle.

CHAPTER TWENTY-TWO

A Do-It-Yourself War:
Homespun, Homemade, and Make-Do

My shoes are gone; my clothes are almost gone. I'm weary, I'm sick, I'm hungry. My family have been killed or scattered. And I have suffered all this for my country. I love my country ... but if this war is ever over, I'll be dammed if I'll ever love another country!

—Confederate soldier during the
retreat to Appomattox, April 1865

The world has seen its iron age, its silver age, its golden age and its bronze age. This is the age of shoddy.

—*New York Times*, April 3, 1861

In the beginning, both sides believed it would be a short war. The North was conceited enough to believe Southern troops would run at the first sound of battle. The South believed one Rebel could whip several Yankees. The U.S. military didn't have enough weapons to go around. The Confederacy didn't have enough of anything. Conditions at times were almost unbearable in the military. No clothing, no food, no weapons or ammunition. And life on the home front wasn't so good, either.

The South believed English mills could not exist without the cotton they imported from Dixie before the war and that Queen Victoria and company would soon recognize the Confederate government. Rebel growers even withheld much of the cotton already picked, cotton packed into bales and taken to ports along the Atlantic Ocean. Much of it sat there, rotting away, and the money it could have brought in escaped to the British colony in India, which increased its own cotton industry to more than meet the English needs.

It wasn't long before the wisest along both sides of the Mason-Dixon Line realized the war would not be an overnight event, and they'd best prepare for it. Up North, machinery began to roll, goods began to pour in and out of its ports. Down South, there were few factories, at least not enough, and the Federal navy became more and more successful at blockading Southern ports.

One blockade runner succeeded for a while. It was the yacht *America,* winner of the 1851 "Queen's Cup" race, which then became known as the "America's Cup" race. The *America* was captured by the Confederacy and used to run the Union blockade until it was sunk off Charleston in 1862.

Near the end of 1863 a Confederate blockade runner slipped out of North Carolina's Cape Fear River, bound for England. One passenger was Mrs. Anna McNeill Whistler, off to visit her artist son. She was the subject of the portrait now known as *Whistler's Mother.*

Which brings to mind a story that may explain Southern society. Years after the war, a young woman went to Europe and, on her return, recounted the visit to her grandmother.

"And to think of it" she bubbled, "when I was in Paris I actually saw Whistler's celebrated painting of his mother."

The Virginia-born, class-conscious older lady wasn't fazed. "Really!" she declared. "I see nothing remarkable about that. After all, she was only a McNeill from Wilmington, North Carolina."

While the North increased its production, the South had to find ways to start their own. Much of what they did, they did at home. In the second year of the war, a young Southern lady wrote new lyrics to the popular "Bonnie Blue Flag."

> My homespun dress is plain, I know;
>   My hat's palmetto, too.
> But then it shows what Southern girls
>   For Southern rights will do.
>   We send the bravest of our land
>   To battle with the foe,
> And we will lend a helping hand
>   We love the South, you know.
> Hurrah! Hurrah!
>   For the sunny South so dear.
> Three cheers for the homespun dress
>   That Southern ladies wear.[1]

Homespun wasn't the only change in Southern life. According to historian Mary Elizabeth Massey:

> *There was nearly always a food shortage in certain areas (of the South). Those near the battle lines were most often swept clean of all food. Foragers from both Confederate and Federal armies preyed upon the land. That section of Virginia, which was a battleground for four years, saw the food problem daily becoming more acute. Here, the battle against starvation was fought during the entire war.*[2]

Confederate War Department clerk John Beauchamp Jones wrote on February 23, 1864, with more than a year left to go in the war:

> *Mean is the only food now attainable, except by the rich. We look for a healthy year, everything being so cleanly consumed that no garbage can accumulate. We are all good scavengers now, and there is no need for buzzards in the streets. Even the pigeons can scarcely find a grain to eat.*[3]

Blame it on Thomas Jefferson. That Virginia genius wanted the whole nation to be made of relatively small, self-sustaining farms. While not totally opposing manufacturing facilities, he believed each section of the country, even each family, should produce not only its own food but its clothing, bricks, steel, iron, leather, you name it. Everything. But, even by Jefferson's times, society had progressed (or regressed, take your pick) beyond a period when one family, even one group of families, could produce everything it needed; therefore, families (or towns or states or even nations) had to look outside their localities. The South depended upon outside sources to supply many of its essentials of life. Not just from Northern factories, either, but from those in Europe as well. A Southerner who lived through America's Civil War later wrote that her defeated people depended on others to supply everything, "from a hair-pin to a tooth-pick, and from a cradle to a coffin."

Today, we go into a room, flick a switch, and the lights come on. In the nineteenth century, you went into a room, struck a match, and a candle would glow, or a gas jet would flare, or a kerosene lamp would burn. Just take the matches, "Lucifer" matches or "Lucifers" they were called at the time, in part due to the smell of sulfur when they were lit. When the shooting war began, the South, for the most part, didn't manufacture its own Lucifers; they came from the North.

You could make them at home, and Southern newspapers even printed instructions for doing so, but it was a complicated process, using materials unfamiliar to most. When Rebel factories did start turning them out, the matches were inferior and there was never enough of them. The Rebel variety came in small blocks, since Southern factories didn't have enough boxes, and were broken off one at a time as needed.

Southern households returned to the practice of banking fires at night to keep the coals going for morning food preparation and, in the colder months, simple warmth. Flint and steel could be used, of course, to strike a spark and start a fire. It was also the process often used by runaway slaves.

Such flint and steel or stone sometimes were handed down to modern times as symbols of what great-grandparents went through in making their way to freedom, carrying fire with them. As they traveled northward, fleeing slaves followed the North Star. To tell others about this route, they sang, "Follow the drinking gourd." The gourd was the Big Dipper, part of *Ursa Major*. The North Star, *Polaris,* is part of the Little Dipper *(Ursa Minor)*. The two outer stars of the Big Dipper point the viewer in the northern hemisphere to Polaris. Slaves hoping to escape to the North might reach safety by following "the drinking gourd."

Where gas was to be found in cities such as Atlanta and Richmond, one gas jet might be left burning all day to use to light others when nighttime came. In the final months of the war, Richmond had trouble with the metal retorts required to burn gas in streetlights. Retorts are that part of a gaslight where the fuel is heated and burned, producing light. In the nineteenth century they were made of iron, and the Confederate secretary of war refused to release material needed by the city of Richmond to manufacture the iron retorts. The retorts wore out just at a time when all metal was going to feed the military maw. There wasn't enough iron to go to civilian needs, even if the civilians were Confederate government officials living in the Confederacy's capital city. At the first meeting of the Richmond City Council in 1865, council members wanted to know why the city was getting darker and darker by the night. "Mr. Compton (the gas works committee chairman) said, because [of] a want of retorts" the lights could not function.[4] The iron to manufacture the retorts may have been made at Richmond's Tredegar Iron Works, but the city couldn't get its hands on it.

An ingenious device sits on the desk in what was President Jefferson Davis's office in the White House of the Confederacy in Richmond. It is, in effect, an extension cord, a tube used to bleed off gas from the overhead chandelier and carry it to a desk lamp.

Much of the coal burned to keep Richmond warm and to make gas so that Richmonders could see, came from neighboring Chesterfield County. But, as with just about everything, as the war continued, coal cost more and more. In the middle of the winter of 1864–65, Richmond officials raised the price of the gas it produced.

There were candles, but in times most recent to the coming of the war, the South had, once again, imported them from the North. So Southerners had to make do with homemade items, items not always such as we today might think of as candles. Some were made of sewn-together rags, twisted, then dipped into liquid wax until something approaching the appearance of a candle resulted. They could be as narrow as a child's finger and as much as two to three feet long. While still soft, the candle might be wrapped around a bottle or jar, even a corn cob.

If they couldn't get beeswax, the Southern candle maker might use berries, boiling them in water to obtain the needed material. Mixing it with tallow from cattle could add to the candle even if it didn't add to the time it burned.

However they were made, whatever was used, it seems no one was ever satisfied with Confederate candles. Not with Confederate oil, either. Oil for prewar lamps came from kerosene, but, like just about everything else in the Civil War South, kerosene was in short supply. A similar, though much smokier, product was made by redistilling turpentine, "terebene oil," it was called. Southerners even tried making substitutes out of sunflower or cotton seeds and from corn or even peas. If you had oil, you might not have a wick for the lamp. As with candles or oil, there never was a satisfactory substitute for wicks.

Another "invention" used even before America's Civil War led to the saying "to light a shuck," meaning to leave rapidly. The "shuck" was a corn shuck and, when dried, often was used to burn as a torch.

So you'd "light a shuck" and move on before the rapidly burning dried-corn sheath expired.

Food was often in short supply, especially in the cities. On April 2, 1863, hundreds of women and children roamed the streets of Richmond, demanding food. It was a bread riot, and while Richmond's bread riot was the most famous, there were similar protests in several other cities. Authorities, of course, blamed it on "outside agitators," a phrase that resurfaced in the riots of the 1960s and 1970s.

Diarist John Beauchamp Jones told about the affair. "A few hundred women and boys," he wrote, "met as by concert" and demanded food. He told of meeting on the street "a young woman, seemingly emaciated, but yet with a smile," who said the crowd was "going to find something to eat." John Beauchamp Jones personally opposed the riot and later testified in court against some of its participants. Yet in telling about the day's events, "I could not for the life of me refrain from expressing the hope that they might be successful." He even pointed the rioters in the "right direction to find plenty in the hands of the extortioners."

They marched on the governor's mansion, demanding Governor "Honest John" Letcher do something about the problem. They carried "pistols, knives, hammers, hatchets, axes, and every other weapon which could be made useful in their defense or might subserve their designs in breaking into stores for the purpose of thieving," young Sallie Brock Putnam wrote.[5] When they didn't get a satisfactory answer from the governor, they rioted.

Sara Pryor, whose husband Roger had declined to fire the opening shot of the war at Fort Sumter, kept a diary during the war and wrote about the Bread Riot. She told about a young woman of about eighteen who marched through the city, demanding bread. The woman obviously was emaciated by hunger.

> As she raised her hand to remove her sunbonnet, her loose calico sleeve slipped up and revealed a mere skeleton of an arm. She perceived my expression as I looked at it (the woman's arm) and hastily pulled down her sleeve with a short laugh. "This is all that's left of me!" she said. "It seems real funny, don't it?"

Apparently, Sara Pryor didn't think so and asked the starving woman where she was going. She was told, "We are going to the bakeries and each of us will take a loaf of bread." The woman believed that was "little enough for the government to give us after it has taken our men."[6]

"Bread! Bread!" The rioters cried that their "children are starving while the rich are rolling in wealth."[7] Not many men took part in the Richmond Bread Riot, according to most reports; they left it up to their wives and mothers, it seems.

When they couldn't get bread, the rioters took whatever they could, clothing, shoes, jewelry, you name it. Finally, and it gets confusing about here, either Virginia Governor Letcher or Confederate President Davis (another report says it was Richmond Mayor Joseph Mayo) put a stop to it all.

Whoever it was, it probably came when the crowd of around five thousand gathered on Main Street, between thirteenth and fifteenth. Letcher or Davis jumped on top of an overturned cart or barrel and ordered the crowd to leave within five minutes or troops would open fire—a quiet speech, but one with a threat. The mob later referred to by Richmond *Examiner* editor John Monclure Daniel as "a handful of prostitutes, professional thieves, Irish and Yankee hags, gallows-birds from all lands but our own" finally left.[8] The army had shown up. Within two hours of its start, the Bread Riot was over. Later that day, the government began issuing rice to local residents.

Forty-four women and twenty-nine men were arrested, but most of the charges were dropped. John Beauchamp Jones even testified in the trial of some of those charged; many of the rioters were found innocent. Only twelve women were convicted, mostly on misdemeanor charges. A few men, however, were convicted of felony charges and sent to prison—or sent home; the area where most of the rioters lived was called "Penitentiary Bottom," because it was around the old jail.

Other rioters demanded food in Atlanta; Salisbury, North Carolina; Mobile, Alabama; and Petersburg, Virginia. While there may not actually have been a conspiracy among the rioters, there was a progression, beginning in Atlanta on March 16, ending in Richmond on April 3. The cities hit were pretty much on a south-to-north line along railroads.

For Southerners who had bread, there was a question of what to put on it. The old family cow (there were still plenty of cows raised inside Richmond and Atlanta at the time) gave milk for butter. Honey might be available, but in some cases it was being used as a substitute for sugar. Even though the sugarcane fields of Louisiana were among the largest in the world, much of the cane area was under Union control. No hope of getting maple syrup or sugar from the North, but the South did have maple trees and the mountain areas of Dixie produced a supply. Not enough, however, reached the market to meet the demand.

You might have milk, you might have sugar, but you likely didn't have coffee; it was denied the South by the Union's blockade of Southern ports. Some people claimed the coffee shortage caused actual discomfort among the people, which could go to prove caffeine is actually habit forming. Rebel troops often traded addiction for addiction, tobacco for coffee. Back home, civilians tried using nearly everything they could stuff down their coffeepots: okra seeds, cotton seeds, corn, rye, wheat, and sweet potatoes. They tried acorns, dandelion roots, rice, peas, beans, and chicory. Folks around New Orleans are still partial to coffee mixed with chicory, a custom hard to understand. Rye was a favorite—boiled, dried, ground, then prepared like coffee. Since rye was and still is used in making some kinds of whiskey, a debate rose whether rye "coffee" was good for you or harmful. In any event, some people swore by it. Rebel Gen. Jeb Stuart, on the other hand, swore by a "coffee" made from dried, roasted, and ground corn. As for the sweet potato "coffee," the leftover sediment was said to be among the best cleaning agents for carpets and rugs, which by itself is enough reason not to try it.

In many cases, individuals made up their own recipes, keeping them secret if they worked and supplies of whatever went into the concoction were scarce, sharing them if the brew didn't work or supplies were plentiful. When a trainload of bootleg coffee wrecked near Sumter, South Carolina, in late 1863, local residents seized, grabbed, scrapped up, stole, and generally made off with bags and bags of beans, drank more unadulterated coffee than they had in years, and probably suffered insomnia more than they could remember.

Usually, no one was satisfied with any substitute for real, honest-to-java coffee, and in truth, the Confederacy never found a substitute for coffee.

Americans, for the most part, lost their taste for tea about the time they kicked out King George III of England, but some people still liked it. Tea drinkers, too, suffered from a lack of their favorite beverage. They substituted blackberries, raspberries, huckleberries, willow, and various other fruits and vegetables.

The South had to lean upon itself to make substitutes for alcoholic beverages they had grown used to importing—wine, whiskey, beer, and brandy. And they returned to the practice of producing "liquid corn." To one extent or other, they've continued to distill this usually crystal-clear elixir, often in the face of Federal revenue agents, but that's another story. A Mississippi newspaper carried a tongue-in-cheek recipe for beer:

> Take an old bootleg, and an old cast-off red flannel shirt, and put in five gallons of rain water. Let it stand for two weeks and ferment well. Then put it into a ten gallon keg, adding two quarts of chinaberries, three gallons of water from a tub used by shoemakers to soak leather in . . . and one pound of assafoetida. Let it stand for one week and add a couple of Florida beans.[9]

The word *Assafoetida* is a variation of *asafetida,* which means "a concreted resinous gum, with a strong alliaceous odour, procured from the *Narthex asafetida,* and so on; used in cookery, and as an antispasmodic in medicine."[10] Something "alliaceous" smells or tastes like garlic, but otherwise we have no idea what this all means and certainly don't want to know what it would taste like in beer of any kind.

Southern home brewers, Civil War style, had to substitute for hops, often using peach leaves, causing a Richmond newspaper editor to scream, "*Mein Gott,* our German friends must raise the blockade."[11] You could make wine out of peaches and brandy out of just about any other fruit; you could make whiskey out of corn or rye. But beer out of peach leaves? Now you know what the fighting was all about.

One item the South had plenty of was (the eventually worthless) Confederate money, more than two billion dollars of it. But even then they imported much of it from the North. The first Confederate money was printed by the National Bank Note Company of New York.

CHAPTER TWENTY-THREE

Singing Through the Pain:
Songs of the Civil War

Oh, how do you like the army,
The brass-mounted army,
The high-falutin' army,
Where eagle buttons rule?
—"The Brass-Mounted Army" 1862

Men in both armies loved music. If letter writing (and letter receiving) was the most popular pastime when Johnny Reb and Billy Yank were not killing each other, music was number two. More songs were written during the Civil War than in any other war America has fought. They wrote new songs, sang old ones, and changed tunes and lyrics. When the men marched off to war, they marched off singing. It was a natural release of emotion and tension.

In the South, the song they frequently marched to was "The Southern Marseillaise":

Sons of the South, awake to glory,
    A thousand voices bid you rise,
Your children, wives and grandsires hoary,
    Gaze on you now with trusting eyes,
    Gaze on you now with trusting eyes;
Your country every strong arm calling,
    To meet the hireling Northern band
    That comes to desolate the land
With fire and blood and scenes appalling,
    To arms, to arms, ye brave;
    Th' avenging sword unsheath!
March on! March on! All hearts resolved on victory or death.

* * *

On April 20, 1862, Confederate troops marched through Richmond, headed for Yorktown to stop Gen. George McClellan as he slowly made his way up the mud-caked Virginia peninsula. As they marched, bands played another favorite song of the South at war, an old Irish drinking song given new words by a New Orleans comedian. It told about the first, and unofficial, flag of the Confederacy.

> We are a band of brothers, and native to the soil,
> Fighting for the property we gained by honest toil;
> And when our rights were threatened, the cry rose
>   near and far,
> Hurrah for the Bonnie Blue Flag that bears a single star!
> Hurrah! Hurrah! for Southern Rights, hurrah!
> Hurrah! for the Bonnie Blue Flag that bears a single star!

Brass bands accompanied many units into battle, especially in the first years of the war. General Robert E. Lee's favorite band was said to be the 26th North Carolina. It was in the thick of things at the Battle of Gettysburg. Lieutenant Colonel Arthur Fremantle of Britain's Coldstream Guards witnessed the fighting at Gettysburg and later wrote of an incident during the battle.

> *When the cannonade was at its height, a Confederate band of music, between the cemetery and ourselves, began to play polkas and waltzes, which sounded very curious, accompanied by the hissing and bursting of shells.*[1]

Of course, the quality of the product produced by many musicians wasn't always the best. Occasionally, musicians of less than top quality were forced into the bands. Frequently, band members were ordered to serve as stretcher-bearers during battle. Often there was a scarcity of good instruments.

Kentucky and Tennessee regiments had a favorite all their own, even though the words told of another country: "Cheer, Boys, Cheer":

> Cheer, boys, cheer! no more of idle sorrow;
> Courage! true hearts shall bear us on our way;

Hope points before and shows a bright tomorrow,
Let us forget the darkness of today;
Then farewell, England, much as we may love thee,
We'll dry the tears that we have shed before;
We'll not weep to sail in search of fortune;
Then farewell, England, farewell forevermore.
Then cheer, boys, cheer! for England, Mother England.

Among the favorite Rebel songs was one more or less about the lowly peanut:

Just before the battle, the General hears a row.
He says the Yanks are coming; I hear their rifles now.
He turns around in wonder, what do you think he sees,
The Georgia militia, eating goober peas.
Peas, peas, peas, peas,
Eating goober peas.
Peas, peas, peas, peas,
Eating goober peas.

Southern troops didn't always sing of peanuts. Sometimes they sang about loved ones, or ones they'd love to love. Take the song about a young woman, one whose favors were frequently sought and apparently frequently available. For a price. She was a real person, a mulatto called "the Yellow Rose of Texas."

Or so one story goes. Allegedly, she'd been around for a while, and was said to be one of Mexican General Santa Anna's favorites. So much a favorite, it was thanks to Rose that, during Texas's fight for independence, the Texans were able to capture Santa Anna. Now, she may or may not have been working for the Texans at the same time she was, so to speak, working for Santa Anna, but she managed to keep the general busy while the Texans surrounded his tent and captured him. Literally with his pants down. Which may explain why she and the song she inspired were such ribald favorites among the Texans. Later, other Confederate troops adopted Rose, or at least the song about her.

Nearly a hundred years later, thanks to movies and sing-along sessions, "the Yellow Rose of Texas" regained her fame and even her virtue. Most Texans today will swear the subject of their favorite song was truly a lady, not a lady of the evening.

True, or not? Was she a real person who helped the Texans catch Santa Anna? It's certainly more interesting than the barebones details listed by some music industry sources. "The Yellow Rose of Texas," music reference books claim, was first copyrighted in 1858, by Firth, Pond, and Company of New York. "Written expressly for Charles H. Brown by J.K.," according to the sheet music. One problem is, no one knows who "J. K." is.[2]

As with most other tunes, the lyrics to "The Yellow Rose of Texas" underwent changes as need arose. The Rebels once sang:

> And now I'm going Southward,
>   For my heart is full of woe,
> I'm going back to Georgia
>   To find my "Uncle Joe."
> You may sing about your dearest maid,
>   And sing of Rosalie,
> But the gallant Hood of Texas
>   Played hell in Tennessee.[3]

Later the "Yellow Rose of Texas" became a favorite of both sides and endures today.

The tune "Gary Owen," however, seems to have been almost strictly Yankee, and strictly the Yankee 7th Cavalry. And who was Gary Owen, you may ask? And we may answer: nobody. It wasn't named for a person, but rather for a bar. Or, to be more accurate, a pub. It was named for Owen's Garden, an inn in Limerick, Ireland, a pub popular with the Fifth Lancers, many of whom wound up in the 7th Cavalry and who brought their favorite song along with them. The phrase "Gary Owen," it seems, is a somewhat loosely Americanized pronunciation of the Gaelic for "Owen's Gardens"; in Gaelic, garden is *garrai*, and the Irish troops just turned it around, Owen's Gardens becoming Gary Owen.

Later, "Gary Owen" often was sung in Irish minstrels, enduring well into the twentieth century:

O, young Rory O'More,
> He came out of the West;
In all of the land,
> His harp was the best.

The Irish also donated one of the Civil War's most lasting songs, one sung by both sides. In the original Gaelic, it's called Shule Aroon (*siubhail a rúin*) and goes like this:

I would I were on yonder hill,
'Tis there I'd sit and cry my fill,
And every tear would turn a mill,
Is go d-teidh tú, a mhúrnín, slán!

> *Siubhail, siubhail, siubhail, a rúin!*
> *Siubhail go socair, agus siubhail go ciúin,*
> *Siubhail go dtí an doras agus eulaig liom,*
> *Is go d-teidh tú, a mhúrnin, slán!*

Americans gave it different lyrics:

When Johnny comes marching home again,
> Hurrah! Hurrah!
We'll give him a hearty welcome then,
> Hurrah! Hurrah!
The men will cheer, the boys will shout,
The ladies they will all turn out.
> And we'll all feel gay,
When Johnny comes marching home.

Johnny Reb and Billy Yank had many songs in common, but a particular favorite of the North was one written and composed by a New England songwriter, Walter Kittridge.

We're tenting tonight on the old camp ground,
> Give us a song to cheer
Our weary hearts, a song of home,

And friends we love so dear.
Many are the hearts that are weary tonight,
    Wishing for the war to cease;
Many are the hearts that are looking for the right,
    To see the dawn of peace.
Tenting tonight, tenting tonight,
Tenting on the old camp grounds.

And the final lines:

Dying tonight, dying tonight,
Dying on the old camp ground.

While it was a favorite of many, "Tenting Tonight" was also one of the most despised songs. A New Hampshire solder said it was "dedicated to the grave and stalwart home-stayers."

After they'd taken a beating in the brush and trees of the Virginia Wilderness, a Union soldier began singing a song written by George Frederick Roote. It had only two stanzas and a brief chorus. It also carried the promise of a better future.

Yes, we'll rally round the flag, boys, we'll rally once again,
    Shouting the battlecry of freedom,
We'll rally from the hillside, we'll gather from the plain,
    Shouting the battlecry of freedom.
The Union forever, hurrah! boys, hurrah!
Down with the traitor, up with the star,
While we rally round the flag, boys,
Rally once again,
Shouting the battle cry of Freedom.

The song cheered up the Federals in the Wilderness and later became the title of a Pulitzer prize–winning history of the Civil War.

In the North, regimental bands became too popular for their own good. In July 1862, the U.S. War Department discovered that Union armies had one musician for every forty-one fighting men. The bands were so popular they had to be abolished in order to get more fighting men on the field of battle.

The Civil War also saw the writing of a new and unforgettable bugle call. The story goes that Union Gen. Daniel Butterfield and his bugler wrote it while sitting on the banks of the James River, in Virginia, at Harrison's Landing. The bugler used it to signal lights-out at the end of the day. "Taps" remains one of the most poignant songs of the Civil or any other war.

In late December 1862, Union and Confederate armies sat on opposite sides of Stones River, near Murfreesboro, Tennessee. The Yankee band began playing "Yankee Doodle," and the Rebel band answered with "The Bonnie Blue Flag." "Hail Columbia" from one side, then "Dixie" from the other. Finally, one of the bands began playing "Home Sweet Home." The other joined in, then troops on both sides began singing.

> Mid pleasures and palaces,
>> There's no place like home.

The same song-singing event reportedly happened a few days earlier in Virginia, along the Rappahannock River. The two versions of the story are so much alike, one wonders if they both really occurred, which one really happened, or did either? Perhaps both stories were fabricated. In any event, it's a good story, illustrating the mutual feelings of the two sides.

"Home Sweet Home" and "Auld Lang Syne" stirred such deep feelings that the Union army brass actually banned the songs from being played. Too much of a good (or at least sentimental) thing. "Auld Lang Syne," however, *did* get at least one additional playing. As General Grant wrote up to the Mclean house in Appomattox, the Union band struck up the old Scottish tune.

A song apparently loved by both Union and Confederate troops was written either by a former minstrel performer named Dan Emmet or by two freed slaves living in Mount Vernon, Ohio. Take your pick.

Rebel bands played it as they marched to war. At the Battle of Shiloh, Union General Grant has his regimental band play "Dixie."

> I wish I was in de land ob cotton,
> Old times dar am not forgotten;

Look away, look away, look away, Dixie Land.
In Dixie Land where I was born in,
Early on one frosty mornin',
Look away, look away, look away, Dixie Land.
    Den I wish I was in Dixie, Hooray! Hooray!
    In Dixie Land, I'll took my stand,
    To Lib and die in Dixie;
Away, away, away down South in Dixie;
Away, away, away down South in Dixie.

Another version was sung by Rebel troops while fighting off the Yankees' "On to Richmond" move.

From home and friends we all must go,
To meet a strong but dastard foe.
    Look away, look away, look away to Richmond town.

And ere again those friends we see
We vow to die or all be free;
    Look away, look away, look away to Richmond town.

Another Union-adapted "Dixie," this by one John Savage:

Oh, the Starry Flag is the flag for me;
'Tis the flag of life, 'tis the flag of the free,
Then hurrah, hurrah, for the flag of the Union.

Oh, the Starry Flag is the flag for me.
'Tis the flag of life, 'tis the flag of the free.
We'll raise that starry banner, boys,
Where no power or wrath can face it;

O'er town and field—
The people's shield;
No reason can erase it;
O'er all the land,
That flag must stand,
Where the people's might shall place it.

Frankly, all sentiment, causes just or otherwise aside, the Union lyrics never quite caught on. They lack the fire of the Southern version; maybe that's why both Johnny Reb and Billy Yank sang the original.

When Robert E. Lee's surrender at Appomattox was announced in Washington, crowds gathered at the White House. Bands played and people cheered. When someone asked Abraham Lincoln what he'd like to hear, he replied:

I have always thought "Dixie" one of the best tunes I have ever heard. Our adversaries over the way attempted to appropriate it, but I insisted yesterday that we fairly captured it. . . . I now request the band to favor me with its performance.

"Dixie" is controversial even among its adherents. Around the turn of the century, the Alabama division of the United Daughters of the Confederacy wanted to change the original lyrics. Some didn't like the African-American dialect and said it was more fitting for slaves than white Southerners. Some others thought "Dixie" wasn't genteel enough. By then, the U.D.C. was decidedly middle-class and wanted something more "chaste," more "educated and refined." "Dixie," they claimed, had more to do with battlefields, blood, and gore. When the issue came up among the veterans themselves, they sang their song. Unchanged. The U.D.C. backed down.

During Civil War church services between battles, troops of both North and South recalled and sang childhood favorites: "Nearer, My God, to Thee," "Rock of Ages," and one, often played in the twentieth century by Scottish bagpipers, "Amazing Grace." It was an old Negro spiritual that both sides, including those pro- and anti-slavery, took to heart.

Causes, heroes, events, and emotions, all were themes of the Civil War. People wrote songs and poems about Stonewall Jackson, William Tecumseh Sherman, and other leaders. They also told of individuals whose roles many have been relatively minor but who themselves became well-known. One such person was the town constable of Gettysburg, Pennsylvania, John L. Burns.

When war came to Gettysburg in July of 1863, the seventy-two-year-old Burns picked up his trusty if somewhat ancient musket, clothed himself in a blue swallowtail coat and a yellow vest, topped it off with a bell-crowned, broad-brimmed hat, and went to war. He'd fought in the War of 1812 and the Mexican War, but when he volunteered for the Civil War he was rejected as too old. "I know how to fight," he said, "I have fit (sic) before." Burns walked up to Union Maj. E. P. Halstead of the 7th Wisconsin and demanded to know, "Which way are the Rebels?" When Halstead only stared at him, Burns tried again: "Where are our troops?"

The Wisconsin troops suggested he might hide in the woods and fight, but Burns objected and joined a line of skirmishers in the open field. The soldiers quit, but he didn't. He joined up with another unit, which also quit the field. Once more John Burns stayed on, this time until he was wounded three times and captured by the Rebels. The Confederates released him, and John Burns returned home to recuperate. Later, author Bret Harte wrote the following:

> *Have you heard the story that gossips tell*
> *Of Burns of Gettysburg? No? Ah, well;*
> *Brief is the glory that hero earns,*
> *Briefer the story of poor John Burns:*
> *He was the fellow who won renown,—*
> *The only man who didn't back down*
> *When the rebels rode through his native town;*
> *But held his own in the fight next day,*
> *When all his townsfolk ran away.*
> *That was in July, sixty-three—*
> *The very day that General Lee,*
> *Flower of Southern chivalry,*
> *Baffled and beaten, backward reeled*
> *From a stubborn Meade and a barren field.*

> . . .

> *Just where the tide of battle turns,*
> *Erect and lonely, stood old John Burns.*
> *How do you think the man was dressed?*
> *He wore and ancient, long buff vest,*
> *Yellow as saffron,—but his best;*
> *And buttoned over his manly breast,*
> *Was a bright blue coat with a rolling collar,*

And large gilt buttons,—size of a dollar,—
With tails that the country-folk called "swaller."

. . .

So raged the battle. You know the rest;
How the rebels, beaten and backward pressed,
Broke at the final charge and ran.
At which John Burns—a practical man—
Shouldered his rifle, unbent his brows,
And went back to his bees and cows.

This is the story of old John Burns;
This is the moral the reader learns:
In fighting the battle, the question's whether
You'll show a hat that's white or a feather.

Burns died nine years later, an old man who had become a national hero. On the fortieth anniversary of the Battle of Gettysburg, the state of Pennsylvania raised a statue to him.

Abolitionist Julia Ward Howe wrote a poem in 1870 after the death of Robert E. Lee, the man who, perhaps, best symbolized the romantic South:

A gallant foeman in the fight,
  A brother when the fight was o'er,
The hand that led the host with might
  The blessed torch of learning bore.

Thought may the minds of men divide,
  Love makes the heart of nations one,
And so, they soldier grave beside,
  We honor thee, Virginia's son.

But it was another of her poems that, more than most others, reminds us of the Civil War. More than a century later it was so famous, so well loved, Britain's Winston Churchill asked that it be played for his funeral.

The music was first written by William Steffe of Richmond in 1852 as a march. The tempo was slowed, and it became a camp meeting song. At one point, a quartet from the 12th Massachusetts Volunteers, commanded by Daniel Webster's son Fletcher, added a comic stanza to the march version. It teased one of their own, an army sergeant named John Brown, apparently no kin to the fire-breathing abolitionist later hanged for the Harpers Ferry raid, but just simply Sgt. John Brown.

About this point in time, the sometimes camp meeting song, sometimes marching song with lyrics joking about an army sergeant, was given new words. This time they *were* about John Brown the abolitionist.

> John Brown's body lies a-mouldering in his grave:
> His soul is marching on!

Then came America's Civil War, and a final adaptation gave the tune the meaning it has today, one entirely different from its original.

One night not long after the Union defeat at Manassas, Julia Ward Howe visited Union troops bivouacked over the Potomac River in Virginia. While there, she heard a regimental band playing the tune, and it stuck with her. She hummed and sang about John Brown's mouldering body all the way back to the Willard Hotel in Washington. A church official riding with Mrs. Howe suggested she write better lyrics to the song. She couldn't sleep that night and, as she lay awake, felt the lines of a poem running through her head. As she later put it, "I did not write them; they wrote themselves." A friend gave the poem to the *Atlantic Monthly* magazine, which paid Mrs. Howe four dollars for the rights to print it in its February 1862 issue. Within weeks, Federal troops had the new lyrics memorized. The tune to "John Brown's Body" became "The Battle Hymn of the Republic."

> Mine eyes have seen the glory of the coming of the Lord:
> He is trampling out the vintage where the grapes of wrath
>   are stored;

He hath loosed the fateful lightning of his terrible swift
    sword:
His truth is marching on.

Glory! Glory! Hallelujah!
Glory! Glory! Hallelujah!
His truth is marching on.

The sixth stanza is slightly different and very seldom heard.

He is coming like the glory of the morning on the wave,
He is wisdom to the mighty, He is honor to the brave,
So the world shall be his footstool, and the soul of wrong his slave,
Our God is marching on!

CHAPTER TWENTY-FOUR

Outlaws and Terrorists:
Random Acts of Unkindness

My God, is it possible that all the people are gone mad? The civil war now being inaugurated will be as horrible as his Satanic Majesty could desire.

—Sam Houston
March 19, 1861[1]

If Benjamin Butler and Nathan Bedford Forrest were scoundrels, there are others who justly deserve the pejorative "renegades." They came out of the conflict between Kansas and Missouri, slave and anti-slave factions. Worst of all, these renegades turned what may be considered honest differences of opinion into theft and murder.

Long before the American Civil War began at Fort Sumter, territory west of Missouri came to be called "Bleeding Kansas." The Compromise of 1820 kept an even number of free and slave states; Missouri would be allowed into the Union as a slaveholder, with Maine entering free. The rest of the Louisiana Purchase territory would forever be closed to slavery. When Kansas asked to be admitted to statehood, it wasn't certain whether it would go free or slave. In 1854, U.S. Senator Stephen A. Douglas of Illinois called for repeal of the Missouri Compromise. He proposed dividing the remaining portions of the Louisiana Purchase into two states—Kansas and Nebraska—and giving "popular sovereignty" to residents. They would be allowed to vote whether they wished to be free or slaveholding. "Popular sovereignty" polarized the state of Kansas and led to a Kansas-Missouri civil war before America's Civil War.

Abolitionist Senator William Seward of Massachusetts got into the act, saying, "We will engage in competition for the virgin soil of

Kansas, and God give the victory to the side that is stronger." With the lines drawn, pro- and anti-slavery factions set the land on fire.

It's not really accurate to call Bill Quantrill a true-to-the-Stars-and-Bars Confederate. He is best described as a bandit with sometimes pro-Southern leanings, or you could say that, psychologically, he was dissatisfied with his life and wanted to be somebody else. Who that somebody turned out to be was a killer only slightly attached to a cause, any cause.

Bill Quantrill was only nineteen years old when the blood began to flow on the Kansas-Missouri border, and at first he was nowhere near the action. He was born in Canal Dover, Ohio, the son of a schoolteacher. Bill followed in his father's "booksteps," so to speak, teaching school when he was just sixteen, first in Ohio, then in Illinois, on to Indiana, and, in 1859, Kansas City. Three jobs in three years could mean several things. Either he wasn't a very good teacher, or he simply didn't want to teach.

Meanwhile, abolitionists from the East rushed in to claim residence in Kansas, hoping to push the coming free-or-slave vote their way. Slaveholders from Missouri weren't far behind.

Most of Missouri's slaves were in the western part of the state, where owners feared it would be too easy for runaways to cross into a free Kansas and claim freedom. They pushed hard for Kansas as a slave state, and that's the way the vote went. It didn't stop the violence. On May 22, 1856, a band of pro-slavery riders, called Bushwhackers, shot up the abolitionist stronghold of Lawrence, Kansas, just over the state line from Missouri.

Abolitionist John Brown took it upon himself to "regulate" matters; he and his gang captured a group of pro-slavers living in a log cabin community called Pottawatomie Creek. Brown claimed his actions were "declared by Almighty God," and he literally chopped his opponents to pieces.

Bill Quantrill gave up teaching and took up fighting; first, with the anti-slavery Kansas Jayhawkers. That didn't last long, and he quickly changed to the pro-slavery side, the Bushwhackers. Just as quickly, he took command of the gang. Quantrill reportedly asked several things of his men: "Will you follow orders? Will you be true to your fellows? And will you kill those who support the Union?" If they did, they were the kind of men Bill Quantrill wanted for his Bushwhackers. He said he could not abide the abolitionists, so he and his Bushwhackers set out to rid the area of them.

The term *Bushwhacker* originally was an honorable expression, one describing backwoodsmen, part of America's folklore, but soon the word took on a new definition. They were Confederate guerrillas, and the name brings to mind private plundering, burning, and murder. At first, most of the new-definition Bushwhackers were young farm boys, volunteers who wanted to defend their homes and take revenge for things done to them and their families. Later on, a more restless breed flocked to Quantrill's black silk banner, riders who would just as soon fight as frolic, and likely as not couldn't tell the difference between the two if you asked them. If anything, plundering and murder were more important to them than were state's rights.

Quantrill's pro-slavery Bushwhackers included James and Cole Younger, sons of Judge Henry Younger of Lee's Summit, Missouri. Earlier, a band of Jayhawkers burned Judge Younger's farm and then brutally murdered Cole's father. To show how virtually nonpolitical this whole mess was, Judge Younger had been a pro-Union, anti-slavery man, but he was killed by anti-slavery, pro-Unionists.

Frank and Jesse James also rode with Quantrill, raiding homes and towns and farms on both sides of the border. For the four—the Youngers and the James boys—riding with Bill Quantrill was something of an apprenticeship. The trades they learned were bank robbery, murder, and destruction. The four continued working their new trades more or less successfully long after the Civil War was over.

Perhaps the most vicious of all Bushwhackers was William "Bloody Bill" Anderson.[2] Not much is known about Anderson's birth, other than that this questionably blessed event apparently occurred in Randolph County, Missouri. As a young boy Bill, along with his brother, Jim, and their three sisters, Josephine, Mary, and Jennie, moved with their father to Council Grove, Kansas. Bill was said to be tall, handsome, and slim—*sinewy* is the word often used to describe him—with long curly dark hair that reached his shoulders. He also had large, piercing blue eyes that one writer claimed "literally blazed with emotion." He was said to be an elegant, dashing man who went into battle "frothing at the mouth."

Friends said Anderson went crazy when his sister Josephine was accidentally killed and Mary was injured while in Federal custody. At the time, the Anderson sisters and several female friends and guerrilla family members were being held prisoner in a large three-storied brick building in Kansas City. It's not certain just what happened, but the old and dilapidated building collapsed. Josephine and three other women were killed; sixteen-year-old Mary Anderson was badly injured.

Fans of Bill Anderson can't blame all of his actions on Josephine's death and Mary's injury. Before the incident, Bill apparently had already killed at least one individual and was said to be "fond of the act"; however, what happened to his sisters apparently pushed him over the already close edge. There's not much doubt he lived on the other side of the law and the other side of sanity for the rest of his life.

It's said he often rode into battle with a necklace of Union scalps tied to his horse, just as some Americans allegedly fought the Korean War wearing belts made of Chinese ears. He once wrote to a newspaper, "If you proclaim to be in arms against the guerrillas, I will kill you. I will hunt you down like wolves and murder you. You cannot escape."

Both Bill Anderson and Bill Quantrill took part in the most vicious raid of the border wars. It came at dawn on August 21, 1863, as Quantrill led 450 of his men into Lawrence, Kansas, the town ravaged seven years before, but the 1863 assault was by far the worse. Lawrence was just thirty-five miles from the Missouri border. The night before the raid, red-haired Bill Quantrill gathered his men around a campfire. He stood before them, wearing a black slouch hat with a gold cord, gray pants, and a brown shirt. He carried four revolvers stuck in his belt. He issued a simple order: "Kill every man big enough to carry a gun, and burn every house in Lawrence."

Well before sunup the following morning, Quantrill's men headed for Lawrence, riding in columns of three. With him was a unit under the command of a regular Confederate officer.

It was dawn on a dusty Kansas morning when they reached Lawrence, and Quantrill's band was about to add to its reputation as devils on horseback. Quantrill ordered his men to spread out, and, with a wave of his hand, he unleashed them. The Bushwhackers were like a roaring tide pouring into the still sleeping town, filling the air with that twisting, screaming sound—the Rebel Yell.

The first resident of Lawrence to see this roaring tide was the first to be killed. The Rev. S. S. Snyder was a minister of the United Brethern church in Lawrence. One of Quantrill's men shot Snyder to death as the minister sat milking his cow. Reverend Snyder was the first to die that day, but not the last.

The lazy Kansas morning was shattered by the shooting; half-awake citizens ran to their doors only to be shot as they stood watching the raiders. Some armed themselves and stumbled into the early morning light, where the guerrillas from Missouri cut them down. There was no organized resistance.

Bill Quantrill led a squad galloping up Main Street to the Eldridge Hotel. They robbed the hotel's guests and set up headquarters in the building. While the killing went on outside, Quantrill himself sat back to enjoy a breakfast cooked for him by the hotel's chef.

The howling band carried lists of local citizens to be executed. One squad planned to capture former U.S. Senator Jim Lane, the leader of the Kansas Jayhawkers, but the whoops and howls coming his way awakened Lane, who jumped out of bed. He took time only to rip off the brass nameplate on his door, hoping the Bushwhackers might not know it was his house without the nameplate, then he raced outside where he hid in a cornfield. Nameplate or not, the guerrillas knew where Lane lived, and they ransacked the house and set it on fire. But they never found Lane in his hiding place among the ripening corn.

Quantrill's band wasn't just after Jim Lane, and what followed was a bloodbath. Everywhere in town, houses were looted and set on fire. Saloons were broken into, and the roving horsemen got drunk, ranging up and down the streets. One group ransacked a stationery store and stole dozens of small American flags, tied the flags to their horses' tails, and dragged them through the streets.

In all, Quantrill's men burned 180 buildings, including three antislavery newspapers: the *Journal,* the *Tribune,* and the *Republican.* Most of the town's business district was destroyed along with at least one hundred houses. The damage was estimated at $1,500,000 in Civil War–era dollars.

Some Lawrence residents tried to run from the attack but they were chased down and shot like rabbits. The roving bands tore other men from their homes, dragged them into the open and killed them in cold blood as wives and children looked on. In two hours, 150 men were killed, including several too young to be called anything but young boys. However, not one woman was injured or physically attacked in Lawrence, Kansas; the code of the West would not have permitted it. The code said nothing about leaving widows and orphans, and 80 widows and 250 young orphans were left crying that day.

One guerrilla was wounded, a drunk named Larkin Skaggs who stayed too long and was shot by a local resident, an Indian. By 9:00 A.M. the bloodbath was over. Scouts left as pickets outside of town rode in with word the Union army was on its way. Quickly, Quantrill ordered a retreat. They left, their horses loaded down with plunder. If they bothered to look back, they would have seen the town they destroyed still burning, its women and children holding on to their dead loved ones. The town the guerrillas hated—Lawrence, Kansas— was virtually wiped off the map.

At the time of the Lawrence raid, Quantrill officially was part of the Confederate army. In 1862 his band had captured Independence, Missouri, as part of a Rebel-led raid. The Confederacy rewarded Quantrill by giving him a captain's commission in the Rebel army. Quantrill himself claimed to be a colonel.

The raid on Lawrence, considered by many the worst atrocity in the Civil War, shocked the country, shocked both countries, really. The Union mounted a manhunt for Quantrill and the Bushwhackers who were then considered outlaws, and the Confederacy withdrew its support. In retaliation, Union army commander Thomas Ewing, William T. Sherman's brother-in-law, issued the now famous Order No. 11. It forcibly removed civilians from large parts of four Missouri counties bordering Kansas.

For a while Bill Quantrill was quiet, but in November 1863, Rebel Gen. Sterling "Pap" Price sent him a letter in which he praised the guerrilla leader. Price commended Quantrill and his men for the hardships they "have so nobly endured [and] the struggle you have made against despotism and the oppression of our state. . . ." Price was convinced Quantrill and the Confederate army would be successful in running what remained of the Union army out of Missouri.

Quantrill went back to work, not for the Confederacy so much as for himself. His band by then was made up mainly of teenagers, and they turned wholeheartedly to shooting and robbery and murder. With General Price, Quantrill's Bushwhackers hit Pilot Knob, Missouri. But Thomas Ewing's Union troops were there with a force of about eleven hundred men. The Price-Quantrill force numbered about seven thousand. Ewing beat hell out of Quantrill's raiders, claiming fifteen hundred Rebel and Bushwhacker casualties to only two hundred Yankees killed or wounded.

Price picked up his army and headed westward, for the capital at Jefferson City. He took with him a Rebel they hoped to inaugurate as the state's new governor. Union forces, however, were growing stronger, and about all Price could do was rape, rob, and plunder. The countryside was used to this; it was exactly what Bill Quantrill had been doing all along.

In October, Bloody Bill Anderson joined up with Price a.d together they began a retreat. Along the way they ran into Union skirmishers.

In his report, Price claimed he and his twelve thousand men had marched fourteen hundred miles into Union-held territory, farther than any other Rebel push into the North. What he didn't mention was that his march, no matter how far, was a disaster. When he returned to Arkansas, he had only six thousand men, half the number he started out with.

Three other things came out of the Price-Quantrill-Anderson raids into Missouri. Quantrill broke forever with the Confederacy. Organized Rebel resistance in Missouri came to an end. And so did Bloody Bill Anderson. He was killed on October 26, 1864, shot down by a unit of the Missouri militia in an ambush near Albany.

Anderson's guerrillas rode head-on into the ambush. When the smoke cleared, men and horses were dead and dying. Most of those who survived the ambush ran for nearby trees. But not so Bill Anderson. He charged back toward the Union militia and broke through the line. Witnesses say that as he did, Anderson threw his arms in the air and fell off his horse. He'd been shot twice in the back of the head.

Late in 1864, Quantrill gathered part of his old gang together and roamed northern Kentucky. While there, he called himself Charlie Hart or Charlie Clarke, after either his mother, Caroline Clarke Quantrill, or his mistress, Kate Clarke, whose name may have been Kate King. Another version is that Quantrill made up the name "Clarke" and Kate later used it herself.

In April, Quantrill's raiders headed east, toward Washington, D.C. They planned to assassinate Abraham Lincoln but turned back when they learned John Wilkes Booth had beaten them to the punch.

A month later, in early May, Quantrill was on his way to surrender his band to the Union commander at the Louisville garrison. Quantrill and his Bushwhackers camped on James Wakefield's farm near Taylorsville in Spencer County, Kentucky. They were surprised by a Union raiding party. As he tried to make his getaway, William Quantrill was shot in the back and paralyzed. He was taken by wagon to the prison infirmary in Louisville.

Quantrill had been converted to Catholicism by a Father Michael Power. Through Father Power, he sent word to a woman in Missouri, Mrs. Olivia D. Copper, who was holding part of his loot, that the money should be given to the priest who would buy a grave plot and headstone for Bill.

The renegade leader lingered for a month but died on June 6, 1865, almost two months after Lee surrendered to Grant. He was just twenty-eight years old.

His mistress, Kate, though she later denied it, used five hundred dollars Quantrill had left her to open a bawdy house.

Father Power bought a plot of land in Louisville's St. Mary's Cemetery. He buried Bill there but ignored the raider's request for a headstone. He claimed he was afraid Quantrill's corpse would be stolen. He was right; even without a tombstone, even with the ground flat and unmarked, Bill Quantrill's bones were dug up and used by friends, family, and enemy alike. Not to mention those just out to make a buck. It's a bizarre and confusing story.

Bill Quantrill's mother was said to be manipulative, quarrelsome, and quick to take offense, in case you wondered where her boy Bill got it. Bill's father died of consumption in 1854, leaving Mrs. Quantrill destitute with four children. One was Bill, one was daughter Mary, who suffered from curvature of the spine; the other two sons were Thomas and Franklin. Franklin died in 1881, leaving a widow of his own and four small daughters. Thomas was little help to Mama; he was irresponsible and unambitious and often turned to his mother for support.

Bill had written home frequently until the war began, then he cut himself off from his family. Apparently, he didn't even write to tell his mother he was dying. That was all right with Mama Quantrill; she didn't want any connection between her family and the notorious guerrilla. She was helped by the frequent newspaper misspelling of Bill's name as "Quantrell."

But four or five years after the war ended, Mama sent ne'er-do-well son Thomas out looking for Bill, or to learn what happened to him. Folks in Kansas received Thomas Quantrill with open arms. He repaid them by stealing whatever he could lay his hands on, showing that sometimes blood (genetics) is thicker than water (environment).

With the help of a local Canal Dover, Ohio, newspaper edito., Mrs. Quantrill finally learned Bill's story and where he was buried. In December 1887, Mrs. Quantrill and editor William Walter Scott persuaded the sexton at St. John's Cemetery (as it was then called) in Louisville to open the grave and place Bill's bones in a zinc-lined box. Mrs. Quantrill wanted to take the bones back to Ohio, but the sexton objected.

With the grave open, not much could be found of the coffin; it had rotted away. Scott removed the skull and took it to a nearby Louisville hotel, where Mrs. Quantrill waited. Mama Quantrill identified her son; he'd had a chipped molar in the lower right jaw. Mrs. Quantrill refused to let Scott return the skull to the graveyard. The sexton, Irish-born Bridget Shelly, took what remained of Quantrill's bones, put them into a box (one, incidentally, not zinc-lined), and reburied them, near the surface of the grave.

While in the area of north central Kentucky where Bill Quantrill had last ridden, Bill's mother decided she'd like to meet some of her late son's friends and fellow renegades. She and Scott wrapped the skull in an old newspaper and left it in the hotel checkroom, hidden in a basket, while they went to meet Quantrill's former comrades. A relative of Frank and Jesse James even invited Caroline Quantrill to spend the winter with his family.

She told William Scott to return to Louisville, pretend he wanted Bill's bones so that he could put them all in a zinc-lined box, then take the bones and the skull back to Canal Dover and bury them next to Quantrill's father in the Fourth Street Cemetery. Later, Scott claimed he didn't like lying to the sexton but said he did as Mrs. Quantrill requested. He may not have liked lying to Sexton Shelly, but he apparently didn't mind lying about burying Bill's bones; he kept them in his newspaper office.

Meanwhile, Mrs. Quantrill talked with Sexton Shelly and told her Scott had taken Bill's bones. And she asked Shelly to sell the now-empty plot where Bill earlier had been buried; apparently her credo was, don't let anything go to waste.

For a year, Bill Quantrill's bones lay wrapped in old paper, stored away in William Walter Scott's Canal Dover, Ohio, newspaper office. Apparently Scott didn't like the way Mama Quantrill had blamed the bone removal on him (not to mention that she had made money on the deal by selling Bill's plot in the Louisville cemetery), and he contacted the secretary of the Kansas State Historical Society. "What," Scott wrote, "would [Bill Quantrill's] skull be worth to your society?" The editor enclosed a lock of the dead man's hair just to prove the offer was real.

> *I'm not speculating in dead men's bones, but if I could get a part of the money I have spent, I see no reason why the skull might not as well be preserved in your cabinet, as to crumble in the ground.*
>
> *Please consider this letter strictly confidential, and mark your answer "Personal." Destroy this letter when read, and I will do the same with yours. No one in the world knows I can get the head, but I can.*[3]

Kansas State Historical Society secretary Franklin Adams ignored Scott's instructions to burn the letter, but he offered to pay twenty-five or thirty dollars for the skull.

Apparently, that wasn't enough. Or maybe Scott thought other newspapers might learn about the deal. He claimed he didn't want Mama Quantrill to hear about it; besides, he said, she was old and things could wait until her death.

In the meantime, Mrs. Quantrill had worn out her welcome

among Bill's old cronies. Her son Thomas was off in Tucson, Arizona, and Mrs. Quantrill had argued with the widow of her other son. She also fell out with Scott, and when Scott gave a newspaper reporter some Quantrill family photographs under a promise not to print anything bad about Mrs. Quantrill, Mrs. Q. furiously attacked her old friend.

Scott died in late 1902. He had planned to write Bill Quantrill's biography, but delayed the job, waiting for Mama to pass on. As it was, she outlived him, not dying until 1905.

Like her late husband, Scott's widow tried to cash in on Bill, offering to sell her late husband's papers along with Quantrill's skull. An official of the Kansas Historical Society purchased the papers and three of Quantrill's arm bones and tried to make money on Bill by trading Quantrill's bones for Jesse James's gun. No deal. Another time this same official offered the bones in return for Wild Bill Hickok's revolver, holster, and gunbelt. Again, no deal, and the official finally donated the bones to the historical society. They were put on display in Kansas after Mrs. Quantrill's death. In a glass case along with them, much to the regret of some local ministers, were relics of the Lawrence, Kansas, massacre of August 21, 1863.

A couple of years after Mama Quantrill joined her son in death, a group of Canal Dover teenagers formed what was known as the D.J.S. Club—no one is certain what the initials stood for—which became the Zeta Chapter of the Alpha Pi fraternity. William Scott's son, Walter, gave the fraternity William Quantrill's skull, and for the next thirty-two years, the skull was used in initiation ceremonies—shellacked and nicknamed Jake, with candles glowing through the eye sockets.

During World War II, fraternity membership was at an all-time low, and Zeta Chapter was disbanded. A fraternity trustee bought the skull and kept it in a box in his cellar until 1960, when it was displayed at the fiftieth anniversary of Zeta Chapter. Afterward, "Jake" was returned to his box and, sent back to his cellar, where he remained until 1972, when he was given to the Canal Dover Historical Society.

Finally, a wax head was made by the anthropology department at Kent State University. They used glass eyes (blue, just as Bill's were said to be) and a wig (red, as Bill's hair was said to be, but it's doubtful Bill Quantrill's real hair was as weird-looking as the wig), and they put it on display alongside Quantrill's skull, his powder horn, and a couple of nineteenth-century dime novels about the renegade.

Over the years, stories grew, not only about Quantrill and his Bushwhackers but about Bill Quantrill's bones, stories of how vandals exhumed the body and scattered his remains around the country. Bones said to be his often turned up at carnival side shows. Apparently, the stories were not true.

James Henry Lane was to Missouri what Quantrill was to Kansas: feared and loathed. He was a cadaverous former U.S. senator from Kansas and the leader of the Union guerrillas, the Jayhawkers. They also were called "Red Legs" for the red leather leggings they usually wore.

Lane was tall and gaunt; he had a hatchet face with noticeably bad teeth. Once, he announced he considered everyone from Missouri to be "wolves, snakes, devils, and, damn their souls, I want to see them cast into a burning hell." He did his best to send them there himself. Lane was one of the reasons Bill Quantrill's Bushwhackers attacked Lawrence, Kansas, that fateful August morning, but the Bushwhackers were disappointed when they didn't catch the Jayhawkers leader asleep in bed.

Lane seemed to take special pleasure in harassing one particular farm, that of Solomon and Harriet Louisa Young near Independence, Missouri. The Jayhawkers may have known that one of Young's daughters was married to a member of Quantrill's Bushwhackers, James J. "Jim Crow" Chiles, but Solomon Young himself was an avowed Unionist. That didn't stop Lane. Over the spring and summer of 1861 Lane's gang stole at least fifteen mules and thirteen horses from the prosperous Young farm, shot 400 Hampshire hogs and, when they butchered the dead animals, took only the hams, leaving the rest of the meat to rot. They made Harriet Louisa cook biscuits for the Jayhawkers to eat along with the hams. After the war, the Youngs sent the U.S. government a bill: $21,442, what would amount to a quarter of a million dollars today. Years later, the story of Jim Lane and his Jayhawkers was remembered and talked about often by Harriet Louisa and Solomon Young's grandson, Harry S Truman.

Charles "Doc" Jennison, a bantam-size, Wisconsin-trained medical doctor, took command of the Jayhawkers. Jennison claimed there was more money in horse-stealing than medicine, and that's why he switched careers. He also made a career of hanging people who disagreed with his politics. Catching two men who had ridden into Kansas to kidnap and return a group of runaway slaves to their Missouri masters, Jennison hanged the bounty hunters. It was Jennison who instituted a scorched-earth policy in Kansas, burning anything he believed would be useful to slaveholders, three years before U.S. Army Gen. Phil Sheridan tried the tactic in the Shenandoah Valley of Virginia, long before Sherman howled through Georgia.

Eventually, just as the Bushwhackers were made official by the Confederate government, the Jayhawkers were cloaked with authority by the Union army, becoming the 7th Kansas Cavalry. Still, they were little more than thieves, murderers, and arsonists. Jennison and his men, under the authority of Union Gen. Thomas Ewing's Order No. 11, forced everyone in four Missouri counties to vacate their homes. Order No. 11 gave residents fifteen days to vacate their property, then Jennison and his men murdered, looted, and burned everything in sight. He so often burned houses in the area that, for years after, residents said they lived in "the Burnt District." The counties of Jackson, Cass, Bates, and half of Vernon were left with only stumps of chimneys showing from once prosperous houses and farms. Colonel Bazel Lazear, commander of the Union post at Lexington, was horrified by the condition of the six hundred women, old men, and young children banished from Missouri. He wrote his wife, "It is heart-sickening to see what I have seen since I have been back here. A desolated country and men & women and children, some of them allmost (sic) naked. Some on foot and some in old wagons. Oh God."[4]

Eventually, Doc Jennison was court-martialed for his actions. He had gone too far, and he was drummed out of the Union army in 1865.

Before and during his reign of terror with the Jayhawkers, Jennison had raised (and stolen) horses. After his court-martial he made a fortune raising horses, and for generations people claimed their best horses were "out of Missouri by Jennison." He died of heart disease at age fifty, near the Kansas-Missouri border he raided so many times.

Over the years, attempts have been made to see the Bushwhackers and Jayhawkers as latter-day Robin Hoods. They weren't. They stole from the rich only because the poor had nothing the raiders wanted. They gave away very little, keeping almost everything for themselves. After the war, many turned into outright outlaws (notably the Youngers and the James boys), robbing banks, trains, and anything or anyone else with money.

Time passed, and when things began to settle down after the war, veterans of both the Union and Confederate armies started holding reunions. For a while, however, the Bushwhackers and Jayhawkers stayed away. After all, it wasn't safe; many of those still alive were on the run from the law. But in 1889, Quantrill's men began meeting annually. In 1910, Cole Younger showed up after serving sixteen months in the Minnesota Penitentiary for his part in robbing a Northfield bank. He was something of a celebrity and was the guest of honor. He gave a talk entitled "On What Life Has Taught Me." The few gray-haired boys who were still around received it well.

Don't forget William Quantrill. When last we left him, a wax model of Bill's head, based on the Kent State University anthropology department's study of the Bushwhacker's skull, was on display at the Dover, Ohio, Historical Society. More or less on display. For years, the skull and the wax head sat side by side in a glass case. Summers, however, can get hot in Ohio, and the Dover Historical Society's building is an old Victorian mansion. The air-conditioning isn't the best. Until they could raise funds for a better cooling system for the case, the wax head was removed for safekeeping and kept in a more secure place, one not so hot, kept back among the society's display of a 1920s-era kitchen. There sits a working refrigerator where society workers often store their lunches. Resting alongside soft drinks and sandwiches is Bill Quantrill's wax head, the hairs of its cheap wig sticking out due to electricity and cold air.

In 1989 the Kansas legislature passed a law requiring state museums to rebury the remains of Native American Indians. The Dover Historical Society saw it as a good way to get rid of Bill's skull and bones. They were about to bury them when officers of the Missouri Sons of Confederate Veterans (by now great-grandsons of the vets) objected. The historical society's plans were to bury Bill's remains at a by-invitation-only ceremony; the Missouri Sons said this was like trying to "bury the bones at midnight." They lobbied to get the bones and skull, but the Dover Society refused to give up the skull.

With "full military honors"; however, the Sons buried Bill Quantrill's five bones and a vial containing a lock of his hair at the Confederate Memorial Cemetery in Higginsville, Missouri. No zinc-lined box this time. A handmade oak casket, draped with a Confederate battle flag, held the bones, which were now wrapped in acid-free bubble plastic. About six hundred people were on hand for the October 24, 1992, ceremony, including a five-man squad of cadets from a nearby military academy. One cadet was African-American, and it's ironic he would be there. As "border ruffians" before America's Civil War, Bill Quantrill and his Bushwhackers frequently stole slaves and ransomed them to their owners. The raiders also were careful to kill any black soldier captured in a Union uniform.

In his eulogy at the interment, the commander in chief of the Missouri Sons of Confederate Veterans said Quantrill's bones should not be buried "where people are ashamed of him, where no one remembers or cares to recall the brutality of a partisan warfare that created men like Captain Quantrill and those who rode with him.[5] All but one of the pallbearers were direct descendants of Quantrill's Bushwhackers. Present also was a man who claimed to be Bill's great-great-grandson, though it's not certain Bill Quantrill ever fathered a child. Later, the casket was sealed with cement to deter would-be grave robbers.

A week later, Quantrill's skull also was buried, not in a handmade oak coffin, but in a white fiberglass coffin originally meant for a child. Twenty-two people attended the burial of the skull, and then they sang "Amazing Grace." It's a favorite tune to play at wakes, funerals, Scottish gatherings, and gatherings of any other nature where they wish to bring a tear to the eye and can't find anything more appropriate. In this case, it may have been singularly *inappropriate*, since it originally was a Negro spiritual.

The new burial spot is the same location where Bill Quantrill was interred in 1889. This time the small casket holding his skull was buried only three feet below ground to avoid uncovering any further remains of the Bushwhacker and, more importantly, causing a stir that might lead to a lawsuit by Quantrill's descendants. Attendants lowered the coffin by hand, shoveled in the dirt, packed it down, and left.

William Quantrill, Bill Anderson, James Henry Lane. All renegades of the Civil War.

The wax head stored in the Dover Historical Society's 1920s refrigerator? It's still there, but a while back someone in a hurry to grab a cold drink slammed the door on it. Bill's nose was broken and there are cracks all over the face. The wax skull is still brought out for special occasions, and, at Christmas time, garlands of red and green are tied around it. Real festive-like.

CHAPTER TWENTY-FIVE

Fame:
Some Have it, Some Don't

The halls of fame are open wide
And they are always full;
Some go in by the door called "push,"
And some by the door called "pull."
—Quoted by Prime Minister Stanley Baldwin
in a speech to the British House of Commons

In Shakespeare's *Twelfth Night*, Malvolio, the servant striving to be more than he really is, proclaims, "Some are born great, some achieve greatness, and some have greatness thrust upon them." The Civil War thrust greatness upon many who served. It brought out the best in them, but it also brought out the worst in some others.

America's Civil War thundered and roared in the East but hesitated and whimpered west of the Allegheny Mountains. It was nearly seven months after the First Battle of Manassas that the war was felt along the Mississippi River. To that area, a little-known, little-thought of officer was assigned.

He was thirty-nine years old at the time, five foot seven inches tall with blue eyes, short, light brown hair and a close-cut beard. All his life he'd been skinny. A long-time friend called him "delicate."

So far in his life, he hadn't done much except fail. From the beginning, things didn't look good for him. When he was appointed to West Point, his sponsoring congressman even mixed up his name, giving the cadet his mother's maiden name instead of his own. As a cadet, he was, at best, undistinguished. Good at math, his worst subject was French. He was an excellent horseman.

His friends called him "Sam," and said he was sensitive and withdrawn, certainly not very outgoing. It's believed that not once while at West Point, did Sam attend a school dance. He really didn't want to make the army his life, and his only real interest while at West Point was painting—watercolors, often copying the works of European artists. He graduated well down in his class.

For the most part, the West Point corps of cadets was not made up of aristocrats of the Robert E. Lee nature but of middle-class, middle-of-the-road sons of farmers who saw the academy as a way of getting ahead—and getting a job for life, if they liked the army. Sam didn't. He planned to quit after serving his obligatory time, a practice not uncommon in the nineteenth century. After graduation he served as a lieutenant in the Mexican War and showed some promise. In an official report his commander, Capt. Robert E. Lee, commended Sam for his role in the attack on Mexico City.

Sam served alongside many other newly minted officers in the Mexico campaign—Pierre G. T. Beauregard, Thomas J. Jackson, George B. McClellan, John C. Pemberton, and James Longstreet. Longstreet even served as best man on May 22, 1848, when Sam married Julia Dent. The marriage apparently was a close one, lasting through good times and bad. One of their problems was one experienced by many other couples then and now—money. They faced it early and they faced it late.

After the Mexican War, Sam was sent to California and Oregon. On a lieutenant's pay, he couldn't afford to have his wife with him, and without his wife, he was miserable, lonely, and depressed. He began drinking and had to resign his commission.

Back East he worked a hardscrabble farm Julia's father gave them. He failed as a farmer. Trying to support his family, he worked as a bill collector, then sold real estate, even peddled firewood on the streets of St. Louis; all failures.

One Christmas he had to pawn his watch to buy presents for Julia and their three children.

Sam's father offered him a job at the family leather goods store in Galena, Illinois. He was failing there as well when the Civil War started. It was, he thought, a way to begin anew. So he applied to a former fellow officer from the Mexican War days, asking for the command of a regular army regiment. He failed there as well. The former fellow officer was George B. McClellan, Abe Lincoln's newly appointed commander of the Union's Army of the Potomac, but

McClellan was too busy to see a man who had given up his commission because of a drinking problem.

Finally, the governor of Illinois made Sam a colonel of volunteers. Ulysses S. Grant had failed and failed and failed again, but then he got on track. That track led him to the White House for two terms as president of the United States.

John Charles Fremont, Lewis Wallace, and Henry Halleck are among many who came out of the war much different from the way they went in.

At the very least, you can say John Charles Fremont lived an interesting life. He gained prominence and the nickname "the Pathfinder" by exploring the Rockies. Residents of California elected him governor after he stepped in to save the territory for the United States. He was convicted of mutiny, however, when he disobeyed the officer Washington had sent to head the government in California. Rather than dismissing Fremont, President Polk let him resign his commission.

Fremont went on to serve two terms as U.S. senator from California. In 1856 he ran for president under the new Republican party; he lost to Democrat James Buchanan. Back in the army in 1861 as a major general, Fremont seemed to attract what can only be described as people from the fringe areas of life. In *Lincoln and his Generals,* historian T. Harry Williams describes Fremont as "weak and unstable . . . [but gave] the impression of wise maturity and beyond youth. . . . [H]is every action was dramatic. . . ."

As the Union's military commander in Missouri, Fremont freed the state's slaves long before Lincoln issued his Emancipation Proclamation. The president asked Fremont to modify the emancipation; Fremont refused. Lincoln revoked the order himself.

Whether he sent her, or she went on her own, Fremont's wife, Jessie Benton Fremont (the daughter of Senator Thomas Hart Benton) pleaded her husband's case before President Lincoln. By all accounts she did John Charles Fremont more harm than good.

He ran for president again in 1864, this time with the backing of radical Republicans; he withdrew two months before the election. After the war Fremont turned to building railroads. He proposed building a line from San Francisco, California, to Norfolk, Virginia.

That idea died when he was accused of swindling the French government, which had partially financed the plan.

John Charles Fremont was commander of the U.S. Army's Department of Missouri when America's Civil War began. Seven months after Fort Sumter, Lincoln replaced him with Henry Wager Halleck.

Halleck was as successful in life and as unsuccessful in war as Sam Grant was the opposite. He was called "Old Brains" and graduated third in the West Point class of 1839. Halleck's talents lay in military tactics, and he wrote the book on them: *Elements of Military Art and Science*. While other officers served in the Mexican War and learned the nitty-gritty part of battle, Henry Halleck was stationed in California. He resigned as captain in 1854 and went into law, heading up a major New York firm. He also wrote two law books.

Halleck was pop-eyed, flabby, cantankerous, shrewd, and almost totally lacking in charm. He was an able organizer and administrator but a pretty bad field commander; *incompetent* is a word frequently used about his ability in the field. He demoted Ulysses S. Grant because he was jealous of Grant's victory at Fort Donelson. Halleck then took over Grant's command and marched on the town of Corinth, Mississippi. He marched so slowly and stopped so frequently to build fortifications against an expected Confederate attack, that when he got to Corinth, the Rebels were gone. But Halleck claimed a major victory.

Lew Wallace later wrote about Halleck's "victory." "We marched into deserted works," Wallace claimed, "getting nothing, not a sick prisoner, not a rusty bayonet, not a bite of bacon. Nothing but an empty town and some Quaker guns."

Lewis Wallace was one of many known as "political generals," words that became a synonym for incompetency. Henry Halleck liked Wallace no better than Wallace liked him and once complained that it was little better than murder to give an important command to a political general such as Lew Wallace. In this case, Halleck may have known what he was talking about.

Wallace had trouble at the Battle of Shiloh: He got lost. He was stationed five miles away from the fighting, left to guard supplies. At the close of the first day of battle, General Grant sent for Lew

Wallace. Wallace, however, took the wrong road, and by the time he reached the battlefield, it was too late. It was all over.

Lew Wallace hated school, apparently because he was more intelligent than his fellow students, probably more intelligent than his teachers. He was precocious and a voracious reader who gobbled up anything he could find to read.

Wallace was a newspaper reporter and a lawyer; he fought in the Mexican War and was appointed adjutant general in Indiana. After Fort Sumter, he was named colonel and commander of the 11th Indiana. Five months later, he became brigadier general, then major general in March of 1862. Henry Halleck removed him from command not once but twice; the first time Lincoln restored Wallace's authority; the second time Grant did the honors.

Lew Wallace was an atheist, a soldier who couldn't stand the sound of cannon fire. He wanted to form a regiment of black recruits but use them only "for digging ditches and driving mule teams." After the war, he served on the court-martial of Lincoln's assassins and presided over the trial in which Andersonville Prison commander Henry Wirz was convicted.

Wallace resigned his commission in late 1865 but raised a corps of volunteer veterans to fight in Mexico against the Emperor Maximilian. Later, he was governor of New Mexico for three years. It was then, as they say, Lew Wallace got religion. Got religion and wrote one of the most famous novels ever about Christianity—*Ben Hur.*

John Rowlands didn't get religion; he got lucky—lucky enough to find a man everyone thought was missing but who really wasn't.

Rowlands enlisted in the Confederate army, but after he was captured he decided he liked the other side better. He joined the Union army. He quit the army and joined the Union navy. Finally, he gave it all up, deserted, and sat out the rest of the war in Canada.

When the Civil War ended, John Rowlands returned to the United States, changed his name, and became a newspaper reporter, first in Kentucky, then in New York City. It was while he was working in New York that the former John Rowlands went to Africa to search for a man the public presumed was lost, an explorer who had gone off to find the head of the Nile River. The explorer knew where the Nile was, and he even knew where *he* was. He wasn't lost at all, but it took months for John Rowlands, now known as Henry Stanley, to find him, to walk up to the not-so-lost explorer and declare, "Dr. Livingstone, I presume."

During the American Revolution, Thomas Paine wrote, "These are the times that try men's souls. The summer soldier and the sunshine patriot will, in this crisis, shrink from the service of their country." And he added, "He that stands it *now*, deserves the love and thanks of man and woman."

Henry Halleck, it might be said, was very much a summer soldier. As were Lew Wallace and John Rowlands (or Henry Stanley). John Charles Fremont remains a mystery. Sam Grant did not "shrink from the service" of his country. The greatness that was thrust upon Ulysses S. Grant was well accepted and well used.

Charles Shiels Wainwright was a New York farmer until the Civil War came along. As these things happened during America's Civil War, promotion came fast for Wainwright. First a major in the 1st New York Artillery in October 1861, then a lieutenant colonel six and a half months later; he became a full colonel on June 1, 1862. He was breveted a brigadier general in August 1864. Like many others of the day, Wainwright kept a diary. On December 12, 1861, less than a full year after the firing on Fort Sumter, he wrote this:

> It is astonishing how little snap men have generally. I suppose we have as good a lot of officers as any regiment among the volunteers; . . . yet I have not come across more than half a dozen in the lot who can get fairly wakened up.[1]

Charles Wainwright was among the majority of those who served in America's Civil War, too busy to be afraid and equally too busy to worry about gaining his fifteen minutes of fame a later generation was taught to expect.

After the war Wainwright returned to farming and died in 1907. Fame never quite found him, and he probably liked it that way.

CHAPTER TWENTY-SIX

In the End:
A Heap of Men Gone Home

The "Bureau" (of conscription) to-day calls upon everybody between the ages of sixteen and fifty to report at certain places named, and be registered and state the reasons why they are not now in the army and in the field. What nonsense! How many do they expect to come forward, voluntarily, candidates for gunpowder and exposure in the trenches?

—John Beauchamp Jones
Confederate War Department Clerk [1]

On Saturday, July 9, 1864, the *Richmond Dispatch* carried a front page story about members of the local guard deserting to the enemy.

Attempting to Cross the Lines—*The following parties, belonging to local defense companies of this city, some of them . . . detailed workmen at the Tredegar Iron Works, were arrested yesterday while attempting to go to the enemy. . . . While our state forces were in the neighborhood of Bottom's Bridge, three men obtained permission to go a short distance from camp, but as soon as they got out of sight, they changed their direction and struck a bee line for the Yankee camp on the other side of the river a few miles below. Meeting with some of our cavalry, however, a short distance after they started, they were compelled to take to the woods, where they skulked about till yesterday, when they again fell in with our scouts, about three miles from their old camping ground and were captured.*

If anything was unusual about the occurrence, it was that the men tried to go over to the enemy. Normally, they just wandered off, or went home. And the worst things got, the more likely it was that someone, from either side, simply decided it was time to check up on Maud or Sue or the kids, time to plant a crop or harvest one.

Sometimes the men were encouraged by their wives and loved ones. In April of 1863 a woman wrote North Carolina Governor Zebulon Vance.

[A] crowd of we Poor women went to Greenesborough yesterday for
something to eat as we had not a mouthful of meet nor bread in my
house what did they do but put us in gail in plase of giveing us aney
thing to eat. . . . I have 6 little children and my husband in the armey
and what am I to do?

When appeals to authorities failed to gain the husbands' discharges, the husbands often discharged themselves. A Mississippi soldier, one who did not desert, wrote his wife that "there is a heap of men gone home and a heap says if their families get to suffering they will go [too]." Desertion, what one author calls "unwarranted absentees," increased after every loss in battle. In 1862, when the Confederate government announced that all soldiers between 18 and 35—those with one-year enlistments about to expire—were being held over, the list of Johnny Rebs going AWOL greatly increased.

As Robert E. Lee headed for Antietam, one-third of his army headed home. Lee didn't return to Virginia just because he lost the battle. In a letter to Jefferson Davis he said that "desertion and straggling . . . were the main causes of . . . retiring from Maryland."

Many troops saw it as a rich man's war and a poor man's fight, and they wanted no part of it. Some just wanted to go home, and others apparently preferred operating on their own. They left the regular army and formed bands of guerrillas in the countryside, raiding, looting, resisting Confederate authority, and sometimes joining with peace groups to protest the war.

The "dog-catchers," as the guards are called, are out again, arrest-
ing able-bodied men (and sometimes others) in the streets, and lock-
ing them up until they can be sent to the front. There must be ex-
traordinary danger anticipated by the authorities to induce a resort
to so extreme a measure.

—*John Beauchamp Jones*
Confederate War Department Clerk[2]

Following the fall of Atlanta in 1864, an elderly former slave insisted on seeing Union Gen. William Tecumseh Sherman. "I just wanted," he insisted, "to see de man what made old massa run." Sherman not only made "old massa run," he scared the hell out of him and a lot of other Southerners along the way.

Sherman's men called him "Uncle Billy," and in November he ordered the sixteen hundred Southern citizens remaining in a captured Atlanta, Georgia, to evacuate the city. On the fourteenth Sherman also left. With him were sixty-two thousand troops and thirteen thousand mules and horses.

It was his "March to the Sea," and it drove a path of destruction sixty miles wide and three hundred miles long from Atlanta to Savannah. Behind him, Sherman had cut the telegraph lines. He had Ulysses S. Grant's reluctant approval, but he didn't want any interference from Grant or any Washington bureaucrat who might object to what he was doing. As he'd once predicted, he made Georgia howl. Sherman punished the South into submission.

Along with Federal forces came another army made up of deserters, criminals, crooks, and the scum of the earth. They were called "Bummers," a word that in the nineteenth century, had a totally different meaning from the one given it by a seventies drug culture. Elias Smith of the New York *Tribune* was with Sherman and wrote about this second army.

> *In the rear of each Division followed the foragers, or "bummers," as they are called by the soldiers, constituting a motley group which strongly recalls the memory of [Shakespeare's] Falstaff's ragged army. . . . Here came men strutting in mimic dignity in . . . old swallow-tailed coat[s], with plug hats, the tops kicked in; there are a group in seedy coats and pants of Rebel grey, with arms and legs protruding beyond all semblance of fit or fashion. . . .*
>
> *The procession of vehicles and animals was the most grotesque description. There were donkeys large and small, almost smothered, under burdens of turkeys, geese and other kinds of poultry, ox carts, skinny horses pulling in the fills of some parish doctors, old sulkies, farm wagons and buggies . . . all filled with plunder and provisions.*
>
> *There was bacon, hams, potatoes, flour, pork, sorghum, and freshly slaughtered pigs, sheep, and poultry dangling from saddle tree and wagon, enough, one would suppose, to feed the army for a fortnight.*[3]

It wasn't so much Sherman's regular army troops who devastated Georgia; it was the Bummers, the deserters. And they did a thorough job of it.

Did Sherman care how much devastation this band of deserters wreaked on the citizens? Apparently not. He said the South might regret the fall of Richmond but would scream when all of Georgia was destroyed.

On Sunday, April 2, 1865, from his headquarters near Petersburg, General Lee sent Maj. Gen. George Pickett a note, telling the long-haired, perfumed officer to "Protect [the] road to Ford's Depot and prevent Union forces from Striking the South Side Railroad."

Pickett thought Robert E. Lee was panicking. Besides, he hadn't liked the leader of the Army of Northern Virginia since that mile-long, open-field charge at Gettysburg, which saw the South reach its "high water mark" and Pickett's division devastated. So instead of worrying about Ford's Depot and Union troops, Pickett had lunch. Pickett and Lee's nephew, Fitzhugh Lee, were off with Maj. Gen. Thomas Rosser, eating fried shad under the towering pine trees along Hatcher's Run Creek. It wasn't far away, just far enough. That's when the Union army broke through the Rebel lines.

George Pickett and Fitzhugh Lee later claimed they never heard the nearby fighting, and it's possible they didn't. There are numerous reports from America's Civil War of incidents when the sounds of battle went unheard less than half a mile from where cannon roared. There also are reports of individuals hearing rifle fire and cannon, sometimes feeling the ground shake, when a battle took place fifty miles away. There is no ready explanation for these phenomena.

By the time Pickett and Fitzhugh Lee finished lunch and rejoined their units, it was too late. The Union army had broken the Rebel lines around Petersburg; more than five thousand Confederate soldiers had been taken prisoner, and other Rebel troops were streaming away, never to return. After four long years, the way to Richmond was open. At last, the Union army could make the move it hoped to make in 1861; they could resume their "On to Richmond" charge.

The physically failing Gen. A. P. Hill had spent increasingly more time on sick leave with his wife and two young daughters at their home in Petersburg. When the Confederate lines broke, Hill hurried back to his troops. Accompanied only by his favorite courier, Sgt. George W. Tucker, the general made a personal reconnaissance into the wooded area beyond the Rebel fortifications. They saw a

squad-size band of Union stragglers, and against Tucker's suggestion, Hill rode toward them. He ordered the Yankees to surrender,
yelling, "If you fire, you'll be swept to hell." *You are surrounded,* the
general claimed, but the Yankees didn't believe him and opened fire.

General Ambrose Powell Hill was described as "genial, approach-
able, and affectionate in private life, (and) restless and impetuous
in action." In that single volley he fell from the saddle, but before
he died he told Tucker to take his horse and go tell General Lee what
had happened. Leaving Hill where he'd fallen, Sergeant Tucker
grabbed the reins to Hill's dapple-gray mount and rode off. Away
from the action, the sergeant changed over to Hill's faster horse and
rode toward Lee's camp. Seeing Tucker riding Hill's horse, Robert
E. Lee immediately knew what was wrong. Barely able to control
himself, Lee said, "He is at rest now, and we who are left are the ones
to suffer."

On Monday, April 3, 1864, Richmond Mayor Joseph Carrington
Mayo rode out, trying to find some Federal officer to whom he could
hand-surrender the fire-racked city. Confederate forces were gone,
and he hoped Union troops could protect the city's civilians. Finally,
he located Maj. Atherton H. Stevens, Jr., and the 4th Regiment, Massachusetts Cavalry.

A Northern band marched into town playing "The Year of Jubilee."

Major Stevens's regiment rode through the crowded streets until they reached the Virginia state capitol, the building which, for
almost four years, had served as the capital of the Confederate States
of America. Stevens couldn't find a regular flag, so he used a
guidon, the small flag carried by his cavalry unit. No matter; the flag
of the United States of America once more flew over Richmond.
Union troops stood on the capitol's white marble steps, looking
down on the destruction not they but Rebel troops had inflicted on
Richmond.

A reporter from the New York *World* walked through the tortured
city and wrote:

> *There is a stillness, in the midst of which Richmond, with her ruins,*
> *her spectral roofs . . . and her unchanging spires, rests beneath a*
> *ghastly, fitful glare. . . . We are under the shadow of ruins. From the*
> *pavements where we walk . . . stretches a vista of devastation. . . .*

Ahead lay Saylor's Creek, where six thousand retreating Confederates were captured by Grant's advancing army. On April 7, five days after the Union breakthrough at Petersburg, Brig. Gen. Thomas A. Smyth was wounded. He died two days later, the last Federal general to be killed in the war.

The day Smyth died was Palm Sunday, April 9, 1865. Robert E. Lee stood a short distance from his staff that morning, looking off into the distance where Union troops surrounded his remaining small army. "How easily I could be rid of this," another officer heard Lee say, "and be at rest." His troops once derisively called him "Granny"; later they affectionately referred to him as "Marse Robert." He said, more to himself than to anyone around him, "I have only to ride along the line and all will be over." He rejected that thought, turned to his men, and reminded them, and himself, of the people of the South. They faced troubled times; they would need help to recover, and he must offer whatever help he could give.

Later that morning—boots gleaming, dress sword at his side, wearing a brand-new full-dress uniform he'd carried throughout the war as if waiting for the moment, Confederate Gen. Robert Edward Lee rode to Wilmer McLean's house at Appomattox Courthouse to meet Union General Ulysses S. Grant. Lee arrived first and waited patiently.

Then came Grant. As he arrived, the Union army band played "Auld Lang Syne." Grant wore a private's blouse and muddy boots; he was stoop-shouldered, with no sword at his side. A few words, signatures scratched on a hurriedly written document. Lee offered Grant his sword; Grant declined to take it. They saluted each other, and it was over.

Lee later rode among his troops, now down to as few as 20,000, many barefoot, all near starvation. *Say it isn't so,* they cried. And Robert E. Lee cried with them.

The group of Union officers inside the McLean house slowly dispersed, with more than one grabbing a souvenir as he left. The next day, the always self-effacing Gen. George Armstrong Custer wrote his wife.

I respectfully present to you the small writing-table on which the conditions for the surrender of the Confederate Army of Northern

*Virginia were written by Lieutenant General Grant—and permit me
to say, Madam, that there is scarcely an individual in our service
who has contributed more to bring this about than your very gallant
husband.*[4]

There's still confusion over the "surrender table." Apparently, there
were three tables in the McLean house parlor when Lee and Grant
met, two small wooden oval tables, and one larger, square one with
a marble top. The Chicago Historical Society has on display the mar-
ble-top table. The Smithsonian Institution in Washington owns one
of the oval tables, and in 1995, a Wisconsin resident purchased the
second small table for a private collection. It's not positive which, if
any, of these three tables was used by which of the participants at the
surrender. About the only certain thing is that the two men did not
sit together during the discussions and signing. That, and the fact
Wilmer McLean never was paid for anything stolen from his house
by the conquering Yankees.

The day after the signing, remnants of the Army of Northern Virginia marched in final parade at Appomattox Courthouse. Many had
torn up their flags, some as souvenirs, some rather than hand them
over to their conquerors. Many threw down their weapons as hard
as they could, so as to break them and prevent any further use. Union
Brig. Gen. Joshua Chamberlain received the formal surrender of the
Confederate troops. It was Chamberlain who had led Union forces
to victory at Gettysburg's Little Round Top.

As the defeated Confederates walked between rows of conquering Federals, Chamberlain ordered his troops to salute the men who
had fought them so long and so hard with so little chance of winning. The Rebels silently returned the salute and marched off and
broke ranks and went home.

America's Civil War didn't end at Appomattox, and it didn't end with
Lee's surrender of the Army of Northern Virginia. While Confederate troops filed through Union General Chamberlain's ranks, Robert
E. Lee headed for Richmond. He was worried about his ailing wife,
who had refused to leave the city when the Rebel government pulled
out. He found her safe, a Union soldier standing guard outside her
door, making sure no one bothered Mrs. Lee. The soldier was black.

To the south, Joseph Johnston fought on against the Union's William Tecumseh Sherman in North Carolina. A courier rode into Sherman's camp, shouting the news of Lee's surrender. Someone shouted back, "You're the sonofabitch we've been looking for all these four years."

On April 26, Johnston surrendered his Army of Tennessee to Sherman.

Jefferson Davis was on the run, hoping to rally the remnants of the Rebel army somewhere in Texas. A troop of Union cavalry finally caught him in Irwinville, Georgia. Despite Northern newspaper claims, Davis was not wearing a dress, simply a long coat. He was taken to Fort Monroe, Virginia, where the Union held him, often in chains, for two years before he was bailed out by Horace Greeley, who apparently felt sorry for Davis. The only president the Confederacy ever had never went to trial.

Greeley was no fan of Abraham Lincoln's. When secession talk began, Greeley advocated letting the Southern states go in peace. When war broke out, he joined the anti-slavery forces pushing Lincoln hard to free the slaves. He was so impatient that, in August of 1862, he scolded the president in an open letter in the New York *Tribune*, saying Lincoln was

> *strangely and disastrously remiss with regard to the emancipating provisions of the new Confiscation Act. Those provisions were designed to fight Slavery with Liberty. . . . We think you are unduly influenced by the councils, the representations, the menaces of certain fossil politicians hailing from the Border Slave States. . . .*

Lincoln replied,

> *I would save the Union. I would save it the shortest way under the Constitution. The sooner the National authority can be restored, the nearer the Union will be 'the Union as it was.' . . . My paramount object in this struggle is to save the Union. . . . If I could save the Union without freeing any slaves, I would do it; and if I could save it by freeing all the slaves, I would do it; and if I could do it by freeing some and leaving others alone, I would also do that. . . .*

On May 8, Gen. Richard Taylor surrendered his army to Union forces at Citronell, Alabama. Or, at least, Taylor says it was on the eighth. Union Gen. Edward Canby says Taylor surrendered to him on May

4, 1865, and that is the generally accepted date. Taylor himself says that on the fourth he and Canby merely met to talk about surrender, that the surrender did not become official until four days later, on the eighth. The fourth, the eighth. Does it matter? Only to old soldiers remembering what they may have done and what they did not want to do any sooner than they were forced to do.

A group of five hundred Rebel soldiers stationed in San Antonio, Texas, learned that the war was over and immediately confiscated $80,000 in Confederate-owned silver. They divided it up, about $160 each, then went home. They were, in effect, the only Confederate soldiers to receive mustering-out pay when the war ended.

At Palmito Ranch, Texas, the final death of the Civil War came when Pvt. John J. Williams of the 34th Indiana was killed in a skirmish with Rebel troops. It was May 13, 1865, and for what it's worth, the final skirmish is listed as a Confederate victory.

Confederate Gen. Edmund Kirby Smith surrendered forty-three hundred men, the remaining Rebel forces in the Trans-Mississippi Department. The Union officer was the same man who had accepted Richard Taylor's surrender, Gen. Edward R. S. Canby. It was June 3.

It was August 23 when the last Confederate ground troops surrendered, troops under the care of Surgeon Maj. Aaron B. Brown of the Georgia, State Line. He operated a field hospital in Upson County, Georgia, until he was captured and forced to give up.

And on November 6, 1865, Capt. James Iredell Waddell, commanding the Rebel raider *Shenandoah,* hauled down the Confederate flag. He surrendered, not to a Yankee, but to the British in Liverpool, England. It was the final time the Confederate flag would be flown.

Almost.

With their cause lost, many Rebels were emotionally depressed. In those pre-Prozac days, many withdrew into the haze of alcohol or drugs rather than admit defeat. Drunkenness became common among many demoralized Southerners. Excessive drinking had not been uncommon in the *Old* South; the *New* South saw even more. But former Rebel soldiers weren't the only ones turning to alcohol and drugs.

In 1877, a New York opium dealer said that "since the close of the war, men once wealthy, but impoverished by the rebellion, have taken to eating and drinking opium to drown their sorrows."[5] Medical corps of both Union and Confederate armies used pain killers such as opium to ease the suffering of those badly wounded. Many who were helped by such drugs soon became addicted to them. This was especially so in the North, where pain killers were more readily available and, thus, used more often to ease distress.

William Tecumseh Sherman died in 1891. One of his pallbearers was his old Confederate adversary, Gen. Joseph E. Johnston. Johnston said Sherman would have done the same for him. The men who had been worst enemies in the war had become best friends in peace. Sherman almost got the chance to carry Johnston to his grave. Six weeks after Sherman's death, Johnston also died. He had been bareheaded while serving as a pallbearer to Sherman. The old Confederate caught pneumonia and joined his Union foe-turned-friend.

In 1898, as American troops under soon-to-be-president Theodore Roosevelt stormed up San Juan Hill outside Santiago de Cuba in the Spanish-American War, former Confederate Gen. "Fighting Joe" Wheeler led the way. U.S. Brigadier General Wheeler forgot where he was and what war he was fighting. He cried out, "We've got the damn Yankees on the run!" He finally retired in 1900.

On the eve of America's entrance into World War I, Maj. Gen. John Lincoln Clem resigned from the United States Army. He had joined the 22nd Michigan as a drummer boy when he was only nine years old. At the Battle of Shiloh, an artillery shell destroyed his drum. Clem survived, and they called him "Johnny Shiloh." As a ten-year-old at the Battle of Chickamauga he fought off a Rebel soldier, and they called him the "Drummer Boy of Chickamauga." He was a major general when he retired in 1916.

One year later, on April 5, 1917, former Cpl. Henry Lewis and former Pvt. Henry Peters of Company B, the 47th Ohio, were awarded the Congressional Medal of Honor. Not for anything they had recently done, but for heroism back at the siege of Vicksburg, fifty-three years, eleven months, and two days earlier. They were the last to be awarded the Congressional Medal of Honor for service during the Civil War.

As America entered World War II, the army suddenly realized its recruits no longer needed perfect teeth. During the Civil War, it took good teeth to bite open cartridges in order to load a rifle. With the days of muzzle-loading rifles gone, a soldier no longer needed perfect teeth, and suddenly, thousands of men whose draft board had deferred them because of malocclusions became 1-A and were sent off to war.

In Norfolk, Virginia, in June of 1951, the United Confederate Veterans held their final reunion. Only three of the twelve surviving veterans who fought for the Confederacy attended, but those three had the time of their lives. Local, state, and federal officials marched in parades, made speeches, held memorial services, and even staged a reenactment of the battle between the *Monitor* and the *Virginia*.

It was 96 degrees on the final day of the reunion. At least fourteen marchers collapsed during the parade. Heat prostration. One young drummer boy, however, did double duty; as soon as the band he was with finished the parade, he changed uniforms and drums and joined another marching unit. His mother thought she saw a mirage in the heat when her son marched by the second time.

Just as in the real battle between the first ironclads, the mock fight between the *Monitor* and the *Virginia* saw the two ships almost sink before they could have a go at each other. The make-believe *Virginia* listed to port as she sailed out into the Elizabeth River, southeast of Hampton Roads where the real battle took place in 1862. The make-believe *Monitor* listed to starboard, her bow high out of the water. Unlike the real battle, the 1951 venture saw a special boat carrying members of the press, photographers onboard urging the skipper to "get us in closer" to the action.

The two fake ironclads fired shot after shot. The press photographers took picture after picture. A newsreel cameraman asked a member of the *Virginia*'s crew to provide some noise. Two shots went screaming over the press boat, and the cameraman yelled, "That's too close."

After the five-day gathering, the veterans met no more. That same year, 1951, Union veteran Albert Woolson died, the last surviving Yankee soldier. One year later, in 1952, death claimed Walter Washington, the last Confederate veteran, the last veteran of America's Civil War.

* * *

Now, more than 130 years after the official end of the unofficially named Civil War, the Confederate flag still flies. Not just as parts of state flags in Georgia and Alabama or among dissidents who sow hatred. Not just as bumper stickers or on T-shirts proclaiming "Forget Hell!" The Confederate flag flies in Brazil.

Shortly after Lee surrendered at Appomattox, some diehard Rebels chose to leave the country rather than remain in the United States as a defeated people. Others left to avoid what they felt would be either prosecution or persecution by the new order. They headed, first, for Mexico or Cuba, later going on to England or France or Canada. Most who settled in Canada did so along the border and watched developments in the United States; when the political situation looked favorable, they returned South.

By the summer of 1865, the individual flight of emigrants had become an exodus of thousands. Where they went, they often chose to live alone, not assimilating with the natives. They built insulated colonies that were mirror images of their lost plantation lives.

Former Confederate naval leader Matthew Fontaine Maury recruited Virginians to emigrate to Mexico. They called him the Imperial Commissioner of Colonization for Mexico, and he specifically targeted descendants of the so-called "First Families of Virginia." Maury envisioned a colony of 200,000 to 300,000 white planters who would take with them a proportional number of blacks—"skilled laborers in agriculture." Former American slaves would become Mexican peons. These Confederates and their faithful peons would build a "New Virginia" in Mexico. Maury said the area he had chosen near Vera Cruz reminded him of Virginia's Shenandoah Valley.

Other emigrant Southern planters hoped to recruit local labor, assuming the Mexican peasants were a "gentle and docile race," more compliant and steady than had been the blacks of the Confederacy who, after all, had been the cause of the war that had caused the downfall of their original plantation society. But New Virginia never made it. In 1866, Maury's experiment failed when Mexican Emperor Maximilian, who approved of the plan, fell to rebellion.

Other unrepentant Rebels went farther south, taking their families, their beliefs and culture, and their flag to South America, Argentina, Venezuela, British Honduras. And to Brazil. Backers of the

Brazil plan placed ads in Southern newspapers, extolling a paradise south of the Amazon. These citizens of the late Confederacy went to Brazil, as one author puts is, "because of its dazzling resources, its rich soil, and the presence there of slavery."[6] Virginia planter Henry M. Price joined the flight to Brazil, saying his "belief in the orthodoxy of slavery is as firmly fixed as my belief in [the] Bible."

Very quickly, however, Brazil lost favor with adherents to the Lost Cause. It was too remote, the natives spoke a different language, professed a different religion, and wanted nothing to do with the diehard Rebels.

Not only that, but there were blacks in Brazil, and freedom for them came in 1888. That would leave the emigrant Rebels surrounded by millions of blacks who were freer than those they'd left in the doomed Confederacy. So, by the thousands, they left their new country to return to their old. Only a few stayed on.

Colonel William Hutchinson Norris, a former Alabama state senator, founded the city of Americana, Brazil, eighty miles northwest of São Paulo. Norris lured others to an area whose brick-red soil was reminiscent of good old Georgia red dirt. The natives called them the "Confederados." When the Southerners arrived in Brazil, they took with them the sewing machine and the plow, neither seen before in their new home. The also took watermelons, pecans, and new strains of cotton.

At first they kept to themselves, married their own, and ran their own schools with teachers imported from the United States. Ostracized by the locals in the beginning, they spoke only English at home. But more and more they had to incorporate words of the Portuguese language of Brazil, because it was the language they had to use while conducting business with the world beyond their gates.

What the progenitors revered, their progeny honor. In 1954 they founded the Fraternity of American Descendants, and it now boasts four hundred members. There's a Confederate cemetery in Americana, Brazil, and only descendants of those original "Confederados" may be buried there. Pine trees and palms, and grass seed imported from Alabama, are tucked deep among thousands of acres of South American sugarcane. One tombstone marks the grave of W. S. Wise, the great-uncle of former U.S. First Lady Rosalynn Carter. Another grave is that of Robert Stell Steagall, born in 1899 of a Confederate emigratee; in 1932 he fought in the rebellion when the State of São Paulo tried to secede from Brazil. That rebellion, like the Confederacy before it, failed. His tombstone bears the epitaph: "Once a rebel, twice a rebel and forever a rebel."

Every year the Fraternity of American Descendants holds a reunion and picnic in the graveyard: dancing in hoop skirts and Confederate gray uniforms; hot dogs, candied apples; Southern fried chicken and cold beer; cornbread, biscuits, and gravy. No grits, though. Apparently grits didn't translate into their new lifestyle. They pick pecans and listen to Dixieland jazz. Alongside the yellow and blue flag of Brazil, they fly the red, white, and blue Confederate battle flag. They fly it proudly, but not as an endorsement of slavery, because some of the Descendants have more than just a tinge of nonwhite blood, the result of intermarriage with native Brazilians and freed slaves. But they fly the flag with pride, preferring to look at its good qualities, its virtues. They do not wait for the South to rise again. For them, she has never fallen, merely slipped along the way.

Americana, Brazil, is more than five thousand miles south of Dixie. Truly, as the song says, it is "way down yonder." Way, *way* down yonder.

Down where they speak a mixture of Portuguese and English with a Southern drawl thrown in.

EPILOGUE

⚔

I have had enough of the glory of war. I am sick of seeing dead men and men's limbs torn from their bodies....When the war ends, If I am alive, no one will return to peaceful avocations more willingly than I.

—Private James M. Binford
August 13, 1862
21st Virginia[1]

A few years ago, I read an ad in a medical journal that intrigued the hell out of me. It stated that for seventy-nine cents the life oɪ silent screen actor Rudolph Valentino could have been saved. That was, the ad writer claimed, the cost of an injection of penicillin. Valentino apparently died of pneumonia and, if it had been available, penicillin may have saved his life. Intriguing, as I said.

Penicillin was not around, of course; just another in the many "what ifs" of history.

Take the death of George Washington. On Thursday morning, December 12, 1799, Washington did what he did on most other days; he went for a ride at his Virginia plantation, Mount Vernon. This time, however, he rode out in a combination of snow, hail, and freezing rain. He was sixty-seven years old at the time. Biographer Noemie Emery says that Washington returned to Mount Vernon about three that afternoon, "his cloak soaking, his neck wet and damp snow clinging to his hair."[2] The next day he complained of "a hoarseness, which increased in the evening; but he made light of it." By Saturday, his throat was raw and aching; he had a violent cough. It may well have been that Washington, like Valentino, had pneumonia. And like "the Great Lover," "the Father of His Country" likely could have been saved by seventy-nine cents worth of penicillin. But, of course, they didn't have penicillin back in 1799 either.

Instead, they gave Washington a mixture of molasses, butter, and vinegar, which, says Emery, "brought on convulsions and a near choking fit." They tried another remedy: a mixture of tartar and calomel, mercury. They poisoned the poor man! President Washington's doctors poisoned him!

But they weren't satisfied with that; they bled him. I know, I know; it was standard procedure for the time, but remember we're just playing "what if" here. In fact, they bled him four times, draining a total of thirty-two ounces of blood, beginning early Saturday morning and ending about four-thirty in the afternoon. That's two pints of blood they drained from him. The reports say the flow at 4:30 was "slow." No wonder. A 150-pound man has about five quarts of blood, ten pints. Here, the doctors had taken one-fifth of his blood. Washington by now had three doctors, one of whom, according to Noemie Emery, later wrote that he didn't think bleeding the man was the proper thing to do. She quotes doctor number two, James Craik, as saying doctor number three, Elisha Dick, "was averse to bleeding the General, and I often thought that if we had acted according to his (Dr. Dick's) suggestion . . . 'he needs all his strength—bleeding will diminish it' . . . our good friend might be alive." But they didn't have penicillin; instead, they gave him poisonous mercury. They didn't take Elisha Dick's advice; instead, they bled Washington of 20 percent of his blood.

What if, what if?

And now comes a debate surrounding the death of Abraham Lincoln. A Rye, New York, doctor says it may not have been John Wilkes Booth who killed the president but, rather, the doctor who treated Lincoln after the president was shot by Booth. Dr. Richard Fraser is a prominent neurosurgeon and an expert on brain injuries. Writing in the April 11, 1995, issue of *American Heritage*, Dr. Fraser says Dr. Charles Leale, the attending physician after Lincoln was shot, used his unwashed hand to feel around inside the president's skull, contaminating the wound. If not for the contamination, he claims, Lincoln might have lived. Dr. Fraser says it wasn't Booth's bullet but Dr. Leale's dirty hands that killed Lincoln.

Another physician disagrees with Dr. Fraser. He's Dr. John K. Lattimer, chairman emeritus of the department of urology at the College of Physicians and Surgeons at Columbia University. He says

Lincoln's wound was fatal, which puts us back to what they've taught us all along. Dr. Lattimer believes the good Dr. Leale may even have prolonged Lincoln's life by removing a blood clot from the president's head, allowing him to live another nine hours.

He says similar bullet shots to the head would leave the skull so jagged, Dr. Leale could not have inserted his finger deeply enough to contaminate the wound. Doing so, he says, would have ripped Dr. Leale's finger to shreds, and there's no evidence that this happened.

Back to Dr. Fraser. He says Dr. Leale was inexperienced, fresh from medical school, and that he even gave the president brandy and water, something Dr. Fraser claims is a "sure way to cause instant pneumonia in gunshot victims."

Fraser and Lattimer obviously disagree, and Fraser goes so far as to say, "I hope that none of you who ever suffers a brain injury will choose a urologist (referring to Dr. Lattimer) instead of a brain surgeon."

To which Dr. Lattimer replies, "Never insult your urologist, because he will get you in the end."

Notes

Introduction

1. James McPherson, *Battle Cry of Freedom: The Civil War Era* (New York: Oxford University Press, 1988).
2. U.S. Department of Defense figures, quoted in *The World Almanac and Book of Facts* (New York: Funk & Wagnalls, 1994), 163; U.S. Parks Service figures.
3. Burke Davis, *Our Incredible Civil War* (New York: Holt, Rinehart, and Winston, Inc., 1960; republished in 1994 by Wings Books of Random House as *The Strange and Fascinating Facts:*), 79.

Chapter One

1. Quoted in Darryl Lyman, *Civil War Quotations* (Conshohocken, Penn., Combined Books, 1995), 14.
2. There are many versions of Mary Boykin Chesnut's diary. This is taken from C. Vann Woodward, ed., *Mary Chesnut's Civil War* (New Haven, Conn.: Yale University Press, 1981), 46.

Chapter Two

1. This and other monologues by former slaves are taken from Belinda Hurmence's *My Folks Don't Want Me to Talk About Slavery* (Winston-Salem, N.C.: Blair, 1984) and *Before Freedom: When I Just Can Remember* (Winston-Salem, N.C.: Blair, 1989).
2. See Douglas Deal, "A Constricted World: Free Blacks on Virginia's Eastern Shore, 1680–1750" in *Colonial Chesapeake Society,* Carr, Morgan, and Russo, eds. (Chapel Hill: University of NC Press, 1988); Carl Brindenbaugh, *Jamestown: 1544–1699* (New York: Oxford, 1980); and Winthrop D. Jordan, "Enslavement of Negroes in America to 1700" in *Colonial America: Essays in Politics and Social Development,* Katz and Murrin, eds. (New York: Knopf, 1983).
3. See Robert William Fogen and Stanley L. Engerman's "Property Rights in Man" in *American Negro Slavery: A Modern Reader,* Weinstein, Gatell, and Sarasohn, eds. (New York: Oxford, 1979), third edition.

4. Herbert G. Gutman, *Slavery and the Numbers Game: A Critique of "Time on the Cross"* (Urbana, Ill.: University of Illinois Press, 1975), 15–25, 34–35, 37–39.

5. See Edwin Adams Davis, "Plantation Life in the Florida Parishes of Louisiana: 1836–1846," as quoted in Weinstein, Gatell, and Sarasohn's *American Negro Slavery: A Modern Reader* (New York: Oxford, 1959).

6. See Bobby Jones, "A Cultural Middle Passage: Slave Marriage and Family in the Antebellum South," Ph.D. dissertation, University of North Carolina, 1965, 57–58.

7. Stanley M. Elkins, *Slavery: A Problem in American Institutional and Intellectual Life* (Chicago: University of Chicago Press, 1959, 2d edition, 1968), 82.

8. Bryan Edwards, *The History, Civil and Commercial, of the British Colonies in the West Indies* (Philadelphia: James Humphreys, 1806), vol. 2, 252. Quoted in Elkins *op. cit.*, 90.

9. Bruno Bettelheim, "Individual and Mass Behavior in Extreme Situations," *Journal of Abnormal Psychology* (October 1943). Quoted in Elkins, *op. cit.*, 106, 111.

Chapter Three

1. Written to his wife during the Atlanta campaign. Quoted in Lyman, *op. cit.*, 59.

2. This comment was attributed to Lincoln by Gen. Irvin McDowell, not known as a McClellan fan. Quoted in Lyman, *op. cit.*, 148.

3. Robert Hunt Rhodes, ed., *All for the Union: The Civil War Diary and Letters of Elisha Hunt Rhodes* (New York: Mowbray, 1985; reprinted by Orion Books, 1991), 97.

Chapter Four

1. Quoted in James I. Robertson, Jr., *Soldiers Blue and Gray* (Columbia: University of South Carolina Press, 1988; reprinted in 1991 by Warner Books).

2. *Ibid.*

3. Robertson, *op. cit.*, 88.

4. See Chapter Fourteen, "Sex and the Single Soldier."

5. From November 1862: *Official Records of the Union and Confed-*

erate Armies (Washington, D.C.: 1880–1901), series I, XIX, part 2, 722, hereafter *O.R.* The *Official Records of the Union and Confederate Armies* is one of the most important works about the Civil War. Its 128 volumes carry information relating to the life of the common soldier. As others have noted, however, wading through the many volumes of the *Official Records* is a rather daunting task.

6. Quoted in Bell Irvin Wiley, *The Life of Johnny Reb: The Common Soldier of the Confederacy* (Baton Rouge, La.: Louisiana State University, 1943; reissued in 1978), 39.

Chapter Five

1. Written May 22, 1862, to Henry P.; letter in possession of Mary C. Fugate, Danville, Va. Quoted in James I. Robertson, Jr., *op. cit.,* 111.

2. Samuel Beardsley to his son, Freddy; written September 12, 1861. In the Lewis Leigh, Jr., Collection, Department of the Army, U.S. Army Military History Institute, Carlisle Barracks, Penn.

3. Constantine A. Hege to his father; written August 13, 1862, at Petersburg, Va. Lewis Leigh, Jr., Collection, Department of the Army, U.S. Military History Institute, Carlisle, Penn.

4. Constantine A. Hege, written near Fredericksburg, Va., December 18, 1862, *op. cit.*

5. J. H. Puckett to his wife, June 27, 1862; manuscript in the University of Texas Library.

6. Quoted in Bell Irvin Wiley, *The Life of Johnny Reb, op. cit.,* 196.

7. *Ibid.*

8. Frank Moss, written to his sister, Mrs. A. E. Rantfrow, December 6, 1864; manuscript owned by the University of Texas.

9. *Ibid.*

10. An ad in the Richmond *Dispatch,* December 31, 1864.

11. Richmond *Enquirer,* Friday November 11, 1864.

12. Wiley, *The Life of Johnny Reb, op. cit.,* "Dear Folks."

13. For more such words, phrases, and general nineteenth-century usage see Marc McCutcheon, *The Writer's Guide to Everyday Life in the 1800s* (Cincinnati: Writer's Digest Books, 1995). McCutcheon even informs us of the cost of a doctor's office visit in rural New York: 50¢. And, yes, he says, physicians even made house calls at the same price. Truly, the good old days.

Chapter Six
1. Mark M. Boatner III, *The Civil War Dictionary* (New York: David McKay Company, 1959; reprinted by Vintage, 1991).
2. See Chapter Twenty, "Battlefield Medicine."

Chapter Seven
1. G. F. R. Henderson, *Stonewall Jackson and the American Civil War* (New York: Longmans, Green, 1936, a reprint from the 1898 edition), 12.
2. Douglas Southall Freeman, *Lee's Lieutenants: A Study in Command*, 3 vols. (New York: Charles Scribner's Sons, 1942), vol. 1, xlii.
3. Morris Fishbein, M.D., *A History of the American Medical Association 1847 to 1947* (Philadelphia: W. B. Saunders Company, 1947), 661.
4. See the Epilogue for more on pneumonia and how a cure for the disease might have changed history.
5. Joseph T. Glatthaar, *Partners in Command: The Relationships Between Leaders in the Civil War* (New York: The Free Press, 1994), 92.
6. *Ibid.,* 237–238.
7. For a good account, see Stephen W. Sears, *Landscape Turned Red: The Battle of Antietam* (New York: Houghton Mifflin Company, 1983).

Chapter Nine
1. Quoted in John Macdonald, *Great Battles of the Civil War* (New York: Macmillan, 1988), 36.
2. Boatner, *op. cit.,* 552.
3. Quoted in Wiley, *The Life of Johnny Reb, op. cit.,* 123.
4. Helen Jones Campbell, in the Norfolk *Virginian-Pilot,* May 27, 1951, written as part of a series for the final reunion of Confederate veterans held in Norfolk that summer.
5. The *New York Times,* October 20, 1862.

Chapter Ten
1. Quoted in Lyman, *op. cit.,* 165.

Chapter Eleven
1. Quoted in Lyman, *op. cit.,* 41.
2. George Green Shackelford, *George Wythe Randolph and the Confederate Elite* (Athens, Ga: University of Georgia Press, 1988), 2.

Chapter Thirteen

1. John Beauchamp Jones, *A Rebel War Clerk's Diary at the Confederate States' Capital* (Philadelphia: J. B. Lippincott, 1866), 25.

2. *Ibid.*, June 27, 1861.

3. *Ibid.*, June 28, 1861.

4. *Ibid.*, April 5, 1861. For more, see Mike Wright, *City Under Siege: Richmond in the Civil War* (Lanham, Md.: Madison Books, 1995), 266–267.

Chapter Fifteen

1. William Marvel, *Andersonville; The Last Depot* (Chapel Hill N.C.: University of NC Press, 1994), 144.

2. For a much more complete look at this remarkable person, read Stephen B. Oates, *A Woman of Valor: Clara Barton and the Civil War* (New York: The Free Press, 1994).

3. Dr. C. E. Godfrey, *Sketch of Major Henry Washington Sawyer* (Trenton: MacCrellish & Quigley, Printers, 1907), 6.

4. Richmond *Dispatch,* July 7, 1863.

5. G. E. Sabre, *Nineteen Months a Prisoner of War* (New York: American News Company, 1865), 23–24.

6. Quoted in Emmet Dedmon, *Fabulous Chicago* (New York: Random House, 1954), 70.

Chapter Seventeen

1. Quoted in Lyman, *op. cit.,* 39

2. Richmond *Dispatch,* April 29, 1864.

3. Richmond *Dispatch,* February 15, 1865.

4. Ella Lonn, *Desertion in the Civil War* (New York: The Century Co., 1928), 28.

5. Quoted in Lyman, *op. cit.,* 18.

Chapter Eighteen

1. From an interview with Mrs. McEva Bowzer, quoted in David D. Ryan, *Cornbread and Maggots, Cloak and Dagger: Union Prisoners and Spies in Civil War Richmond* (Richmond: The Dietz Press, 1994), 141. A "living history" actress portraying Mary Elizabeth Bowzer's mother appears during the summer months at the restored White House of the Confederacy.

Chapter Nineteen
1. Phoebe Yates Pember with Bell I. Wiley, ed. *A Southern Woman's Story: Life in Confederate Richmond* (St. Simons Island, Ga.: Mockingbird Books, Inc. 1974), reprinted in 1984, 98.
2. Pember and Wiley, *op. cit.*, 94.

Chapter Twenty
1. Harry Lewis Papers, Southern Historical Collection, University of North Carolina, Chapel Hill.
2. Written June 24, 1863, to T. W. Meighan. Quoted in Lyman, *op. cit.*, 34
3. Quoted in Oates, *op. cit.*, 7.
4. Quoted in Percy H. Epler, *The Life of Clara Barton* (New York: The Macmillian Company, 1915), viii.
5. See Chapter Eighteen for Senator Wilson's alleged entanglements with Confederate spy Rose Greenhow.
6. John R. Brumgardt, ed., *Civil War Nurse: The Diary and Letters of Hannah Ropes* (Knoxville, Tenn.: University of Tennessee Press, 1980), 68.
7. Diary, April 13, 1862; April 24, 1862, quoted in Lyman, *op. cit.*, 63-64.
8. Quoted in Robertson, *op. cit.*, 161.
9. *Ibid.*

Chapter Twenty-One
1. Sgt. Achilles V. Clark to his sister, April 1864. Quoted in Lyman, *op. cit.*, 57.
2. Richmond *Sentinel*, April 18, 1864.
3. Brian Steel Wills, *A Battle from the Start: The Life of Nathan Bedford Forrest* (New York: HarperCollins, 1992; reprinted by Harper Perennial, 1993).

Chapter Twenty-Two
1. Quoted in Mary Elizabeth Massey, *Ersatz in the Confederacy: Shortages and Substitutes on the Southern Homefront* (Columbia, S.C.: University of South Carolina Press, 1952; reprinted 1993), 89.
2. *Ibid.*

3. Over the years, there have been many reprints, reediting, and revivals of Jones's Diary. One of the latest is "Condensed, edited, and annotated by Earl Schenck Miers," the book's cover proudly proclaims. Originally published in 1958 by Sagamore Press, the Miers edition was reprinted in 1993 by the Louisiana State University Press. It's the "condensed" part that is bothersome about this edition. With annotation it runs to 545 pages; strange, since the original, non-condensed version was published in two volumes, with a total of 480 pages.

4. Louis H. Manarin and Robert W. Waitt, Jr., eds., *Richmond at War: The Minutes of the City Council, 1861–1865* (Chapel Hill, N.C.: University of NC Press, 1966), 543.

5. Sallie A. Brock Putnam, *A Lady of Richmond: Richmond During the War. Four Years of Personal Observations* (New York: G. W. Warleton, 1867), 208. Sallie Brock was just sixteen when the war began; her diary was published after the war and after she married.

6. Sara Agnes Pryor, *Reminiscences of Peace and War* (New York: The Macmillan Company, 1905), 238.

7. Quoted in Hudson Strode, *Jefferson Davis: Confederate President* (New York: Harcourt, Brace & World, 1904–1905), 381.

8. Richmond *Dispatch,* April 3, 1863.

9. Natchez *Daily Courier,* April 15, 1863, as quoted in Massey, *op. cit.*

10. *The Oxford Universal Dictionary on Historical Principles* (London: Oxford University Press, 1933), 108, 104.

11. Richmond *Enquirer,* August 3, 1861.

Chapter Twenty-Three

1. Lt. Col. Arthur James Lyon Fremantle, Sr., *Three Months in the Southern States: April–June 1863* (New York: John Bradburn, Co., 1864; reprinted by the University of Nebraska Press, 1991), 260.

2. James J. Fold, *The Book of World Famous Music* (New York: Dover Publications, 1985), 661. Roger Lex confirms this in *Great Songs Thesaurus* (New York: Oxford University, 1898), 2d edition, 427. Lex says "Words and music by J.K. Adapted by Dan George in 1958 for the film *Night Stage to Galveston.*

3. Quoted by Wiley, *The Life of Johnny Reb, op. cit.,* 122.

Chapter Twenty-Four

1. Quoted in Lyman, *op. cit.*, 115

2. See Richard S. Brownlee, *Gray Ghosts of the Confederacy: Guerrilla Warfare in the West 1861–1865* (Baton Rouge, La.: Louisiana State University, 1958), 139.

3. Edward E. Leslie, "Quantrill's Bones," in *American Heritage* (New York: Forbes, July/August 1995), 53.

4. *Ibid.*, 127.

5. *Ibid.*

Chapter Twenty-Five

1. Quoted in Lyman, *op. cit.*, 236.

Chapter Twenty-Six

1. Jones, *A Rebel War Clerk's Diary, op. cit.*, September 19, 1864.

2. *Ibid.*, October 28, 1864.

3. New York *Tribune,* March 1865. Quoted in John R. Carey, ed., *Eyewitness to History* (New York: Faber and Faber, Ltd., 1987).

4. Quoted in Lyman, *op. cit.*, 66.

5. Quoted in Gaines M. Foster, *Ghosts of the Confederacy: Defeat, the Lost Cause, and the Emergence of the New South* (New York: Oxford University Press, 1987), 18.

6. James L. Roark, *Masters Without Slaves: Southern Planters in the Civil War and Reconstruction* (New York: W. W. Norton, 1977), 124.

Epilogue

1. Written to his sisters; quoted in Lyman, *op. cit.*, 39.

2. Noemie Emery, *Washington: A Biography* (New York: G. P. Putnam's Sons, 1976), 372.

Bibliography

General

Bettelheim, Bruno. "Individual and Mass Behavior in Extreme Situations." *Journal of Abnormal Psychology*. vol 38 (October 1943).

Boatner, Mark, III. *The Civil War Dictionary*. New York: David McKay Company, Inc., 1959; reprinted by Vintage Civil War Library in 1991.

Brindenbaugh, Carl. *Jamestown: 1544–1699*. New York: Oxford University Press, 1980.

Brownlee, Richard S. *Gray Ghosts of the Confederacy: Guerrilla Warfare in the West: 1861-1865*. Baton Rouge, La: Louisiana State University, 1958.

Brumgardt, John R., ed. *Civil War Nurse: The Diary and Letters of Hannah Ropes*. Knoxville, Tenn: University of Tennessee Press, 1980.

Carey, John R., ed. Eyewitness to History. New York: Faber and Faber, Ltd., 1987.

Davis, Burke. *Our Incredible Civil War*. New York: Holt, Rinehart, and Winston, Inc. 1960; later published as *The Civil War: Strange and Fascinating Facts*. New York: Wings Books, 1994.

Davis, Edwin Adams. "Plantation Life in the Florida Parishes of Louisiana: 1836–1846." In *American Negro Slavery: A Modern Reader*. edited by Allen Weinstein, Frank O. Gatell, and David Sarasohn. New York: Oxford University Press, 1979.

Deal, Douglas. "A Constricted World: Free Blacks on Virginia's Eastern Shore, 1680–1750." In *Colonial Chesapeake Society*, edited by Lois Green Carr, Philip D. Morgan, and Jean B. Russo. Chapel Hill, N.C.: University of North Carolina Press for the Institute of Early American History and Culture, Williamsburg, Va., 1988.

Dedmon, Emmet. *Fabulous Chicago*. New York: Random House, Inc. 1954.

Edwards, Bryan. *The History, Civil and Commercial, of the British Colonial West Indies*. Philadelphia: James Humphreys, 1806.

Elkins, Stanley M. *Slavery: A Problem In American Institutional and Intellectual Life*, 2nd edition. Chicago: University of Chicago Press, 1959; reprinted in 1968.

Emery, Noemie *Washington: A Biography.* New York: G. P. Putnam's Sons, 1976.

Fogel, Robert W. and Stanley L. Engerman. "Property Rights in Man." In *American Negro Slavery: A Modern Reader,* edited by Allen Weinstein, Frank O. Gatell, and David Sarosohn. New York: Oxford University Press, 1979. Extracted from *Time on the Cross: The Economics of American Negro Slavery,* Boston: Little, Brown and Company, 1974.

Foster, Gaines M. *Ghosts of the Confederacy: Defeat, the Lost Cause, and the Emergence of the New South.* New York: Oxford University Press, 1987.

Fremantle, Lt. Col. Arthur James Lyon, Sr., *Three Months in the Southern States: April–June 1863.* New York: John Bradburn, Co., 1864, reprinted by the University of Nebraska Press in 1991.

Glatthaar, Joseph T. *Partners in Command: The Relationships Between Leaders in the Civil War.* New York: The Free Press, 1994.

Godfrey, Dr. C. E. *Sketch of Major Henry Washington Sawyer.* Trenton: MacCrellish & Quigley, Printers, 1907.

Gutnam, Herbert G. *Slavery and the Numbers Game: A Critique of "Time on the Cross."* Urbana, Ill.: University of Illinois Press, 1975.

Hurmence, Belinda. *Before Freedom: When I Can Just Remember.* Winston-Salem, N.C.: Blair, 1989.

———. *My Folks Don't Want Me to Talk About Slavery.* Winston-Salem, N.C.: Blair, 1984.

Jones, John Beauchamp. *A Rebel War Clerk's Diary at the Confederate States' Capital.* Philadelphia: J. B. Lippincott and Company, 1866.

Jordan, Winthrop D. "Enslavement of Negroes in America to 1700," In *Colonial America: Essays in Politics and Social Development,* edited by Stanley N. Katz & John M. Murrin. New York: Alfred A. Knopf, 1983.

Leslie, Edward E. "Quantrill's Bones," In *American Heritage.* New York: Forbes, July/August 1995.

Levy, George. *To Die in Chicago: Confederate Prisoners at Camp Douglas, 1862–1865.* Evanston, Ill.: Evanston Publishing, Inc., 1994.

Lonn, Ella. *Desertion in the Civil War.* New York: The Century Co., 1928.

Lyman, Darryl. *Civil War Quotations.* Conshohocken, Penn.: Combined Books, 1995.

Manarin, Louis H., and Robert W. Waitt, Jr., eds. *Richmond at War: The minutes of the City Council, 1861–1865.* Chapel Hill, N.C.: University of North Carolina Press, 1966.

Massey, Mary Elizabeth. *Ersatz in the Confederacy: Shortages and Substitutes on the Southern Homefront.* Columbia, S.C.: University of South Carolina Press, 1952; reprinted in 1993.

McCutcheon, Marc. *The Writer's Guide to Everyday Life in the 1800s.* Cincinnati: Writer's Digest Books, 1995.

McPherson, James M. *Battle Cry of Freedom: The Civil War Era.* New York: Oxford University Press, 1988.

Oates, Stephen B. *A Woman of Valor: Clara Barton and the Civil War.* New York: The Free Press, 1994.

Pember, Phoebe Yates, with Bell I. Wiley, ed. *A Southern Woman's Story: Life in Confederate Richmond.* St. Simons Island, Ga.: Mockingbird Books, 1974; reprinted in 1984.

Pryor, Sara Agnes. *Reminiscences of Peace and War.* New York: Macmillan & Co., 1905.

Putnam, Sallie A. Brock. *A Lady of Richmond: Richmond During the War, Four Years of Personal Observations.* New York: G. W. Warleton, 1867.

Rhodes, Robert Hunt. *All for the Union: The Civil War Diary and Letters of Elisha Hunt Rhoses.* New York: Mowbray, 1985.

Roark, James L. *Masters Without Slaves: Southern Planters in the Civil War and Reconstruction.* New York: W. W. Norton & Company, Inc. 1977.

Robertson, James I., Jr. *Soldiers Blue and Gray.* Columbia, S.C.: University of South Carolina Press, 1988: reprinted by Warner Books in 1991.

Ryan, David D. *Cornbread and Maggots, Cloak and Dagger: Union Prisoners and Spies in Civil War Richmond.* Richmond: The Dietz Press, 1994.

Sabre, G. E. *Nineteen Months a Prisoner of War.* New York: American News Company, 1865.

Sears, Stephen W. *Landscape Turned Red: The Battle of Antietam.* New York: Houghton Mifflin Company, 1983.

Shackelford, George Green. *George Wythe Randolph and the Confederate Elite,* Athens. Ga.: University of Georgia Press, 1988.

Strode, Hudson. *Jefferson Davis: Confederate President.* New York: Harcourt, Brace & World Inc., 1904–05.

Weinstein, Allen; Frank O. Gatell; and David Sarasohn, eds. *American Negro Slavery: A Modern Reader.* New York: Oxford University Press, 1979.

Wiley, Bell Irvin. *The Life of Billy Yank: The Common Soldier of the Union.* Baton Rouge, La.: Louisiana State University, 1952; reissued in 1992.

————. *The Life of Johnny Reb: The Common Soldier of the Confederacy.* Baton Rouge, La.: Louisiana State University, 1943; reissued in 1978.

Wills, Brian Steel. *A Battle from the Start: The Life of Nathan Bedford Forrest.* New York: HarperCollins, 1992; reprinted by Harper Perennial in 1993.

Woodward, C. Vann, ed. *Mary Chesnut's Civil War.* New Haven, Conn.: Yale University Press, 1981.

Wright, Mike. *City Under Siege: Richmond in the Civil War.* Lanham, Md.: Madison Books, 1995.

Manuscripts

Beardsley family papers in the Lewis Leigh, Jr., Collection, Department of the Army, U.S. Military History Institute, Carlisle Barracks, Penn.

Constantine A. Hege papers, U.S. Army Collection, Department of the Army, U.S. Military History Institute, Carlisle Barracks, Penn.

Moss family papers, University of Texas Library, Austin.

J. H. Puckett papers, University of Texas Library, Austin.

Newspapers

Natchez *Daily Courier*
New York *Times*
New York *Tribune*
Norfolk *Virginian-Pilot*
Richmond *Daily Dispatch*
Richmond *Enquirer*
Richmond *Examiner*
Richmond *Sentinel*
Richmond *Whig*

Unpublished Dissertation

Jones, Bobby. "A Cultural Middle Passage: Slave Marriage and Family in the Antebellum South," Ph.D. dissertation. Chapel Hill, N.C.: University of North Carolina, 1965.

Other Sources

Axelrod, Alan. *The War Between the Spies: A History of Espionage During the American Civil War.* New York: Atlantic Monthly Press, 1992.

Bradford, Ned, ed. *Battles and Leaders of the Civil War.* New York: G. P. Putnam's Sons, 1956; reprinted by Meridian in 1989. This is an abridgement of the original four-volume edition edited by R. U. Johnson and C. C. Buel and published in 1887–1888.

Brooks, Noah and Herbert, Mitgand eds. *Washington, D.C. in Lincoln's Time: A Memoir of the Civil War Era by the Newspaperman Who Knew Lincoln Best.* (Original title, *Washington in Lincoln's Time.* New York: The Gramercy Co., 1895.) Chicago: Quadrangle Books, 1971; reprinted by the University of Georgia Press in 1989.

Committee of Hospital Physicians of the City of New York. *A Manual of Directions Prepared for the Use of Nurses in the Army Hospitals.* New York: Baker & Godwin, 1861; reprinted by John M. Bracken and the New Market Battlefield Museum in 1994.

Current, Richard Nelson. *Lincoln's Loyalists: Union Soldiers From the Confederacy.* Boston: Northeastern University Press, 1992; reprinted by Oxford University Press in 1994.

Denney, Robert E. *Civil War Prisons & Escapes: A Day-by-Day Chronicle.* New York: Sterling Publishing Co., Inc., 1993.

Donald, David, ed. *Why the North Won the Civil War.* Baton Rouge, La.: Louisiana State University Press 1960; reprinted by Collier Books in 1989.

Dowdy, Clifford. *Lee's Last Campaign: The Story of Lee and His Men Against Grant—1864.* New York: Barnes & Noble Inc., 1994; reprint of the 1960 original edition.

Foner, Eric. *Reconstruction: America's Unfinished Revolution, 1863–1877.* New York: Harper & Row, Publishers, 1988; reprinted by Harper Perennial in 1989.

Freeman, Douglas Southall. *Lee's Lieutenants: A Study in Command,* 3 vols. New York: Charles Scribner's Sons, 1942–1946.

————. *The Centennial History of the Civil War,* 3 vols. Garden City, N.Y.: Doubleday & Company, 1961–1965. 3 Vols.

Hansen, Harry. *The Civil War: A History.* New York: Penguin Books, Inc., reprinted by Mentor in 1991.

Hesseltine, William B., ed. *Civil War Prisons.* Kent, Ohio: Kent State University, 1962; originally published in *Civil War History,* vol. 8, no. 2, under the general editorship of James I. Robertson, Jr.

Hill, Lois, ed. *Poems and Songs of the Civil War.* New York: Gramercy Books, 1993.

Hoehling, A. A. *Thunder at Hampton Roads: The U.S.S.* Monitor—*Its Battle with the* Merrimack *and Its Recent Discovery.* New York: Da Capo, 1993; originally published in 1976.

————. *Women Who Spied: True Stories of Feminine Espionage.* New York: Dodd, Mead & Company, 1967; reprinted by Madison Books in 1993.

Kolchin, Peter. *American Slavery: 1619–1877.* New York: Hill and Wang, 1993.

Larson, Rebecca D. *Blue and Gray Roses of Intrigue.* Gettysburg, Penn: Thomas, 1993.

Lee, Richard M. *General Lee's City: An Illustrated Guide to the Historic Sites of Confederate Richmond.* McLean, Va.: EPM Publications, Inc., 1987.

Leech, Margaret. *Reveille in Washington.* New York: Carroll & Graf, 1986, reprinted by Harper & Row, Publishers, in 1989.

Marvel, William. *Andersonville: The Last Depot.* Chapel Hill, N.C.: University of North Carolina Press, 1994.

McFeely, William S. *Grant: A Biography.* New York: W. W. Norton & Company, Inc., 1981.

Monaghan, Jay. *Civil War on the Western Border: 1854–1865.* Boston: Little, Brown and Company, 1955; reprinted by the University of Nebraska in 1984.

Official Records of the Union and Confederate Armies. Washington, DC: 1880–1901.

Oxford Universal Dictionary on Historical Principles. London: Oxford University Press, 1933.

Price, William H. *Civil War Handbook: A Civil War Research Associates Series.* Fairfax, Va.: Prince, Co., 1961.

Reid, Mitchell. *Civil War Soldiers: Their Expectations and Their Experiences.* New York: The Viking Press, Inc. 1974, reprinted by Touchstone in 1989.

Robertson, James I., Jr. *Civil War Virginia: Battleground for a Nation.* Charlottesville, Va.: University of Virginia Press; reprinted in 1993.

Rogers, J. L. *The Civil War Battles of Chickamauga and Chattanooga.* Chattanooga, Tenn.: Rogers, 1942. This is a 40-page pamphlet, interesting primarily for its 79-year-old perspective and pictures of tourists on the battlefields.

Ross, Ishbel. *Rebel Rose: Life of Rose O'Neal Greenhow, Confederate Spy.* St. Simons Island, Ga.: Mockingbird Books, 1954.

Sears, Stephen W. *To the Gates of Richmond: The Peninsula Campaign.* New York: Tichnor & Fields, 1992.

Shaara, Michael. *The Killer Angels* (A novel of the Battle of Gettysburg.) New York: McKay, 1974; reprinted by Ballantine Books in 1989. This is the basis for the Turner Entertainment, Inc., movie *Gettysburg* of 1993.

Sommers, Richard J. *Richmond Redeemed: The Siege At Petersburg.* Garden City, N.Y.: Doubleday & Company, Inc., 1981.

Trudeau, Noah Andre. *Bloody Roads South: The Wilderness to Cold Harbor, May–June 1864.* Boston: Little, Brown and Company, 1989.

Ware, Geoffrey with Ric Burns and Ken Burns. *The Civil War.* New York: Vintage Civil War, 1994. Originally published in illustrated form by Alfred A. Knopf, Inc. 1990. This came out of the PBS television series *The Civil War,* produced by Ken Burns.

Witt, Col. Jerry V., USA, Ret. *Escape from the* Maple Leaf. Bowie, Md.: Heritage Books, 1993.

Womack, Bob. *Call Forth the Mighty Men.* Bessemer, Ala.: Colonial Press, 1987.

Woodworth, Steven E. *Jefferson Davis and His Generals: The Failure of Confederate Command in the West.* Lawrence, Kan.: University Press of Kansas, 1990.

Magazines
America's Civil War. Leesburg, Va.: Cowles History Group.

American Heritage Civil War Chronicles. New York: Forbes, Inc.

American History. Leesburg, Va.: Cowles History Group.

Blue & Gray Magazine. Columbus, Ohio. Blue & Gray Enterprises, Inc.

Civil War Times Illustrated. Leesburg, Va.: Cowles History Group.

Civil War: The Magazine of the Civil War Society. Berryville, Va.: The Civil War Society.

Great Battles. Leesburg, Va.: Cowles History Group.

Historic Traveler: The Guide to Great Historic Destinations. Leesburg, Va.: Cowles History Group.

MHQ: The Quarterly Journal of Military History. New York: American Historical Publications, Inc.

Military History. Leesburg, Va.: Cowles History Group.

Southern Partisan. Columbia, S.C.: Southern Partisan Corporation.

The Civil War News: For People With an Active Interest in the Civil War Today! Turnbridge, Vt.: Historical Publications.

Index

Gilmore, Brawley
  former slave, 36
Glassells, CSA Lt. W. T.
  designs David, 103
"Goober Peas," 237
Gosport Navy Yard
  and CSS Virginia, 111
  burned by Union, 111
  evacuated by Confederacy, 117
Grand Wizard of K. K. K.
  see Forrest, 225
Grant, Julia Dent, 265
  and slavery, 23
Grant, U.S. Gen. Ulysses S., 48
  accepts Lee's surrender, 275
  and Butler, 220
  and Lee, 122
  and McClellan, 265
  and Mexican war, 122
  and uniforms, 133
  at Fort Donelson, 267
  described, 264
  early problems, 265
  militia appointment, 266
"graybacks," 130
"Great Locomotive Chase"
  see "The General," 92
Greeley, Horace
  and Davis, 277
Greenhow, Rose O'Neal
  and Manassas, 181
  and Davis, 183
  Confederate spy, 180
  death of, 183

H. L. Hunley

Confederate submarine, 104
Halleck, U.S. Gen. Henry W. 46, 266
Hammond, U.S. Surgeon Gen. Dr. William A.
  and medical practices, 201
Hampton Roads, Virginia
  and ironclads, 111
Hancock, US Gen. Winfield S.
  and Gettysburg, 123
Hart, Charlie
  see Quantrill, 255
hats, 133
Hawks, Dr. Esther H., 208
Herburt, Thomas
  and Andersonville, 155
"High water mark"
  and Gettysburg, 124
Hill, CSA Gen. Ambrose P.
  death of, 273
  and Ellen McClellan, 85
Hollywood Cemetery, Richmond, Virginia, 193, 205
Holmes, Oliver W.
  and war photography, 108
"Home Sweet Home"
  and Stones River, 241
honey as sugar substitute, 233
Hood, CSA Gen. John B., 43
Hooker, U.S. Gen. Joseph
  "Fighting Joe," 48, 171
  and prostitutes, 148
Horry, Ben
  former slave, 33
hospitals, 202, 205, 206, 210, 214
  Antietam wounded, 89